WILD PLACES

20 JOURNEYS INTO THE
NORTH AMERICAN OUTDOORS

Edited by Paul McHugh

Foghorn Press

BOOKS BUILDING COMMUNITY

ISBN 0-935701-41-9

51595

9 780935 701418

This book may not be reproduced in full or in part without the written permission of the publisher, except for use by a reviewer in the context of a review. Inquiries and excerpt requests should be addressed to:

Rights Department
Foghorn Press
555 DeHaro Street, Suite 220
San Francisco, CA 94107
foghorn@well.com

Credits and copyright notices for the individual stories in this collection begin on page 304. Foghorn Press has made every effort to trace the ownership of all copyrighted material and to obtain permission from copyright holders. Should there be any question regarding the ownership of any material herein, we will be pleased to make corrections in future printings.

Foghorn Press titles are distributed to the book trade by Publishers Group West, based in Emeryville, California. To contact your local sales representative, call 1-800-788-3123. To order Foghorn Press books, please call: 1-800-FOGHORN (364-4676) or (415) 241-9550.

Although the authors and publisher have made every effort to ensure that the information in this book was correct at press time, the authors and publisher do not assume and hereby disclaim any liability to any party for any loss or damage caused by errors, omissions, or any potential travel disruption, whether such errors or omissions result from negligence, accident, or any other cause.

Library of Congress Cataloging-in-Publication Data:

Wild places : 20 journeys into the North American outdoors / edited by Paul
  McHugh.
       p.   cm.
   Includes index.
   ISBN 0-935701-41-9 (paper : alk. paper)
   1. United States—Description and travel—Anecdotes. 2. Wilderness
areas—United States—Anecdotes. 3. Outdoor life—United States—
Anecdotes. 4. United States—Guidebooks.
I. McHugh, Paul, 1950–
E169.04.W52   1996
917.304'929—dc21   96-45105 CIP

The Foghorn Press Commitment

Foghorn Press is committed to the preservation of the environment. We promote Leave No Trace principles in all of our guidebooks. Additionally, our books are printed with soy-based inks on 100 percent recycled paper, which has a 50 percent post-consumer waste content.

Printed in the United States of America

WILD PLACES

20 JOURNEYS INTO THE NORTH AMERICAN OUTDOORS

Edited by Paul McHugh

Richard Bangs
Tim Cahill
W. Hodding Carter
Paula J. Del Giudice
Gretel Ehrlich
Pam Houston
Bob Marshall
Linda Watanabe McFerrin
Paul McHugh
Tom Wharton

For my mother,
Delphine Genevieve Villemaire.
She taught me early, and taught me continuously,
why kindness, steadfastness, and humor are virtues.

CONTENTS

Prologue

A t this point in the late twentieth century, I think rather too much is made of the adrenaline-fueled, solo outdoor adventures. They are fine, but gentler, shared outings can have just as much depth and consequence—if not more. The strong mental focus that's triggered in response to risk can also be summoned by the simple presence of natural beauty. Wilderness epiphany is not the sole possession of epic adventurers; folks of equal inspiration have been setting pen to paper (or keystroke to disk) for years.

Enter the ten authors whose work is assembled in this book. These folks are not just "travel writers"; they are adventure, outdoor, and nature authors. In some cases their stories are about having a rollicking good time; in other instances they border on the visionary and the profound. If you let them, they can inspire you. They are used to doing this job. And once they carry you away, you'll find yourself in good hands. You can circle in the dark skies above Newfoundland with Paula Del Giudice, then descend to a rendezvous with an elusive Atlantic salmon. Or you can canoe down the Potomac with Richard Bangs, at the dawn of his globe-rambling career; or walk through a Pacific Northwest rain forest in the footsteps of Pam Houston; or see whether or not the mystic power of Sedona, Arizona, is grounded in fantasy as you roam the desert with Linda Watanabe McFerrin.

It has been a great pleasure to work with these writers. Many already have a national reputation; some are still comers—not yet enjoying the recognition they deserve. All are adept, sensitive researchers, their accounts rich in both natural and human historical detail. This is more important than ever because these days, to paraphrase Lincoln, we meet as though on a great battlefield, testing whether any civilization so conceived can long endure. We must realize that our economy and ecology stand on the same ground—and that no matter how impressive our technologies may grow, we already live amid the most fantastic technology on earth: one that continuously transforms sunlight into life. So when Gretel Ehrlich takes us on a stroll on the deck of the *Peace* as the Channel Islands sail into view, and when she helps us hear the songs of Chumash native oarsmen, we are not just being guided to a wild place; we are also brought further into understanding.

While you live, walk this earth. Find as much beauty in the desolation of the Great Salt Lake as Tom Wharton did. Paddle Louisiana's bayous in the wake of Bob Marshall's boat, and peer through the swamp mists to glimpse scenes of past and future. Admire the ghostly glide of beluga whales under Hudson Bay at the mouth of the Seal River, just like Hodding Carter. And gallop on horseback through the silver-green sage in the billowing dust of Tim Cahill.

To help you get there in the pragmatic sense, factual how-to trip notes accompany each story, enabling you to physically go to the twenty wild places featured in this book. Compare your experiences to those of the authors. And let them inspire you to discover other wild places of your own. Or, in the words of Ulysses, as imagined by Tennyson: "Come my friends, 'tis not too late to seek a newer world. . . ."

—*Paul McHugh*

"You Are Cowboy"

by Tim Cahill

F our or five years ago, I was interviewed by a Swedish photographer who leveled a bizarre accusation at me. "You are cowboy," he said.

Hey, smile when you say that, pardner. The man was visiting the small Montana town where I live. He was working on a photo essay about the American West and seemed to believe that anyone who'd want to live in some tumbleweed tank town had, of necessity, to be a cowboy.

I tried to set my Swedish friend straight on those individuals who labor in the field of bovine animal husbandry. "Cowboys," I said, "are men and women who work with cattle on horseback. Such persons tend to share a certain philosophy, a courtesy, a prickly pride, and a tendency to, oh, sometimes exaggerate events, often to humorous effect. Many of my neighbors are, in fact, ranchers or working cowboys, and yes, you can tell them by their outfits. Wannabe buckaroos always get it wrong: wrong hat, wrong length pants, wrong boots, wrong life, big pathos.

"So no," I told the Swedish photographer, "I am not cowboy. Oh sure, I ride horses now and again, but the awful truth is, I keep falling off the sons of bitches." It happened again just last spring. For reasons that have never been satisfactorily explained, I failed to stop when the horse did. I just kept going right over the horse's neck and landed, boom, on my back in a cloud of dust.

It occurred to me then that I was rather like those English seamen of a century ago who, shipwrecked in the Arctic, failed to adopt Inuit survival techniques and consequently froze to death. Just so. If I ever wanted to ride a horse with any degree of dignity, I was going to have to learn from a cowboy.

Which is how, some months later, I made my way to the All 'Round Ranch in Utah, where Al Brown runs a kind of horseman's clinic on the sage-littered slopes of the Blue Mountains. You don't need any experience, and you don't need to know the first thing about horses. Al swears he can have you galloping around barrels in an arena within a week. He'll have you herding cows. Rounding up strays in brushy draws. Running down obstreperous calves at a gallop, through knee-high sage.

So there I was in Utah, three months after my spring horse-wreck, galloping along on Josh, a horse that had once run at Ruidoso Downs, home of the richest horse race in the world. Josh was a quarter horse gelding, 11 years old, and just coming into his prime as a saddle horse. He was easily the finest and fastest horse I had ever ridden—*Dios mío*, was he fast.

It was pouring down rain on the Blue Mountain plateau, near the border of Utah and Colorado. There was a rainbow behind us to the east, some blue sky to the south, and a black thundercloud directly ahead. Bolts of lightning danced on a distant ridge that marked the horizon. The trail was a narrow rut, running with water, and the horse's hooves threw up clods of mud. Al Brown, galloping easily beside me, shouted some words of welcome instruction. "Settle down a little deeper into the saddle," he called. I did that, and it smoothed out the ride some.

Josh was steadily gaining speed, however, and I was steadily losing confidence. Unfortunately, I know this drill well: The horse just keeps running, faster, then faster still—it's really a barely controlled runaway—until a kind of dumb terror informs me that it's time to stop or die. The stopping process involves pulling back on the reins and shouting "whoa" several dozen times as the horse shifts down through several bone-jarring gears to a final stop.

It's like driving some kind of hot sports car, a Ferrari, for instance, but the car is rigged in such a way that once you punch the accelerator, you either have to run it all the way up to 180 or hit the brakes in a panic stop. There's no cruise control, no way to drive the beast at a safe and sane 85 miles an hour.

As Josh gained speed, Al said, "Hey, give him a little tap." By which he meant: Pull back once, quickly, gently, on the reins. I did, and Josh immediately settled back into his previous pace. If the horse had been a Ferrari, we'd be doing, oh, 55 or 60, and—hey, what's this?—I could keep him right there, with only an occasional tap on the reins.

"All right," Al shouted, "now touch his ribs." That's what you do on a horse like Josh. No need to kick. You just touch his ribs with your boot heels. When I did, my head snapped back and we were doing a figurative 85, instantly.

"You get unbalanced," Al shouted, "grab your saddle horn." Al didn't buy into the dictum that a "real cowboy" never grabs his saddle horn. He'd worked with cattle, had been "a-horseback" all his life, and was, he said, always grabbing the saddle horn.

He pointed off to the right, at a place where the trail probably branched to the north. We were going to turn "just beyond that big stand of sage." Which was probably hiding the trail.

And I thought about what Al had said about turns, about how a running horse, in the wild, turns in a sinuous curve, winding its body into the motion. In contrast, a horse carrying a rider will turn stiffly, all in a block. The back end of the animal tends to come around too far, like a car losing traction on an icy curve. "A-horseback," as Al would say, you correct the tendency to come around by touching the animal far back on the ribs on the outside of the turn.

Which is what I did, and pretty well, too. Josh wound around the stand of sage, which stood five feet high, wrapping the turn so tight that stiff branches scraped against the outside of my thigh, and I was glad, for a moment, that I was wearing leather chaps. I say for a moment, because rather quickly after that, I wasn't glad about anything at all. We weren't on any trail, but were galloping at 85 over a gently rising plain littered with sage so thick that if I fell off, no part of my body would actually hit the ground.

You can't ride horses through thick sage. This ought to be evident to anyone. It's not possible. The horse is going to get his feet tangled up; he's going to go down, hard, and take you with him. This was dangerous. It was irresponsible. I was maybe a little scared.

Al Brown was about 50 yards ahead, shouting cowboy shit like "Yee-hah" and "Yah-hoo," and he wasn't on any trail either. Rain was sluicing off his oilskin slicker, and his horse was moving smoothly, splashing through standing water and kicking up dry dust underneath. Thunder rumbled in the distance and there was no way, at this speed, that I could direct Josh through the sage.

He was making tiny adjustments that I could feel in my inner thighs, moving miraculously through the heavy brush, and I kept my right hand close to the saddle horn, just in case. It occurred to me, in a panicky way, that I ought to discuss responsibility with Al, and I touched Josh once, gently, on the ribs so that, instantaneously, we were doing 120 and closing in on Al Brown. I realized, with a start, that Josh had at least two more gears in him and that he could do 180, easy. Even through the sage.

Josh wanted to run, to leave Al's horse in the rain and dust, but I tapped back on the reins so that Al and I were riding side by side at about 100 miles an hour, through the deadly sage. I wanted to tell him that what we were doing was impossible. It didn't occur to me at the time that such a statement is ridiculous.

"Al," I shouted. "Hey, Al!" He turned to look at me: Al Brown with the front brim of his cowboy hat blown flat against the crown, Gabby

Hayes style; Al Brown with his goofy mop of a mustache mostly covering a maniacal grin; Al Brown with the rain in his face, the rain running in sheets down his slicker; Al Brown at 100 miles an hour, sitting his horse like he was part of the animal. We were topping a gentle ridge, and out ahead, in the distance, a sea of silver-green sage fell down toward the Green River in a series of long, gentle swells.

"Al," I shouted into the wind. "There's no damn trail!"

The man regarded me for a moment. He was squinting against the wind and rain, but there was a strange luminescence in his eyes, something that seemed to transcend joy altogether and to rise up into realms of spiritual ecstasy.

I thought perhaps he had misunderstood me. "No trail here," I screamed. "Yeah," he shouted back, "ain't it grand!"

The point here is that I completely missed the point. There were seven of us riding with Al Brown that week, including three women from Switzerland. One of them was a good rider, the other two were experts, and they had all read about the All 'Round Ranch in a German magazine specializing in, yes, Western riding. The style, they said, was all the rage in Europe. In Switzerland, the women rode English saddles. In the English tradition, folks ride with their legs folded up under them like jockeys; they hold their reins up under their chins, in the manner of a squirrel with a nut.

It's a tough, demanding way to ride, very stylized, but the women wanted to learn Western riding—the buckaroo style—because it allowed you to sit in the saddle all day. It seemed to them "more natural." In Switzerland, they told me, there are plenty of places to ride, but it's all trail riding. What the western United States offered was vast tracts of prairie and desert and mountain meadow. It was ranch land or public land, and you could ride anywhere. You were not confined by trails. This was a freedom not available anywhere in Europe.

So the women had come to "ride the range"—to do the very thing that had frightened me that day, which is to say, they wanted to get off the trail and go loping at 150 miles an hour through the sage.

We were sitting around a campfire, discussing the matter, and Polly Golins, Al's business partner, pointed out that wild horses live, and run, through sage-littered landscape every day. Horses didn't get tangle-footed in sage any more than Br'er Rabbit got tangled up in the briar patch. Sage was a horse's natural medium.

Oh, sure, you had to look out ahead. But while the rider made major decisions in terms of direction, the horse micromanaged the ride. Which meant, in essence, that if there was a big stand of sage looming up in front, you had to be prepared for the horse to zig right, zag left, or simply jump the brush. You had to pay attention.

If I was embarrassed by my expressed fear of off-trail riding, Polly and Al pretty much made me feel at ease. They did this by purposefully making complete fools of themselves in the bad joke department.

"Say Polly, I heard you had to shoot your dog." "Yep." "Was he mad?" "I reckon he weren't too pleased."

The next morning, our third with Polly and Al, we were all up at about seven o'clock, building the fire and making ourselves breakfast.

At the All 'Round, clients are not called dudes. Dudes, Al explained, get waited on. By contrast, we enjoyed the privilege of setting up our own canvas tepees, digging rain trenches around them, and making breakfast. Help was always available, but in general, we caught our own horses in the corral, cleaned their hooves, and checked the animals for saddle sores and suspicious swellings in the legs. We saddled them ourselves, and there was none of this single-file trail riding, with the horses all bunched up nose to butt.

The first two days we had walked our horses, mostly in deference to John, a young insurance executive from New Jersey who had never ridden before. The afternoon of the second day, Al had taken me out for the run through the sage. My stirrups seemed to be too short. I had figured this out when Al said, "Your stirrups are way too short."

In buckaroo-style riding, the stirrups are run long, leaving just an inch or two between you and the saddle. I had always ridden with the balls of my feet in the stirrups, carrying a lot of the weight of my body in the knees. My knees have always ached after riding.

With the longer stirrups, the knees barely bend, and they never ache afterward. If you have a good pair of boots made with heavy leather, a steel shank in the sole, and heels at least an inch high, you can use hoop stirrups, which are simple metal rings. Slip the smooth-soled boot into the ring, right up to the heel. When you stand to smooth out the ride, you are standing on the bottom of your foot, on the steel shank.

With good boots, hoops, and stirrups adjusted at the proper length, you feel welded into the saddle. Secure. There's no talk about posting or cantering at the All 'Round. Al and Polly start you off in a slow lope, riding beside you, offering advice—"settle back a little deeper into the saddle"—and things seem to progress naturally.

This day, we'd be riding mostly at a stiff trot, a gait that has always been problematic for me. Al explained that it was, in fact, the gait favored by men and women who work cattle on horseback. Walking's too slow to get anything done, a gallop will tire any horse, but the animals can trot all day long. You smooth out the jarring ride by watching your mount's shoulder. It's a little like dancing. The horse sets the beat, and you adjust from side to side, walking along in your stirrups to a rhythm that is more easily felt than described.

We were trotting out over the range when a half a dozen sage hens rose before us and fluttered off to the east. Al and I were chatting about hats. I asked him why he seemed to disdain stampede strings, strips of rawhide that are tied under the chin to keep the hat from blowing off at full gallop.

Al Brown thought for a moment, than launched into a full half hour on the philosophy of cowboy hats. The shape of the crown and brim, the curl, would all be expressive in some way of a rider's personality. And, although Al didn't precisely say it, there is an element of initiation—of real pain—involved in any hat. They are purchased small, and should feel like a band tightened around the skull. A week of constant headaches will stretch the thing out a bit, especially if there are rainstorms involved, or sleet and hail.

The hat becomes a part of the rider. It keeps the rain and snow out of his face, shades him from the sun, and keeps him warm in the cold. If the rider has to do some brush popping, that is to say, ride through high, thick brush—with serviceberries or chokecherries rising up over his head—he ducks down, holding the hat on his head with one hand. The wide brim protects his face from snapping branches.

The hat, as Al saw it, was a mystical thing. Kings wear crowns, Indians wear feathered headdresses, proper Englishmen wear bowlers. There was a weight of symbolism invested in any hat, a character and a philosophy. Cowboys understand this and associate their headgear with good fortune. No buckaroo ever lays his hat brimside down: Hey, the luck just runs out of it that way.

When there's difficult work to be done, a cowboy wants to pull the hat down low, tight. If it still blows off his head, he has to understand that nothing is accidental. The missing hat is a matter of some significance, a signal to him from the cosmos. Maybe it blew off because he was cocky or unprepared. Maybe he didn't need to be in that particular place at that particular time. When a cowboy's hat blows off, he is obliged to think about it. To philosophize.

However, with a stampede string, Al said finally, your hat never blows off. Therefore there is never any need to review your life, such as it is. Al seemed to believe that people who wear stampede strings fail to live sufficiently contemplative lives.

A cowboy's outfit is all cotton and wool and leather. Nothing much has changed in 150 years, primarily because the system works. This is a lesson those shipwrecked English seamen never learned from the Inuit. There's a reason and a purpose for everything. Cowboys wear boots, for instance, because boots slide off the foot. This won't seem important until you fall off a galloping horse with one lace-up shoe caught in a stirrup.

Frankly, the functionality of the gear surprised me. I wore the Wrangler jeans Al recommended because the inseam is stitched on the outside and doesn't cause saddle sores. My hat and ankle-length riding slicker kept me bone dry in heavy rains. The way my boots fit the stirrups had a lot to do with my new confidence in my mount, Josh. The leather chaps I wore, provided by the ranch, took a lot of punishment from snapping sage. I liked they way they felt against the saddle—leather on leather—and imagined they contributed to the extraordinary fact that in more than 50 hours of riding, I had failed to fall off my horse once.

Some of the riding was even a little demanding. The seven of us learned to herd cattle, ride drag and swing, and read brands. John, the novice in our group, learned to ride at a gallop and on our last day, we competed in an arena, racing around barrels and passing mailbags to teammates at a full gallop. The arena work seemed almost easy after a week of range riding, and I found myself doing things "a-horseback" that I thought only rodeo cowboys could do.

This is not to say that I am, or ever will be, a cowboy. I still have areas of total incompetence on a horse. Tight, galloping 180-degree turns have me bamboozled. Josh never liked the way I did them. He would nearly stop, get all tangle-footed, and sometimes rear up a bit.

Al Brown's advice was to look at it from Josh's point of view. "What do you tell him when you get to the turn?" Al asked.

"I tap on the reins to slow him up a bit."

"Are you perfectly balanced?"

"No, not really."

"What do you do to get your balance?"

And I saw it very clearly: On a tight turn, when I begin to feel unbalanced, I tend to clamp my legs tight around the animal. This causes my boot heels to touch his ribs, which is, of course, the signal to go. Meanwhile, I'm pulling back on the reins. No wonder Josh gets tangle-footed. No wonder he rears up.

I had to look at it from his point of view. What I knew for sure about Josh and his point of view was this: The horse just purely loved to run. In our time together, we opened it up all the way and did 180 miles an hour out there on the range. We did it lots of times, with the rain, sleet, or snow blowing in our faces. There were rainbows or storm clouds or both spread out all across the sky, and the wind blew the brim of my hat back flat against the crown and I was welded into the saddle, shouting "Yah-hoo" or "Yee-hah" or just "Go Josh!" What I felt in those moments was something so far beyond exhilaration that it was, well . . . it was almost cowboy.

TRIP NOTES

Working wrangler ranches offer an authentic experience of the American West. That means a chance to eat dust as well as beans, get your nose rosily sunburnt, and perhaps acquire a scrape or two en route to learning the right way to ride the sage.

When to go

If you want to avoid a less celebrated part of the authentic experience, such as a high plains winter that involves clawing ice out of your mustache and watching your breath-plume freeze and shatter against a barn wall, the best time to go is from mid-spring to early fall. Most operations are also open to guests at that time.

Where to go

Here's a ranch roundup:

- **All 'Round Ranch,** Jensen, Utah. Folks at this 400-square-mile spread in the northeastern corner of Utah will put you on a horse and keep you there for four- to six-day pack trips through the aspen-covered backcountry.
  Capacity: 12 guests.
  Season: April 1 to October 31.
  Cost: A six-day stay is approximately $1,100 per person.
  Phone: (800) 603-8069.

- **Bar H Ranch,** Soda Springs, Idaho. A former Mormon homestead, this working ranch with 2,000 head of cattle in Idaho's Wasatch Mountains is for those who want to have a true-blue cowboy experience.

Capacity: Four to six guests.
Season: May 1 through September 30.
Cost: A five-day stay is about $650 per person.
Phone: (800) 743-9505.

- **Cheyenne River Ranch,** Douglas, Wyoming. An 8,000-acre working cattle and sheep ranch in eastern Wyoming's open prairie, the Cheyenne holds five cattle drives per season, as well as lambing, sheep-shearing, and branding sessions. The family-owned, down-to-earth ranch is deep in the heart of tumbleweed country.
  Capacity: 12 guests.
  Season: May through October.
  Cost: A week's stay is about $850 per person.
  Phone: (307) 358-2380.

- **Homestead Ranch,** Matfield Green, Kansas. For cowgirls only, this ranch maintains 200 head of beef cattle on 5,000 acres in the grasslands of central Kansas. Female guests are invited to participate in all ranch activities, from mending fences to castrating bulls. Those who simply wish to relax can fish or ride horses or mountain bikes.
  Capacity: 20 guests.
  Season: Open year-round.
  Cost: Weekend stays start at $275 per person; five-day stays start at $475.
  Phone: (316) 753-3465.

- **Sweet Grass Ranch,** near Big Timber, Montana. This 20,000-acre ranch in the Crazy Mountains is for guests whose

idea of a good time is a hard day's work—be it feeding hogs or driving a 200-head herd of Angus—followed by a refreshing dip in the snowmelt waters of Sweet Grass Creek.
Capacity: 20 guests.
Season: June 10 to September 5.
Cost: A week's visit starts at $700 per person.
Phone: (406) 537-4477; ask for Sara Corbett.

What to bring

Most outfitters take care of the camp and riding equipment and ask only that you bring personal gear. For trips away from the ranch house, you may want to tote along your own sleeping bag (a bag rated to 20 degrees Fahrenheit is suitable for most summer conditions). For horseback riding, good, durable cotton-canvas clothing and thin leather gloves are appropriate, and men and women should try wearing pantyhose under their jeans to reduce the friction and leg-hair yanking associated with long rides. Also bring synthetic insulating garments to stay warm, a water- and windproof shell, strong mosquito repellent, a large hat, sunblock, and sunglasses.

Additional information

"The Greenhorn's Guide to Cowboy Adventures" is a free brochure with information on campsites, lodgings, and safety issues, and tips on how and where to ride horses. For a copy, contact the All 'Round Ranch at P.O. Box 153, Jensen, UT 84035; (800) 603-8069.

For more information about travel and recreation in Utah, call the Utah Travel Council at (801) 538-1030.

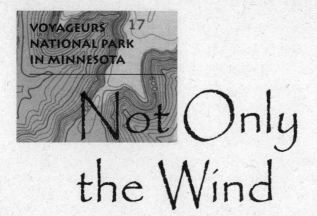

Not Only the Wind

by Tom Wharton

The wolves started howling at 2 A.M. Checking my watch in the still darkness of the family's old canvas tent, I tried to wake up.

Was this for real? We'd driven 1,500 miles from Salt Lake City to savor this moment. Our route had taken us through desolate Wyoming, the cornfields of the Great Plains, and Minnesota's thick North Woods. The ancient orange van, as is its vacation habit, broke down in Duluth, delaying our trip north to Voyageurs National Park, near the Canadian border, for a few hours.

As is also the custom on our family vacations, it had rained almost constantly, ending one of the decade's great droughts. We thought farmers ought to pay us to camp near their property! Thus, we weren't surprised when a summer storm greeted us as we arrived at Voyageurs—a place where, we hoped, we might hear the howl of a wolf.

Unlike western national parks such as Yellowstone or Zion, Voyageurs seems a strange mix of private enterprise and public resource. Dozens of small lodges dot the banks of Kabetogama Lake in the heart of the park.

Judging from the park brochure, however, we would have to own a boat to reach the backcountry and the wolves. So, with the distinct feeling we'd driven a long way for nothing, we began stopping to ask for advice on where we might camp and how we might see this place.

The first two lodge owners examined my old van, unshaven face, four fidgety children, and desperate look, and politely told me they couldn't help me hear wolves. But things changed when we approached Burchell's Moosehorn Resort. The sun even started shining, if only for a moment. A pleasant man with a heavy Minnesota accent greeted me as I walked out on the dock.

"Alan Burchell," he said, offering a hand. I introduced myself, telling him we'd come all the way from Salt Lake City to hear a wolf howl and were now plenty confused about how we might do that. Pulling out a park brochure and pointing to a spot on the map, I told him we were looking for someone to take us across the lake and into the park's backcountry, where we hoped to backpack, fish, and, perhaps, see or hear a wolf. We also needed a campsite that night. Smiling, Burchell offered some advice. "I could take you to this trail," he said, pointing at a spot on the map. "But the rain we've had these past few days is going to make walking difficult for you. We've got bedrock here, and the water hangs around in puddles."

Then he added, "Would you consider another idea? Why don't you let me rent you a 16-foot aluminum boat for a couple of nights? I'll draw you a map and show you where you can likely find a single campsite that can only be reached by boat. Those sites are nice. They have tent pads that drain the water, picnic tables, primitive toilets, and a locker to keep your food away from the bears. Of course, most people don't see bears. That's just a precaution."

After discussing it with my family, I asked Alan what the boat rental might cost. The price was surprisingly reasonable and, in view of what mechanical breakdown the ancient orange van might inflict on us on the way home, something I could afford. In fact, it seemed like a bargain.

Burchell smiled when I asked where I might obtain fishing licenses. He'd been watching my teenage son, Jacob, in the back of the van, who, in turn, had been watching an angler on the dock as he kept catching walleye with amazing ease. While I was trying to figure out where we might camp, my son was itching to fish.

"There's a park service campground at Woodenfrog just up the road," Alan told me. "Why don't you go set up while the rain has stopped and the sun is still out, and then come back later to prepare for tomorrow? And," he added with a smile, "while you're at it, why don't you leave that youngster with me? I'll show him how to rig up a rod to catch walleye and then he'll be able to show you what works here and what you'll need to buy."

My son raced out of the van, moving faster and with more enthusiasm than he had during the entire trip. I watched him follow on Alan's heels as he attended to some other customers.

The lodge owner was right. Even though the rain had ceased, the rocky land didn't drain well. Reading the park brochure, we discovered the reason. The park lies in the southern portion of a geologic formation known as the Canadian Shield. Glaciers had scoured the land of its soil, leaving 2.7-billion-year-old rock, some of the oldest exposed rock in the world. Hundreds of ponds, lakes, and streams now found throughout the park were gouged out by the flowing ice.

As a result, the vegetation around our campsite seemed more lush than we were accustomed to in the dry Great Basin of the Salt Lake Valley. Pitching a tent was difficult because we kept hitting bedrock. And there was water almost everywhere.

After wrestling with the tent, breaking a couple of plastic stakes in the process, I returned to the Moosehorn Resort to pick up my son and put together a shopping list for our Voyageurs adventure.

We purchased insect repellent, fishing licenses, tackle, backcountry-type food, a navigator's map of Kabetogama Lake, and large plastic garbage bags to protect our sleeping bags in case it rained.

"Fishing's been pretty good," said the man in the store. I didn't have the heart to tell him that despite trying for many years, I'd never been able to land a walleye. Where I go, the fishing was mostly good yesterday. Even my son struggled to get a bite from the same place where the angler we watched had caught dozens. Apparently, my teenager was doomed to inherit the famous family fishing curse.

After a night made fitful by lightning and rain, it was easy to get up early. With the weather clearing at last, we examined the Burchells' 16-foot aluminum boat. Trying to figure out where to store camping gear, fishing tackle, and four kids turned into an interesting chore. But having owned a Volkswagen bug in my youth, I'm well trained in the art of using every available inch of space.

"Are you sure this boat will be safe in the open water?" my wife asked. She'd seen me sink more than one canoe and had vowed never to get in a small boat with me again. Fortunately, she also yearned to hear the cry of a wolf, which meant that this time she'd make an exception.

Burchell examined the boat closely and said we'd be fine, especially if all the kids wore life jackets. Getting out my navigational map, I had him show me where we might find some decent fishing, a good camping spot, and, most important, howling wolves.

Why wolves? Why here? At the time of our visit, debate was raging over the reintroduction of wolves into Yellowstone National Park. Ecologists wanted to put large predators back into the wild to complete the ecosystem. It was felt the wolves would help control Yellowstone's burgeoning elk and bison populations.

Yet area ranchers and hunters were successfully lobbying against the reintroduction, arguing that their grandparents had rid the country of this beast at the turn of the century and there was no need to bring it back. The big predator would eat game and livestock and only cause trouble, these opponents said.

To me, a wolf's howl symbolizes all that's wild in the world. I couldn't afford to fly or drive to Alaska or northern Canada, where this creature is more common; I had plans to attend a writers' conference in Des Moines, Iowa, and the trip north to Minnesota seemed an intriguing compromise.

According to the International Wolf Center in Ely, Minnesota, about 2,000 wild wolves roam Minnesota's north country. Though a few also roam Montana's Glacier National Park, and some have been recently reintroduced into the Yellowstone ecosystem, the region around Voyageurs and the adjacent Boundary Waters Canoe Area Wilderness are home to most of the wild wolves in the lower 48 states.

The mission of the Wolf Center, located near one of the main entries into the Boundary Waters, is to support the survival of wolves by offering worldwide environmental education about the animal, its relationships with other species, and its role in human culture. The center tries to provide information that helps people make up their own minds about the value of these creatures.

Visitors to the center can watch employees such as Janice Templeton frolic in an enclosed lot with a pack of captive wolves. They can also study the center's Wolves and Humans exhibit, which shows that despite what you read in fairy tales, there is no record of a wolf ever killing a human being.

At one time, different types of wolves inhabited much of North America. The red wolf, which weighs between 40 and 90 pounds, once inhabited most of the southeastern United States; the gray wolf, weighing between 57 and 130 pounds, once roamed most of the continent. And the Mexican wolf, the fabled lobo, was a native of the United States' Southwest.

Nowadays, though plentiful in Canada and Alaska, the wolf is an endangered species in all the lower 48 except Minnesota, where it is listed as threatened. The animal now occupies about 3 percent of its former range.

Once considered vermin, the big predators were hunted, trapped, poisoned, and killed by settlers. Many groups, including farmers, ranchers, and some hunters, still think the only good wolf is a dead one. Obviously, others disagree. "There is a mystique about being in wolf country," says Walter Medwid, the International Wolf Center's executive director. "Hearing wolves is a life-enriching experience and an incredible treat. It's hard to put a dollar value on that."

Seeking that experience, and armed with a map, a prayer, and a sense of adventure, we left the Burchells' dock and headed toward the unknown.

Was this, I wondered, what the French-Canadian explorers felt like as they set out in their canoes to trap beaver in this area 200 years ago? They called themselves *voyageurs,* and this park was named in their memory in 1975.

Of course, while the voyageurs paddled their birchbark canoes some 16 hours a day and often had only the crudest of maps, we were aided by an outboard motor, a good map, and the knowledge that if we didn't appear back at the Moosehorn Resort in three days, the Burchells would come looking for us.

Still, those facts didn't dim our sense of drama and risk, especially since map reading was the only subject I failed in Army officers' school. Alan had given us a couple of key points to help us find our way, and he clearly knew what he was talking about. About 15 miles up the lake, we started seeing campsites.

We selected one on a tiny island and immediately set up camp. That chore complete, some of us relaxed. I, however, went fishing, determined to catch my first walleye.

And so the stage was set for our first adventure. I failed to catch the walleye, but the fishing for yellow perch and smallmouth bass was fair, with the help of leeches rigged for bait the way Burchell had taught my son.

It was warm, midday, just after a rainstorm, and an easy time to start dreaming. That's why I couldn't believe my eyes when a black bear lumbered across the tip of the island. Burchell had said the chances of a bear encounter were slim. But I was glad we'd carefully followed his instructions to store our food in the bearproof containers.

I was also glad we were on an island. Even though only a few feet of water separated our spot of land from the mainland shore, I doubted a bear would go to the trouble to wade across.

Still, I started screaming at my wife and kids. "Get in the boat! Bear! Get in the boat! Bear!" "But . . ." stammered my teenage daughter. "Listen . . ." added my wife, who had read the brochure about possible bear encounters and what to do. I wasn't in the mood for an argument. "Shut up!" I screamed. "Get in the damn boat this instant!"

Considering the situation, it was easier to comply than to argue with Dad. Leaving all our food and camping gear behind, we leaped into the boat. As the bear watched, no doubt amused at the consternation it had caused, we promptly hung the boat up on a sandbar a few feet from shore, within several yards of the animal.

The boys tried to free us from the sandbar, and I promptly flooded the outboard motor. The engine wouldn't start. At this point, the bear stopped sniffing around for food. Obviously frustrated by his fruitless search, the big, furry animal stood on its hind legs right next to the tent, looking at us. Then, with a quick shrug, it lumbered back into the woods.

That's when my wife and daughter let me have it. "If you would have read the brochure, you would have known that when encountering a black bear in the wild, you're supposed to get into as large a group as possible and make lots of noise," they told me.

"Isn't that what we just did?" I asked innocently. "Yes," they admitted, "but we're not sure that's what *you* had in mind when you started screaming at the top of your lungs, racing around the campground like an idiot, and then flooding the boat engine. It looked to us as if you were panicking."

"Not me," I said. "I was in complete control of the situation." Actually, I hadn't read the brochure. Being more familiar with grizzly bears in Glacier and Yellowstone National Parks, I had been certain that my family was in grave danger.

We instituted a buddy system for the next two days in the event we met up with the bear again. When a family member had to use the open-air pit toilet in the dark outskirts of the camp, he or she was assigned a lookout to stand nearby, just in case.

We decided to take a boat ride for the next few hours in hopes the bear would leave our little island. After quickly grabbing the fishing gear that had been scattered all over the boat and around the campsite, we headed out into Kabetogama Lake.

Fishing was good. My wife hooked a huge smallmouth bass that took 20 minutes to land. The fish kept making runs, much to everyone's delight. Using light tackle, my wife said she'd never had so much fun catching a fish. The smallmouth fought so hard we decided it should live. And so the monster was carefully released.

As the sun set, other creatures started to appear. The distinctive sound of a pair of loons reminded us of this place's wildness. We watched in awe as an osprey dove from a pine tree high above the water, plucked out a fish, and took it back to its nest for dinner. Scanning the lake surface, I spotted a wood duck. Though my wife had embroidered the colorful little bird on the back of a shirt years ago after seeing it in a book, neither of us had ever seen one outside a zoo.

We also looked for bald eagles, which have nested along the lakeshores since 1973, if not longer. National park biologists who have been studying eagles report that the birds like to nest on islands or peninsulas on the northern edges of the park's four major lakes. White-tailed deer, no doubt wary of wolves and humans, could occasionally be seen creeping along the edge of the rocky shores, stopping briefly to sip some water or graze on the grasses.

Disdaining a fire, we sat in camp and watched the sun set. The wind and rain of the past few days died down. It was quiet. As we cooked on an ancient gas stove by the light of a lantern, the hassles of driving cross-country seemed to melt away. We laughed about the bear and examined a map of the lake, planning to hike on a trail that led to other lakes.

Though I didn't say much, I still wondered if we would hear a wolf. It was dark and quiet now. Wary of the bear, we used a flashlight to find the pit toilet in the shadowy woods. The place seemed untamed and foreboding.

"What would the voyageurs think about a night like this?" my wife wondered aloud. "Did they enjoy their lonely, wild excursion as much as we like ours? Of course, they didn't have a car, hot showers, and a grocery store to run to if they got into trouble, did they?"

We tucked the children into their sleeping bags and, for a while, lay awake in the darkness, savoring the quiet, cool summer evening and the smells of the forest. We soon drifted off to sleep. Our tent has large mesh windows that we enjoy keeping open when rain isn't threatening. I like to wake a few times in the middle of the night to look at the stars or moon or simply listen to sounds of the nocturnal world.

And so, at about 2 A.M., I sat straight up when I heard the distant sound. It didn't take long for me to figure out that I was listening to that unmistakable howl.

For a moment, I listened alone, trying to make sure I wasn't dreaming. Then another wolf answered. This was much closer. I nudged my wife awake. She stealthily woke each of the children. We listened for the next 30 minutes. We'd heard wolf sounds before, on tape, in park visitor centers, and in curio shops. But nothing like this. This was the real thing.

How can I describe such a sound? It was lower than the howl of a coyote, a musical treat we'd heard many times when we camped in our beloved southern Utah red-rock country. This was stronger, more plaintive, full of primal, savage lamentation.

Were these wolves trying to speak with other pack members at a distance? Were they establishing turf, warning an invading pack to stay away? Could these be mating calls? Or do wolves, like humans, simply sing to enjoy the sound of their own voices?

Of course, these are the musings of someone trying to ascribe human characteristics to a nonhuman creature. Did a wolf need a reason to howl? Still, why was it so exciting? Why had we traveled so far, enduring mosquito bites and bear scares and boat hassles to reach this point? Why did I suddenly feel so complete, as if another one of my life's dreams had been fulfilled?

Perhaps it had something to do with the reason the voyageurs persisted with their travels so long ago. They could no longer enjoy the life of noisy cities. They needed to escape into the freedom of the deep woods, where they could be tested by nature's forces.

The howl of the wolf symbolized wilderness, the top of a complete food web. It represented all that was good about camping, hiking, and being alive. In a world carpeted with human artifice, the wolf's howl was as real as things get.

Then, as suddenly as the howling had started, it ended. Voyageurs National Park became quiet once again. Happy, I drifted off to sleep.

The next morning dawned clear, cool, and quiet. We woke early, hoping to get in some good fishing and to perhaps catch a glimpse of the wolves we had heard. They had seemed so close. . . .

The sound of the boat's engine was a foul intrusion. I stopped it for a while in the middle of Kabetogama Lake, ostensibly so we could fish, but mostly to enjoy the quiet.

That's when something quite amazing occurred. We heard the high-pitched "yip! yip! yip!" of a wolf cub in the nearby forest. Amazed, we looked at each other. My twin sons, always aggressive and usually willing to take control of a situation, suddenly started yipping. The cub yipped back. This went on for more than a few moments. We started giggling. Hearing the howl of a wolf in the distance was one thing. Hearing your young sons have a conversation with a wild wolf cub was an even mightier marvel.

That was our last wolf encounter. We hiked to a small lake where I actually landed a northern pike. Finding a trail-building crew on the wet path, we told them about our encounter with the bear and the howling.

"There are signs of bears around here, too," one of the workers said. "Be careful."

The footpath finally petered out. More likely, we took a wrong turn on a game trail and got momentarily lost. Whatever the case, knowing there were bears and wolves in the nearby woods seemed to make us feel more alive, more alert to the beauty of the landscape.

We returned to the boat and fished for much of the rest of the afternoon, and then, as the inevitable storm moved over Kabetogama Lake, my wife decided it was time for the kids to take a sponge bath in the tent and change clothes. As it turned out, that was a good idea. Stripping each child down to his or her underwear, she screamed when she saw ticks everywhere. We must have run through a horde of wood ticks on our hike.

Using the tweezers from my Swiss Army knife, we began slowly pulling ticks off our skin. My wife started counting as she removed them. There were 47 ticks in all (not counting the one that leaped from a piece of loose clothing onto her neck as we drove across Iowa two days later).

After taking care of the ticks, we fixed a quick dinner and tried to do some fishing. But the wind began to come up, and the flashes and boom of lightning and thunder filled the northern Minnesota sky. As the rain began to pelt our tent, I quickly put everything away, taking care, again, to lock the food away from bears. The quiet had been replaced by the sound of rain on canvas and rolling thunder. The only howl we heard that night was the wind's.

TRIP NOTES

Voyageurs National Park is in northern Minnesota, on the Canadian border. The 218,055-acre park holds 30 lakes with heavily wooded shoreline and islands laced by trails. These were once used by French-Canadian trappers known as voyageurs, who traded beaver and other goods between Montreal and the Canadian Northwest 200 years ago. About 84,000 acres of the park are water.

When to go

The best time for visitors who want to make use of the open waters for boating and angling is after the thaw, from late spring through early fall. In winter, cross-country skiers, dogsledders, ice anglers, and snowmobilers take over.

How to go

The park is surrounded by 60 resorts in four communities, and many are located right on the lakeshore. That should not present a problem to a family that owns a boat, but even nonowners can hop on a tour boat or rent a powerboat, fishing vessel, houseboat, or canoe from one of many private outfitters. Floatplanes also take visitors into the more remote lakes.

For one of the best experiences of Voyageurs, take a boat to one of the 133 primitive boat-in campsites scattered throughout the lakes. Most offer a tent pad, primitive toilet, picnic table, and fire grate; a few also provide a steel locker to keep food away from bears. Families on a budget can rent a small fishing boat and take tents and camping gear into the park. (Some boat-in sites are temporarily closed to protect local wildlife such as nesting birds.)

For a less rugged experience, consider spending the night at Kettle Falls. A tour boat takes modern-day voyageurs to this historic hotel, located between Namakan Lake and Rainy Lake at the northeast

WILD PLACES

corner of the park; for information on lodging and meals, call (888) 534-6835.

Fishing is one of the park's major activities; there are good populations of smallmouth bass, walleye, northern pike, crappie, and sauger. The season usually opens in mid-May. A Minnesota fishing license is required.

Where to go

There are four major lakes inside the park—Sand Point, Namakan, Kabetogama, and Rainy—in addition to 26 smaller lakes. Most contain several islands.

Park visitor centers are located at Rainy Lake, 12 miles east of International Falls; in the middle of Kabetogama Lake, near the town of the same name; and at Ash River, at the end of the Ash River Trail.

The Rainy Lake visitor center, which also features a nature trail, is open year-round. The Kabetogama Lake and Ash River centers are open only during the busy summer season.

Campers will find an array of public and private facilities. Park-operated campgrounds are located at Woodenfrog, north of the Kabetogama Lake visitor center on County Route 122, and at Ash River, on the unpaved Ash River Trail.

The park's major access points are located along U.S. Highway 53, between Duluth and International Falls. To reach Crane Lake, on the park's east end, take County Route 23 from Orr. Kabetogama can be reached by taking County Route 122 off Highway 53. Rainy Lake is located 12 miles east of International Falls, on Minnesota Highway 11.

Park interpretive programs include the chance to ride a 26-foot-long replica of the voyageurs' North Canoe, with costumed interpreters providing commentary, special children's programs, guided canoe trips, a kids' puppet show, and evening naturalist programs.

One interesting interpretive display is the Rainy Lake Gold Rush exhibit on Little America Island. Here, a quarter-mile trail travels past gold-mine shafts and the Rainy Lake Goldfields. Tour boats also operate out of the Rainy Lake visitor center.

For park information, contact the Superintendent, Voyageurs National Park, 3131 Highway 53, International Falls, MN 56649-8904; (218) 283-9821. Request a park brochure and a copy of "The Rendezvous," a park newspaper.

For additional publications and navigational charts, contact the Lake States Interpretive Association at the above address, or call (218) 283-2103.

Information on International Falls is available by contacting the International Falls Area Chamber of Commerce, 301 Second Avenue, International Falls, MN 56649; (800) 325-5766.

What to bring

From late spring until late June, ticks can be a serious problem. They usually get onto humans from the grass and brush alongside the trails. One method of prevention is to wear light-colored long pants, like chinos, tucked into your socks, then spray yourself from the knees down with strong insect repellent. It's also a good idea for hiking and camping companions to inspect each other periodically. (Ticks always climb upward, so you should have time to spot them before they fasten and bite.)

Some—though not all—ticks carry Lyme disease; the deer tick—about one-sixteenth the size of the more common wood tick—is the carrier. According to the National Park Service, the disease's most common sign is a skin rash or red patch that slowly expands around the bite, often followed by flulike symptoms.

Mosquitoes can also be a problem. One way to avoid bites is not to wear dark clothing or use perfume or scented toiletries. DEET-based repellents work well but should be used with caution.

Additional information

The Boundary Waters Canoe Area Wilderness (BWCAW) and Canada's adjacent Quetico Provincial Park both lie east of Voyageurs National Park. Since the BWCAW is heavily used, permits are required from May to September for overnight stays and day use. For information, contact the BWCAW, Box 338, Duluth, MN 55801; (218) 720-5324.

The Minnesota Travel Information Center offers resort and campground directories and lists of local guides. For details, contact the center at 100 Metro Square, 121 Seventh Place East, St. Paul, MN 55101-2112; (800) 657-3700.

The International Wolf Center in Ely, Minnesota, at the edge of the Boundary Waters, offers some of the world's best displays on the wolf. Staff members explain the natural history of the wolf at regular intervals, and visitors can even enjoy watching a captive pack of wolves live and play in a 1.25-acre enclosure next to the center. For information, contact the International Wolf Center, 1396 Highway 169, Ely, MN 55731-8120; (800) 359-9653.

WASHINGTON'S
WILLAPA BAY
17

On the Trail of Walking James

by Pam Houston

There's a young man in Willapa Bay, Washington, who
goes by the name of Walking James. He's tall and
lanky, young-looking even for his age (18), and a little
shy. He's famous among tree farmers in Pacific County because he's the only tree thinner who will climb all the way to
the top of the Douglas firs and cut the double trunks off. Even
more astounding, to me, is James' other accomplishment: In
the last five years he has walked and mapped every square
mile of five townships in the Willapa Bay area.

His maps are detailed and professional, indicating all the
usual topographic features: buildings, roads, landforms, and
bodies of water. But James' maps are unique because they
include features that are of particular interest to him: the

WILD PLACES

Roosevelt elk's winter grazing ground, a little-known waterfall on the Niawakem River, a red alder grove where he once saw a pair of chestnut-backed chickadees, and the magical remnants of old-growth forest that for one reason or another the logging companies' chain saws have missed.

You don't have to spend much time with James to realize that he is a walking computer: He knows every bird and plant and subspecies found in the area, knows every hill and slough and meadow, knows each indigenous animal's favorite habitat, knows by heart the elevation of every square mile of the places he's been. When he isn't working high in the tree branches, thinning the new forests so they more resemble the ancient ones, he is walking and mapping, looking for rare or endangered species that live in the pockets of old-growth timber he loves.

When I ask him why he's devoted so much of his life to mapping, he tells me he hopes to save the old-growth remnants. He says he has always been interested in exploring the unknown, in recording the things that in the past have been overlooked.

A desire to explore the unknown has taken young people away from their homelands for centuries. But for James, there is plenty of unknown in his backyard. Two years ago, when his parents moved north from the Willapa area to Olympia, on the tip of the Puget Sound, James walked back to Willapa Bay three times (a distance of 90 miles, one-way) before his parents gave in and let him stay in the forest he loves.

Today James and I walk through a young Doug fir forest, and I can't help thinking of *Star Trek,* of Mr. Spock or his more recent counterpart, Data, as James plies me with information—hundreds of plant and animal names, a rapid-fire catalog of local life-forms he has seen, too fast and too numerous for me to write down.

He interrupts himself only to impart more information, to name the Townsend chipmunk who natters at us from a nearby tree, the Wilson warbler several hundred feet above us, the western sword fern that suddenly lines both sides of the trail.

It is clear to me that James adores this forest, that he adores every bit of flora and fauna like another man might adore his Mercedes or his wife, but when I ask him to talk about his emotional investment in saving the trees he looks at me, one eyebrow raised, like an android.

I rethink my question, asking, this time, simply how it makes him feel to be inside the ancient forest, and he lowers his head and says he has no words to describe that feeling.

He smiles, suddenly less alien, more boyish, and suggests that I go into the ancient grove and see how it feels for myself.

It is June 21st, the longest day of the year. My husband and I are standing in the center of a 274-acre ancient cedar grove on 5,000-acre Long Island, the largest estuarine island on the Pacific coast. It's in the middle of 47,000-acre Willapa Bay, the most productive coastal ecosystem remaining in the United States. We have come a long way to be here: a thousand miles in a pickup truck, a four-hour paddle against the wind and the tide in a very old and rickety fiberglass canoe, and a five-mile walk down a logging road to find this large and ancient wood, which has been miraculously preserved.

Lush rain-forest vegetation covers the ground, waist-high bushes with broad, waxy leaves and red and white berries. Birds and birdsong are everywhere, as are fallen trees in various stages of decay.

We have come to this place from the desert, where magic comes from the spareness, the simplicity, the delicate balance between creatures that need almost nothing and a landscape that gives them only slightly more than what they need. But here in this rain forest there is a magic in abundance, in the way the place teems with life, swarms with life, life piled on top of life, so many life-forms trying to occupy the same space.

The four-leaf clovers are as big as daisies. The first moving creature we see is a slug as big as a hot dog.

It is the longest day of the year, and the late-afternoon light seems like it will hang on forever, unwilling to begin its six-month-long losing battle with the night.

At this time between sunset and twilight there is magic in all wild places. In the desert, night falls silently and slowly in an explosion of color in the western sky. Here it comes secretly, in deepening shades of gray and a cacophony of bird sounds, in the footfalls of deer, and in rumbles and whispers that come from the soft shapes just beyond my range of vision.

In the desert, you can watch the rain for miles as it comes toward you, watch it fall out of the sky and disappear, watch it evaporate before it falls far enough to hit the ground where you stand. In the rain forest, you can hear the rhythm of the rain on the canopy minutes before it saturates the leaves and breaks through, minutes before you feel it on your skin.

Under this canopy, it is either raining, or it has just stopped raining, or it is about to rain. And even when it is not raining the wind will rustle the trees and drops will fall from the sky, and the only way I can tell whether or not it is raining is to measure the amount of light coming under the canopy, and to wait for the clean-smelling breath of air that rides on the cusp of a storm.

When Lewis and Clark arrived in the Willapa Bay area at the end of their two-year journey, in the days when the whole region was covered with this magical forest, the rain drove them halfway insane. Their supplies turned to mildew and their clothes rotted to their bodies and they finally retreated inland and south, to winter in a region that was comparatively dry.

The largest tree my husband and I can find in this grove is a western red cedar, nearly 200 feet high and big enough around to build a comfortable house inside. A 150-foot hemlock grows right out of its roots, the two trees entwined like old friends with different natures, the cedar's branches and needles airy and hopeful, the hemlock's melancholy and sad. The roots spread their mossy fingers across the path, over and under much younger trees, and what's left of the daylight filters down through the multilayered canopy.

Night is falling on the longest day of the year, and I find myself wondering how many summer solstices these trees have seen, how many times the sun has risen and fallen in its yearly path, hitting different branches from different angles, sending the trees messages of reproduction, dormancy, and growth. I know the answer for the hemlock could be well over 500 years, for the cedar, well over a thousand.

I wonder what lucky combination of inaccessibility, placement, and latter-day preservation has saved this tree from the logging companies, when 98 percent of the old-growth timber in the Willapa region has been chopped down. I put my hand on the bark of each of the old giants. They are mossy and damp. The hemlock's trunk is surprisingly warm.

When I look way up into the top of these two trees and ask myself how anyone could cut down one of these giants, it is not simply a question of morality. This tree is so massive, so solid, so powerful and permanent that I can't imagine the saw that would go through it, can't imagine the size of the machine that would remove it, can't imagine the sound it would make as it fell, shuddering, can't imagine the size of the hole it would leave if it were gone.

And I know, then, that I am under the trees' power, because all of a sudden I can't imagine the one thing about these forests I know to be true: that thousand-year-old trees this size are felled in them every day.

We have lingered too long in this magical forest, and we are in for a dark walk back to the place where, hours before, we made camp. In the graying half-light, we take a pathway out of the ancient grove and into a grove that was harvested in the 1930s, when loggers were less efficient. Perhaps they didn't take the trees that were gnarled and twisted, perhaps they understood the forest would be healthier if not all the trees were of the same age and height, perhaps a few trees spoke to them as the one in the ancient forest spoke to me, perhaps these remaining old trees asserted their power and were spared.

For whatever reason, the 1930s cut is an only slightly dimmer, slightly less magical version of the old-growth forest. Because so many of the replanted trees are the same age, less sunlight comes through the canopy, and because of the more regular canopy, there is less undergrowth, fewer birds, and fewer signs of life.

Using the branches of a neighboring hemlock, I climb up onto the stump of a big cedar that was harvested in the '30s. It is tabletop smooth up here and, given its 60 years of exposure to the elements in the rain forest, not all that badly decayed. Four couples could dance comfortably on top of this tree trunk. Ten people could sit up here in beach chairs. The canopy rustles above me in a light breeze it won't let me feel. The rain has stopped momentarily, and for just a few moments some bright color of twilight lights the sky.

Surrounding the 1930s cut is a 1960s cut that doesn't even resemble the ancient cedar grove. It is a sickly little forest: thousands of trees all exactly the same height—Doug firs, maybe, planted for their symmetry and short maturation cycle, though they are wedged so close and thick and branchless it is almost impossible to tell.

There is no light coming through the canopy, no ground cover, no birdsong, and, except for the uniform trees that look as if they have already been harvested—that look, if I lean my head sideways, like they are already stacked in piles at the lumberyard—there are no recognizable signs of life.

We walk back the five miles along the logging roads to the camp we have made in a cedar grove on a high cliff overlooking Willapa Bay. On our walk to the ancient grove several hours ago, logging trucks dripping oil rattled past us, louder than thunder, and each truck was loaded to capacity with sweet-smelling, sap-dripping, 60-year-old trees. (Because of a deal between the logging companies and the Department of the Interior, Long Island will never be logged again. The logging companies, knowing the end is near, are working overtime, and as each truck passed us I felt its dark measure of sacrifice.)

Now, however, it is dark—rain-forest dark—and the logging ferry has been put to bed for the evening. We are alone with the creatures and the big trees, the only two humans on the island.

The forest leans over us on either side of the dirt road, and I clutch Mike's hand and swivel fast each time an animal crunches through the forest. In desert darkness that disguises nothing, I am never afraid, but these woods hold too many possibilities; there is too much room in the wet dark for my imagination.

I hear footsteps behind us, heavy and threatening, and I insist that we start singing "My Favorite Things" and "A Hundred Bottles of Beer on the Wall." I move from one song to the next almost without breathing. When we see the yellow glow of our dome tent, I am delighted to shed my wet rain gear and crawl inside.

The trees around our campsite have been logged, but haphazardly and a long time ago. The nighttime woods outside the tent windows feel more like the ancient grove than the tight, airless 1960s forest. The rain comes and goes and we sleep intermittently.

We are a few hours into the shortest night of the year when Mike touches my arm and points toward the tent's roof. A nose, black bear size, is pushing itself into the tent and sniffing. We have brought no food into the tent with us, but in an instant all the bear etiquette I've practiced so diligently in grizzly country comes back to me.

I am suddenly conscious of my toothpaste and cough drops beside me. Even my breath, heavy with lunchtime's fresh Dungeness crab, would be enough to bring a grizzly bear into the tent. We watch the nose as it makes one, two, then three circles around the tent, and then hear the soft falls of padded feet as the bear ambles away.

I am completely asleep again when the ground starts to shake and the sky splits in half and a rattling that is at the same time inside and outside of my brain awakens me. My first thought is "earthquake," but it is, in fact, only thunder.

Adrenaline washes through me and the rumble, louder and more powerful than the most spectacular summer desert thunderstorm, intensifies and diminishes, and rolls over our tent like a big tympanic wave. I catch my breath as the sweet, burnt smell of wood filters through the fly screen. We wait for the crackle of fire, the orange glow of flame that will send us running out onto the tidal mud, but this is just another night in the rain forest, and soon everyone has gone back to sleep.

We wake to a gray light not unlike the gray light of evening and the increasingly familiar sound of light rain. When we arrived by canoe at this bayside campsite the tide was (necessarily) in, lapping at the deep soil of the high bank, leaving seaweed fingers plastered to the orange soil. At this morning's low tide there is mud as far as we can see, in every direction. Mud that would suck us in above our waists and then some if we tried to walk on it, mud that will keep us on this island until the next high tide.

If the mud were solid, we could walk 15 miles to the mouth of the bay and the Pacific Ocean, 20 miles to the north bay town of Tokeland,

25 miles to the bustling port town called South Bend. But we cannot walk on the mud, and so we are happy to play around its edges, picking up the tastiest, freshest oysters in the world as if they were pebbles, cracking them open, washing them in the clear Long Island streams, and throwing them, icy cold and slippery, down our throats.

Our dented yellow canoe looks lonely and ridiculous, beached miles from the nearest water. We make a futile attempt to dry our tent between rain showers, and we watch the hawks dive for tidewater animals and a pair of golden eagles make lazy circles in the sky.

At two o'clock the tide's first wave washes in like a thought and fills a long, narrow channel between us and the Long Beach Peninsula to our west. The channel widens in what seems like time-lapse photography, in minutes the oyster beds where we feasted are covered, and after waiting all day for the tide to turn, our tethered canoe is up and floating before we can even pack our still-damp tent.

We ride the incoming tide to the end of the island but then have to turn northeast, against the tide, and paddle back to the public boat ramp where we've left our truck. The two daily tides in Willapa are not equal: The locals sound Hawaiian when they speak of the tides, which are either high-high, high-low, low-high, or low-low.

Yesterday we fought the high-low tide on the way out to the island, but today it's the high-high tide coming in on the added strength of tonight's full moon, and we make very little progress against the current.

Today, however, the prevailing wind is in our favor, and we hoist our tent's ground sheet for a sail, use our paddles as rudders, and sail the canoe on something between a run and a broad reach toward shore.

Later that day we paddle up the Niawakem, an estuarian river a little farther up the bay. An estuary is a tidewater place where the fresh water and the salt water meet. We come into the Niawakem on the saltwater tide, watching the blue tidewater mix with the brown river water a few miles upstream.

Niawakem, in Chinook, means slow-moving river, which it is, but unlike slow-moving streams in the desert, this river changes its direction four times a day, and I am disoriented by the contradictory marks of movement on the shore.

An estuary is also a breeding ground, as full of life as the ancient forest, and with plenty of magic of its own. It is a nursery that protects all varieties of young crustaceans—shrimp, lobster, crab, and crayfish—sheltering their larvae from the battering surf and hungry predators. It has plants that remove pollutants, taking them into their own systems and making the water more pure. It is the place where young salmon undergo the physiological transformations that allow them to make the change to salt water from fresh. Here they change color, they change the osmotic capabilities of their skin (what once only let fresh water in must now let salt water out), and they receive the estuary's imprint, so that many years later, when they have calculated their return using tide and temperature and daylight patterns, the right amount of seasons gone by, they will smell the fresh water of their particular estuary and know that it is time to come home.

The tides in Willapa Bay give life a constant rhythm, a daily symphony in four parts, and everyone who stays here—the tourists, the oysterers, the fishers, even the man who ferries the logging trucks—has to respect the water's movement.

We paddle up the Niawakem as far as the now-outgoing tide will allow us. A field full of elk raise their heads at us. We decide to listen as the water speaks to us and tells us it is time for us, too, to go home.

Tonight we will stay in Tokeland, at a friendly, weathered old inn that feels, I have to admit, as much a part of Willapa as the ancient trees. Tomorrow we will start the drive back to the desert, and our clothes, our tent, and our skin will dry in increments as we leave this watery place behind. We'll tell our friends about the black bear's visit, the wild clap of thunder, the icy sweetness of the oysters, the serenity and power of the ancient trees.

We will be back home in the desert, but the rain forest, its watery raging fullness, will come to us often, timeless, in our dreams.

In the ancient grove, the sun is filtering through the cedar branches like spiderwebs, a red-breasted nuthatch is collecting berries, the branches of the hemlocks are rustling lightly in an afternoon breeze. A small herd of Roosevelt elk is moving through the ancient grove to the meadows where they graze each evening. A black bear argues the toss with a swarm of honeybees who have made their comb at bear's-eye level. A pileated woodpecker rattles the bark of a grandfather cedar. A dark-eyed junco sings from the branches of a Sitka spruce. Above the symphony, above the canopy, thunder rolls in from the Pacific, louder now than the thunder of the logging trucks, louder even than the crash of the falling trees. Somewhere on the island, Walking James has just discovered a new species of butterfly. Any minute now it will begin to rain.

TRIP NOTES

Willapa Bay is a large estuary in the southwest corner of Washington state, just above the mouth of the Columbia River. The shallow bay waters receive ocean tides and outflow from several streams, creating an environment rich in life and relatively pristine. Some natural areas worth checking out include the beaches of Leadbetter Point, the old-growth forest on Long Island, the dirt roads that traverse Willapa National Wildlife Refuge on the south end of the bay, and the estuaries of the rivers, like the Niawakem, which extend the bay waters far inland.

Such natural areas are scattered between patches of land owned by the timber companies, the cranberry farmers, the fishers, and the tourist industry.

When to go

Willapa Bay is a maritime site, separated from the North Pacific Ocean by a very narrow strip of land. The most predictably decent weather for humans is late spring through early fall. However, one of the best periods for seeing wildlife is winter. Great clouds of brant, Canada geese, and ducks on their annual migrations raft on the bay and area ponds, while shorebirds wade the tide flats. A visit during clear winter weather—if you time it carefully—can combine the best of both seasons.

How to go

There are three important modes of transport in the Willapa Bay area: by foot, by small boat, and by auto. Your car will take you to the town of Ilwaco at the base of the Long Beach Peninsula. A two-mile drive west will take you to the state park; a 20-mile drive north brings you out to the north end of the peninsula. There are short hiking trails in both places. (None of the hiking trails around Willapa are long.)

You must provide your own boat transport to Long Island. A booklet of local tides (available at most bait and tackle stores) will help you figure out the best times to travel. Boat-launching facilities are located at Nahcotta Mooring

Basin and on Highway 101 near the refuge headquarters.

Be careful not to block the private ferry facility, and do not use the refuge dock on the island. Moor your boat carefully to the shore, in full awareness of fluctuating tides.

Where to go

There are four main destinations in the vicinity of Willapa Bay:

• **Fort Canby State Park,** two miles west of the town of Ilwaco, was established on the site of a fortification named for a general who was a casualty in California's Modoc War. It's a 1,880-acre park with 250 campsites. Sixty of these have full hookups, and 27 have water and electricity; the rest are equipped with barbecues and tables. The rest rooms have hot showers. Park beaches can be used for digging clams during spring low tides. There are a number of short hiking trails to the lighthouse and old fortifications; the most interesting is the 1.5-mile Coastal Forest Trail, which circles through a grove that remains essentially as it was during the visit of Lewis and Clark, two centuries ago. Contact the park at P.O. Box 488, Ilwaco, WA 98624; (360) 642-3078.

• **Leadbetter Point State Park Natural Area,** managed for daylight visits only, is at the north end of the Long Beach Peninsula. (Fort Canby State Park is at the southern end.) The skinny peninsula forms the western shore of Willapa Bay. A broad area of sand dunes, grasslands, marshes, and forest, Leadbetter is jointly administered by the state parks and Willapa National Wildlife Refuge. For more information, contact Fort Canby State Park at P.O. Box 488, Ilwaco, WA 98624; (360) 642-3078.

• **The Lewis & Clark Interpretive Center,** located in Fort Canby, is a multimedia center designed to help park visitors understand the great exploratory expedition of Meriwether Lewis and William Clark, which departed Illinois in 1804 and journeyed through uncharted wilderness to the mouth of the Columbia River. The center is three miles west of Ilwaco, on a high bluff on Cape Disappointment—the western terminus of the great Lewis and Clark adventure. Contact the center by calling (360) 642-3029.

• **Willapa National Wildlife Refuge** was established in 1937 to save parts of the area's ecology that were being damaged by the land-use practices of the time. Besides the bay itself and Leadbetter Point at the tip of Long Beach Peninsula, the refuge includes three other "units." The only way to get around on the 11,000 acres of refuge land is by foot. (360) 484-3482.

Other areas worth exploring include:

• **Long Island,** at 5,000 acres, is the largest estuarine island on the West Coast. Home to black-tailed deer, black bear, Roosevelt elk, grouse, and beaver, it also holds a 300-acre remnant of the virgin red cedar that covered the island

WILD PLACES

at one time. Logging has been discontinued, and the plan is to let natural regeneration hold sway on the rest of the island. Camping is allowed only at five primitive campgrounds around the perimeter, available on a first-come, first-served basis. You must provide your own transport to the island.

- **Lewis Unit**, at the south end of Willapa Bay, is an area of freshwater marsh, popular with waterfowl.

- **Riekkola Unit**, also at Willapa Bay's south end, is an area of grasslands, popular with wild geese.

For information, contact the manager at Willapa National Wildlife Refuge, Ilwaco, WA 98624; (360) 484-3482.

What to bring

Come prepared for maritime weather, even in summer. That means bring wind- and rainproof outer clothing shells to deal with fog and wet weather, and sunscreen and hats for the bright days. Binoculars and a field guide to birds of the Pacific Northwest will prove welcome assets, too.

Additional information

A bird-watcher's checklist is available from the Willapa National Wildlife Refuge (see the address at left).

The shoreline is a mélange of private and public property. Some areas are closed to public harvest of oysters and clams. For regulations, call the State Shellfish Lab in Nahcotta at (360) 665-4166.

WYOMING WILDERNESS

17

The Source
of a River

by Gretel Ehrlich

It's morning in the Absaroka Mountains. The word *absaroka* means "raven" in the Crow language, though I've seen no ravens in three days. Last night I slept with my head butted against an Engelmann spruce, and when I woke, it was a many-armed goddess swinging around and around. The trunk is bigger than an elephant's leg. I stick my nose against it. Tiny opals of sap stick to my cheeks where the bark breaks up, textured: red and gray, coarse and smooth, wet and flaked.

I'm looking for the source of the Yellowstone River, and as we make the daylong ascent from a valley, I think about walking and wilderness. We use the word *wilderness*, but perhaps we mean *wildness*. Isn't that why I've come here, to seek the wildness in myself and, in so doing, come upon the wildness every-where, because after all, I'm part of nature, too?

Following the coastline of the lake, I watch how the wind picks up water in dark blasts and drops it again. Ducks glide in Vs away from me, out onto the fractured, darkening mirror. I stop. A hatch of may-flies powders the air, and the archaic, straight-winged dragonflies hang blunt-nosed above me. A friend talks about aquatic bugs: water beetles, spinners, assassin bugs, and one that hatches, mates, and dies in a total life span of two hours. At the end of the meadow, the lake drains into a fast-moving creek. I quicken my pace and trudge upward. Walk-ing is almost an ambulation of mind. The human armor of bones rattles, fat rolls, and inside this durable, fleshy prison of mine, I make a bee-line toward otherness, lightness, like a moth toward flame.

Somewhere along the trail I laugh out loud. How shell-like the body seems suddenly—not fleshy at all, but inhuman and hard. And farther up, I step out of my skin, though I'm still held fast by something, but what? I don't know.

How foolish the preparations for wilderness trips seem just now. We pore over maps, chart our expeditions. We "gear up" at trailheads with pitons and crampons, horse packs and backpacks, fly rods and cameras, forgetting the meaning of simply going, the mechanics of disburdenment. I look up from these thoughts; a blue heron rises from a gravel bar, glides behind a gray screen of dead trees, appears in an opening where an avalanche downed pines, and lands again on water.

I stop to eat lunch. Emerson wrote, "The Gautama said that the first men ate the earth and found it sweet." I eat bologna and cheese and think about eating dirt. At this moment the mouth frames won-der, its width stands for the generous palate of consciousness. I cleanse my taste buds with miner's lettuce and stream water and try to imag-ine what kinds of sweetness the earth provides: the taste of glacial flour or the mineral taste of basalt, the fresh and foul bouquets of riv-ers, the desiccated, stinging flavor of a snowflake.

As I begin to walk again, it occurs to me that this notion of eating the earth is not about gluttony but about unconditional love, an ac-ceptance of whatever taste comes across my tongue: flesh, wine, the unremarkable flavor of dirt. To find wildness, I must first offer myself up, accept all that comes before me: a bullfrog breathing hard on a rock; moose tracks under elk scats; a cloud that looks like a clothespin; a seep of water from a high cirque, black on brown rock, draining down from the brain of the world.

At tree line, birdsong stops. I'm lifted into a movement of music with no particular notes, only wind sounds becoming water sounds, becoming wind sounds. Above, a cornice crowns a ridge and melts into a teal-and-turquoise lake, which, like a bladder, leaks its alchemical potions.

On top of Marston Pass I'm in a ruck of steep valleys and gray, treeless peaks. The alpine carpet, studded with red paintbrush and alpine buttercups, gives way to rock. Now, all the way across a valley I see where water oozes from moss and mud—how, at its source, it quickly becomes a river.

Emerson also said, "Every natural fact is an emanation, and that from which it emanates is an emanation also, and from every emanation is a new emanation." The ooze, the source of a great river, is now a white chute tumbling over brown bellies of conglomerate rock. Wind throws sheets of water to another part of the mountainside; soft earth gives way under my feet; clouds spill upward and spit rain. Isn't everything redolent of loss, with momentary radiance, a coming to different ground? Stone basins catch the waterfall, spill it again; thoughts and desires strung together are laddered down.

I see where meltwater is split by rock—half going west to the Pacific, the other going east to the Atlantic, for this is the Continental Divide. Down the other side, the air I gulp feels softer. Ice bridges the creek when night comes; before the full moon, falling stars have the same look as water falling against the rock of night.

To rise above tree line is to go above thought, and afterward, to descend back into birdsong, bog orchids, willows, and firs is to sink into the preliterate parts of ourselves. It is to forget discontent, undisciplined needs. Here, the world is only space, raw loneliness, green valleys hung vertically. Losing myself to it—if I can—I do not fall . . . or if I do, I'm only another cataract of water.

Wildness has no conditions, no sure routes, no peaks or goals, no source that is not instantly becoming something more than itself, then letting go of that, always becoming. It cannot be stripped of its complexity by CAT scan or telescope. Rather, it is a many-pointed truth, almost a bluntness, a sudden essence like the wild strawberries strung on scarlet runners under my feet. For half a mile, on hands and knees, I eat and eat. Wildness is source and fruition at once, as if this river circled around, mouth eating tail and tail eating source.

Now I am camped among trees again. Four yearling moose, their chestnut coats shiny from a summer's diet of willow shoots, tramp past my bedroll and drink from a spring that issues sulfurous water. The ooze, the white chute, the narrow stream—now almost a river— joins this small spring and slows into skinny oxbows and deep pools before breaking again on rock, down a stepladder of sequined riffles.

To trace the history of a river or a raindrop, as John Muir would have done, is also to trace the history of the soul, the history of the mind descending and arising in the body. In both, we constantly seek and stumble on divinity, which, like the cornice feeding the lake, and the spring becoming a waterfall, feeds, spills, falls, and feeds itself over and over again.

TRIP NOTES

The headwaters of the Yellowstone River lie deep within the Teton Wilderness, a federally designated wilderness area in the Absaroka Range, administered by the Black Rock ranger station of the Bridger-Teton National Forest. That area is north of the town of Dubois, Wyoming. The source of any river, great or small, can be barely recognizable: just an ooze of water from a marshy slope. It takes close study of high-resolution USGS maps to determine even the rough location of a source. The head of the Yellowstone is high up a steep slope of Yellow Mountain. No trail leads to it; no signposts mark the spot. It lies far to the southeast of the boundaries of Yellowstone National Park. After the trickle becomes a river, miles below the source, its cool meanderings are scenic and beautiful.

When to go

The months of July and August, during low-to-moderate snow years, are the only times when it is feasible to ride through the Teton Wilderness.

How to go

The traditional and most effective way to get around in these high, large, and remote mountain wildernesses is with a packhorse and guide. Some recommended outfitters in the general area include:

- **Ed Edmonston.** He offers progressive trips, and works in partnership with outfitter Bob Johnson. (307) 733-6557.

- **Grant Gertsch.** This travel guide stays just a few nights in each camp, covering a lot of ground in the Teton Wilderness. (307) 733-1985.

- **Jiggs Black.** He offers progressive trips, with a permitted base for fall hunting. (307) 856-3047.

- **K Bar Z Ranch.** Located near the Clarks Fork River, this outfitter has a permitted backcountry base camp. (307) 587-4410.

- **Press Stephens.** In summer, write to Stephens at: Dubois, WY 82420; in winter, write to him at: Shell, WY 82441; or call (307) 765-4377.

- **Squaw Creek Ranch and Outfitters.** This organization also has a permitted base. (307) 587-6178.

For a directory of other guide services, call the Wyoming Outfitters and Guides Association at (307) 527-7453.

Where to go

Yellowstone National Park is embraced on all sides by large national forests. Bridger-Teton lies to the south, Targhee and Beaverhead to the west, Gallatin to the north, Custer to the northeast, and Shoshone to the east and southeast. Each of the six federal wildernesses described in the following list are, like the Teton, on the east side of the park; all except the Teton Wilderness are in the Shoshone National Forest. To find out about wildernesses in the other forests, call the appropriate forest headquarters (see "Additional information" on the following page).

- **Absaroka-Beartooth Wilderness.** 23,283 acres in Wyoming and 921,465 acres in Montana, with 900 miles of trails. Call (406) 587-6701.

- **Fitzpatrick Wilderness.** 198,525 acres of rugged grandeur, culminating at 13,804-foot Gannett Peak, the highest point in Wyoming. The wilderness holds 95 miles of trails; the lowest trailhead elevation is 7,600 feet. The area has 44 active glaciers. Call the Washakie Ranger District at (307) 332-5460.

- **North Absaroka Wilderness.** 350,488 acres in Wyoming, with 217 miles of maintained trails. The terrain has rough, volcanic mountains generally ranging in elevation from 7,000 to 11,000 feet; springs and lakes are rare. Call the Wapiti Ranger District at (307) 527-6921.

- **Popo Agie Wilderness.** 101,870 acres, east of the Continental Divide in the Wind River Range. Wind River Peak, at 13,192 feet, is the highest point; the lowest elevation is 8,540 feet. There are more than 300 ponds and lakes and 100 miles of trails. Call the Washakie Ranger District at (307) 332-5460.

- **Teton Wilderness.** 585,468 acres, ranging in elevation from 12,165-foot-high Yount's Peak to a trailhead at 6,900 feet. The area is laced with 450 miles of trails, many of them impeded by a 1987 "blowdown" (windstorm) and a 1988 forest fire. The wilderness includes 11,485-foot-high Yellow Mountain; the source of the Yellowstone River lies high on its western flank. This wilderness has many high plateaus and wide valleys and is particularly well suited to horse packing. Call the Buffalo Ranger District at (307) 543-2386.

- **Washakie Wilderness.** 704,529 acres in Wyoming, sprawling across three national forest ranger districts in the southern Absaroka Mountains. Elevations range from 6,600 to 13,153 feet. The terrain is fissured with many deep, narrow valleys; about 50 percent of it is tree-covered. There are about 400 miles of trails. Call the Wapiti Ranger District at (307) 527-6921.

What to bring

Most outfitters will take care of all necessary camp and riding equipment and ask only that you bring personal gear and a sleeping bag (a bag rated to 20 degrees Fahrenheit is suitable for most summer conditions). For riding, good, durable clothing of cotton canvas is suitable; bring synthetic insulating garments to stay warm, and a water- and windproof outer shell layer. A big hat and sunglasses to screen out intense high-altitude sunlight are wise, as is a high-SPF sunscreen. Riders may wish to bring thin leather gloves. And it would be smart to pack several pairs of pantyhose: For men or women, wearing pantyhose under a pair of jeans reduces the friction and leg-hair pulling associated with long horseback rides. (Even longtime wranglers, when pressed, admit they use this trick.) Also, bring a strong mosquito repellent (and it's a good idea to test it out first for a possible skin reaction).

Additional information

Wilderness means often-rugged natural terrain where elemental forces are more unsheathed than usual and human visitors must take care of themselves. A national park, in contrast, is more managed and provides more services for visitors. For information about the 2.2-million-acre Yellowstone, created as the nation's first national park in 1872, call (307) 344-7381.

For information about wilderness areas in other, adjacent national forests, call: Bridger-Teton, (307) 739-5500; Targhee, (208) 624-3151; Beaverhead, (406) 683-3900; Gallatin, (406) 587-6701; or Custer, (406) 657-6361.

THE TATSHENSHINI RIVER OF THE YUKON AND ALASKA

Ursus Major

by Paul McHugh

These grizzly paw prints are still fresh, and quite large. They sink deeply into the wet sand along the shore of a still pond. They go much deeper than the footprints of a human. The forepaws are two inches wider than my spread fingers.

Foolishly, perhaps, I follow the fresh tracks up onto the the final bulge of a glacial moraine that forms one bank of the Tatshenshini River. This place forms a topographic nexus where the Walker and many other glaciers, both Alaskan and Yukon, add icy melt-off to the river's tawny, churning currents.

The grizzly tracks saunter up to a vantage point above five beached whitewater rafts and our little village of dome tents.

Excitement arises like flame in my blood. I realize the bear probably watched us make camp from this very spot.

Back down on wet sand below the hillock, the imprints are now extremely crisp. One paw has crushed a small plant down into the sand. I kneel to see if any of the plant's juices or fibers are discolored by time, and as I do, *Sproing!* the stem and crushed leaves slowly shake off grains of sand and magically rise up in the center of the imprint of the giant forepaw.

My brain reels. All hair on my body bristles. Electric waves of adrenaline wash down my arms and up the back of my neck. I'm perhaps a minute, perhaps less, behind this monarch of the wilderness. I'd love glimpsing an *Ursus arctos horribilis*—from a distance. The very last thing I want to do is surprise a bear in riparian brush, or climb straight up his backside while tracking him.

Alaska is bear country, some of the last and best of it. There are Kodiak, or coastal brown bears; grizzlies, or inland brown bears; big versions of *Ursus americanus,* the black bear; and even a fabulous variation called the glacier blue bear. Along the northern coast, where pack ice jams against the shore in the long arctic winters, the white polar bear rules supreme.

If you fly into Alaska and land at Juneau, one of the first sights to greet you as you deplane is an eight-foot-high stuffed polar bear, jaws open and forearms and claws outstretched, standing right next to a sign that reads, "Welcome to Juneau." This shows sourdough humor is alive and well in the late twentieth century.

Of course, the fact that he's standing in an airport hallway is what makes the apparition funny. Put that same polar bear, alive and snarling, on an ice floe 20 yards distant from your knocking knees, and you'd find a chuckle harder to summon.

Nature writer and raconteur Ed Abbey once observed, "Wilderness can be defined as a place where humans enjoy the opportunity of being attacked by a wild animal." The 25 million acres of arctic nature preserves surrounding the Tatshenshini River qualify, in spades. But in part because there's so much habitat sprawling every which way, and because there's so much natural food available, combative confrontation between brown bears and humans is infrequent. Sightings, however, are common.

And that's fortunate. No one from either species has to get destroyed.

These big brown bears up north are the same species as the grizzlies that once ranged down the Pacific Coast into California—although the only ones remaining in the Golden State are silhouettes on the state flag. (The last grizz' in California may have been one poisoned by ranchers on the hillsides above Round Valley near the turn of the century.) The fur color of these so-called brown bears can actually vary from light blond to jet black. Up here, in their final stronghold, the coastal bears (commonly called Alaska brown bears) grow extremely large, due to ample food supply—mostly spawning salmon—and sometimes exceed half a ton in weight. Inland bears (commonly called grizzlies) are smaller. The Tatshenshini and Alsek river corridors together constitute most of the widespread and natural brown bear habitat that remains on earth.

Most brown bear charges on humans are "bluff charges"—slobbering, tooth-popping rushes that come within a distance of about 10 feet. These are designed to establish turf and express dominance. If the human does not turn and flee in blind panic, the primary damage will be the laundry bill for soiled trousers. Still, the idea of standing face to face with a half-ton of hurtling, ursine territorial outrage, equipped, on its cutting edge, with three-inch teeth and six-inch claws, is not, on the face of it, attractive—even as a consummate wilderness experience.

These days, the well-equipped visitor to arctic bear country traipses about with a spray can of Alaska Magnum, a capsicum pepper spray about twice as strong as those used to repel your garden-variety mugger in the lower 48. Although these sprays have been proven effective, something still seems wildly optimistic to me about squirting out some yellow mist to deter the onrush of a hairy, fanged locomotive.

One fantasizes that it would be better just to hose down your own body with the pepper spray, in a forlorn hope that the northern bear may harbor at least a mild distaste for "long pig tacos."

On this particular day, unequipped as I was with even a can of pepper spray for tentative counterargument, I pulled myself away from the fresh track of the big bear after following him or her for less than a mile.

My imagination was on overload; it was time to back off. To go sit in the cool winds hustling off the Walker Glacier, and breathe deeply of the scents of spruce and alder. Slow a pounding heart and a busy brain, and simply savor the wonder and privilege of being here, in a canyon of North America's wildest river.

The Tatshenshini corridor is truly a forest primeval, some of the last and best of what remains on earth. The Tatshenshini and Alsek Rivers, both before and after they join, drain some of the roughest peaks in Canada's Yukon, tumbling past many unnamed mountains, trackless forests, and the sapphire seracs of huge glaciers, en route to frigid seas off Yakutat in Alaska's panhandle.

Yet more than these elements make it a place where a lover of wilderness can draw a deep breath. An abiding sense of peace derives from the fact that it is now protected about as well as a major landmass can be by human law. There's a reasonable certainty it can stay in a pristine state through the next millennium.

Let your mind dwell on the fact that the 2.3-million-acre Tatshenshini-Alsek Provincial Park comprises just one, single corner of a gigantic, rough quadrangle of wildlands that's now saved from development. This protected quadrangle includes Kluane National Park in the Yukon and, just within the U.S. border, Wrangell–Saint Elias and Glacier Bay National Parks. The net result: a remarkable, 25-million-acre preserve straddling the U.S.-Canada border. Some consider this a harbinger of international cooperation on other ecosystems that sprawl across borders. Which, of course, means most of them.

A sense of immersion seems pivotal to a true wilderness outing, so it's fitting that I am joining a group of eight visitors to be professionally guided down the "Tat" on a two-week raft trip. It's the summer of 1993, just weeks after some of the planet's most pristine wild turf has been declared the Tatshenshini-Alsek park by the provincial government of British Columbia. I'm awed to feel myself rediscovering a visceral glee I have not known since I was a young boy, growing up at the edge of the Everglades. I feel I am about to peer once again into the deep green eyes of nature's God.

Many find a Tat trip to be among the two or three most exotic and wondrous whitewater voyages possible on the globe. Our chief guide is outfitter James Katz from James Henry River Journeys of Bolinas, California. He's one of those who've worked on the Tat the longest. Katz is a study in contrasts: a bookish intellectual who's most at home with a pair of long raft oars in his callused palms; a seemingly sober man who will suddenly erupt in a string of jokes spiced with Yiddish idiom.

Back in 1972, Katz bolted from the University of Colorado just one day before entering law school, then hitchhiked out to California with a new friend he'd just met at an Orange Julius stand. After his apprenticeship rowing dories down the Grand Canyon, plus a few other whitewater gigs, Katz founded his own river-running outfit.

"I've found true liberty comes from being where the environment is wild and intact," he says. "We are most ourselves where we live instinctually. Where we lose ourselves in a fabric of life the way it was centuries ago. I like trips that are real adventures."

That quest has brought him close to the Arctic Circle. Specializing in rivers of the north—the more remote the better—Katz likes to victual his voyages with insight. On this trip, he has hit pay dirt by inviting along two proxies: Nora Dauenhauer, a full-blooded Tlingit and tribal elder who grew up on the Alaskan coast, and her husband, Richard Dauenhauer, a teacher and the former poet laureate of Alaska.

As our shuttle van departs from the Alaskan frontier town of Haines, climbing toward our put-in in Canada's Yukon, the Dauenhauers lead all of us in a Tlingit paddling chant. *"Hue, hue, we-ah yah hey. . . ."* Ancient, rhythmic syllables resonate inside the vehicle's metal walls.

Outside our van, lush bottomlands of the Chilkat River, the former suzerainty of the Tlingit, slide by. Nora recalls fishing with her family all up and down the wild coast. Her first intimation that the old ways were destined for oblivion came the day her family returned to their hand-split, shake-shingle smokehouses and found they'd been leveled and replaced by Standard Oil storage tanks.

"Nobody asked us," Nora says, as we bump along the forest road. "They just mowed them down. All of a sudden, some guys said they were in charge, and we could no longer come ashore."

A putative cure for dispossession of native peoples was the Alaska Claims Settlement Act of 1971, which divided $962.5 million and 44 million acres of land among 13 native-owned regional corporations. Individuals got shares in these corporations and—supposedly—some say in how the businesses would be run.

"The only way they'd give us anything," Nora says tartly, "was if we'd start thinking and acting like white men."

Instead, Nora devoted herself to saving a spiritual side of her heritage: the legends and stories, dances and songs of her people. Such a crusade is also her birthright. The Tlingit are a matrilineal society. By tradition, property—especially ceremonial objects, capes, coppers, and robes—gets handed down along the female line. Through her work and studies, Nora met and married Richard, a professor of anthropology who had grown enamored of Tlingit culture. They now seem devoted and inseparable.

The tree line in the Yukon is low, around 4,000 feet. Up higher, the long ridges grow swathed with a beige plush of tundra, stunted forest, and matted grasses, a rumpled palimpsest for ice sheets that withdrew a scant 10,000 years ago. To reach the start of our Tat expedition, we descend from this tundra zone into a broad canyon upholstered with alder, aspen, and balsam poplar. Here, the rotted log cabins of Dalton Post—a trade center in Gold Rush days—sag drunkenly into moss and a riot of wildflowers.

Waiting for us at the put-in is Marge Jackson, a snowy-maned, copper-skinned elder of the Champagne-Aishihiks. The first name of this trading area, she tells us, was *Sha'washe*. "Our people came here for centuries to fish for Pacific sockeye salmon and for trading," Marge says. "Jack Dalton (a famed Gold Rush scam artist) was here only three years. Now the place is named for him."

Jackson's voice conveys amusement.

Recently, the Champagne-Aishihik people won a government settlement, giving them legal title to 937 square miles of land (4 percent of their historic acreage); they've also been invited to join in managing nearby Kluane National Park. A similar agreement is pending for parklands in the province of British Columbia.

So these days people from Marge's band greet all rafting parties. It's a way to gradually reassert a role in their ancestral lands. To celebrate Nora's arrival to a trading center where her forebears once traveled, Marge Jackson brings a special gift: a dried Tatshenshini sockeye salmon from her smokehouse. She quietly presents the fish to Nora, elder of the Raven House of the Sockeye Salmon Clan of the Raven Moiety of the Tlingit People.

This encounter between the two female elders is their first. Yet they both know the same ancient trading tunes, sung by ancestors who once met here. On this bright day of blue sky and bronze light, a modern raft trip reestablishes an old link between native peoples.

In return, our native guides help us understand the spirit of those who've gone before, and expand our view of the powers that surface in this wilderness and its denizens.

Almost immediately, upon setting out, we see *Tch'auk,* the bald eagle, perched on an instream snag. Mere yards away, he watches our five rafts sweep by into the Yukon wilderness with the cool aplomb of an experienced border guard. No need to check our documents; the point of a Tat trip is to leave such detritus of civilization behind. He looks us in the eye perhaps only to ensure that we have done so.

Overwhelmingly, impressions of the Tatshenshini's wilderness are of deep, elemental purity and of an unconquerable swiftness. Day flows easily into night and into the next two days as we float downstream, our course gradually bending from north to west to south, shooting down a deep canyon that breaches the Alsek and Carmine Ranges. We are no longer manacled to wristwatches, but cradled and upheld in a river's rhythm.

At night, a campfire crackles and shadows leap between knots of rafters who gather around the tiny red spark, sipping whiskey and talking of their old life and the new sensations they are discovering out here.

Near midnight, green iridescent writing is scrawled across the darkness as the northern lights writhe into visibility from the void. The sight fills me with rapture, though the meaning of this skywriting is hard to grasp. It feels as though the aurora borealis *should* make a sound—a musical blend of steel drum, xylophone, and synthesizer, perhaps. Yet, frustratingly, they remain mute.

I do notice that the writing in my notebook from this point on degenerates into more of a loopy scrawl. What am I trying to capture, fence, or suggest with the mimicry in this inky snare?

At dawn, the shaggy white shapes on the highest slopes are wild mountain goats. Eagles stare fiercely from branches, then take flight with what feels like languid insolence—their certainty axiomatic that this realm is theirs. Out here, humans are neither threat nor prey, so most of the eagles barely deign to notice us.

Katz returns the compliment. So many mature bald eagles sweep by to land on spruce snags that he jokes, "There goes another golf ball. . . ."

We've camped one night upriver, two nights at the broad flats of Sediment Creek—performing a day hike up the brow of a tall hill until we reach high tundra, wolf tracks, and incredible alpine panoramas. Then we launch again upon the twisting brown skein of the Tatshenshini. It continues to heave in turbulence down a canyon of slate, and to bend south between the Carmine and Alsek Mountains —rough sawteeth that claw up into a blue sky fretted with white scratches of cirrus.

"To go down the Tatshenshini is to listen to theme music from the film *2001*, played very slowly," says Tom Meckfessel, one of Katz's crew of lean river guides. We round endless river bends, awestruck, drifting through a succession of calendar-photo fantasy vistas, like Alice diving through looking glass after looking glass.

Almost hourly, on the fourth day after our launch, the river seems to double its flow, reaching 40,000 cubic feet per second ("cfs" is a standard measure of river flow) as major side-streams such as the O'Connor add chocolate whirls and whorls of tribute.

The turbid water reminds me of a pioneer description of the sediment-laden, undammed Colorado: "too thin to plow, too thick to drink." However, in addition to thick, this water is extremely cold. By the time we reach the glacier runoff from the Saint Elias Range, Katz tells us, it will have a temperature of 33, just one degree above freezing. We're talking a canyon full of Yoo-Hoo straight from the icebox.

We are swallowed by the scale of the river and mountains, wrapped up and swept away.

Gusts of untamed wind twirl dust devils off midstream gravel bars. As both wind and the river currents mount, our rafts sometimes feel like hapless pucks in a hockey war, batted about between harsh up-canyon blasts of air and the river's unyielding push to the sea.

A sense of ecstatic surrender grows in my heart. Yes, we could die out here. Yet this would happen, should it occur, in the lap of nature, my green God, and I know there would be no ultimate harm.

It seems surreal that an open-pit mine was once aimed, like a dagger, for the heart of this place. A Canadian consortium, Geddes Resources, plotted that project for Windy Craggy Peak, a mountain at the nexus where the Alsek and Tatshenshini knot their mingling currents.

Had it been built, 124 million tons of tailings and 100 million tons of acid waste rock would have been piled behind two earth-fill dams—in a spot between the Denali and Fairweather Faults that once rumbaed in our continent's strongest recorded earthquake. That 8.6 Richter-scale bell-ringer in 1899 added some 50 feet of altitude to the local peaks in one shot, and squirted huge glaciers a half mile forward in five minutes. It could easily happen again.

Had the mine gone in and those dams failed in a temblor, a toxic slurry would have deluged these pristine rivers, which comprise one of the three most productive wild salmon systems in the Pacific Northwest. Naturally, the toxic curse would have reverberated up the food chain, striking at the eagles and brown bears.

The decision to reject this mining scheme and establish a wilderness park involved such major geopolitical players as British Columbia Premier Mike Harcourt, U.S. Vice President Al Gore, and U.S. Congressman George Miller.

It's clear that an epochal agreement has been forged. The 25-million-acre biosphere preserve created by the new Tatshenshini-Alsek Provincial Park, in combination with Kluane National Park and two Alaskan national parks, is the largest managed wilderness on the globe. It was named a World Heritage Site by UNESCO—the strongest preservation status the United Nations can afford.

"Conservationists fight against impossible odds," muses Rick Careless, a Canadian ecologist whose work was pivotal in saving the Tat.

"Big victories come so seldom, we've got to savor this achievement. If we're to survive on this planet," he adds, "we must establish a network of very large preserves, all around the globe. At best, we'll probably wind up with a half dozen."

We find the place where the Tat meets the Alsek on our fifth day, and as these two mighty streams mingle, the flow grows astronomic. The river's now a behemoth of 100,000 cfs, like the Mississippi, like the Colorado in full flood.

The words of poet T. S. Eliot spring to mind: "I don't know much about gods; but I think that the river is a strong brown god—sullen, untamed, and intractable."

Two days of layover on the broad delta at this confluence give the wilderness a chance to seep further into our bones. I want it to penetrate even deeper. I leave the golden domes of the North Face VE24 expedition tents—an assemblage that Katz dubs River City—to go for a long walk alone in the stunted forest. I cover miles of ground, using my compass, yelling out "Ho, bear!" every few steps to give the grizzlies a chance to avoid me. The cry gradually blends into the tempo of walking, like my heartbeat and breathing. Part of me, however, does not wish for the bears' complete avoidance. I think I'd like to glimpse just one while strolling through their home. . . .

Oceanlike waves pound against the bows of our rafts on the seventh day, nearly defeating all forward progress. We swing around a corner where the river carves irresistibly through the Saint Elias Range. There ascends the immense sprawl of the Walker Glacier, a blue jumble of jagged seracs tumbling into a smooth white fan of ice that pours down between green mountains into the brown river.

This wilderness is so vast, its elemental power so unrelenting, that it boggles the human mind. I can feel it disrupting my normal patterns of thought and socialization. It gets very hard to write. The notebook scrawl seems trivial beside the grandeur I attempt to record. I'm casting a bolo of thread around the ankles of the grizzly.

The river guides expect such effects. To some degree, they foster them. They want the soul of the wild world to ignite behind the eyes of their guests. And they also stand ready to buffer this sea change, to reel back into the fold those folks who lose their grounding, who begin to spin off into fears of the primal.

This feat entails many skills. For instance, 10 days out, the guides are still able to dip into ice chests and pull out near-gourmet meals like magicians releasing doves from their sleeves. But for dealing head-on with that sense of the vastly nonhuman and surreal, their main antidote is clownish humor. At this, none excels more than "Mothra," a.k.a. Mark Lorenzen, who's given to stunts such as twirling a can opener on one side of a breakfast egg, then expressing befuddlement when it fails to open. One morning, he rejects Chapstick in favor of crimson lipstick borrowed from one of the ladies, then spends the rest of that day making shameless, pouting moues from his perch atop a rowing seat.

At the Walker Glacier, led by the guides, we bushwhack up a bear trail that leads to a high, flowered knoll, which overlooks all compacted snowfall from millennia past. After hiking back down on the glacier itself, we prop each other up on the slick ice as we gaze down into deep crevasses, looking into the glacier's sapphire heart.

"Your senses get completely engulfed by arctic wilderness," says fellow rafter Mary Marcus. She says that being a Hewlett-Packard process analyst from Roseville, California, may be what she does for a living, but it's not what she does to live.

"You're tantalized by the vibrant colors of flowers, all the smells in the air," she adds. "Beyond that is the vastness, all this majesty of peaks and glaciers. It's a landscape of the imagination, almost like a cheap piece of romantic art painted on velvet, something that I would never buy. Yet out here, it's real. And I feel humble to find myself in the midst of it."

Something has shifted inside all of us. The primal strength, the awesome beauty, the profound wilderness have worn away barriers and loosely bound us all—guides and guided—into a sort of tribe. The soft voices of the Dauenhauers—Richard reading his poetry of animals and Alaska, Nora relating legends and songs from her people—remind us that this tribe is much larger than our immediate company.

We hear of *Yaelth,* or Raven, who stole water from *Ganook,* the Petrel, and eventually escaped through the smoke-hole of Petrel's lodge to bring fresh, sweet water to all peoples of the earth. We hear how Tlingit ancestors poled and dragged cottonwood dugouts upriver for the epic journeys to those trading centers far inland—and then, on their return, dared to paddle through tunnels under the ice when they found that glaciers blocked their way. And we hear how once a young girl broke a taboo focusing on respect for the great bears, only to discover her fate was now to marry a bear, and then to become one. . . .

As we lay over for a few days at the Walker, camped on a moraine at its base, more passengers discuss their passages.

"This is a life trip for me," says Richard Dauenhauer's brother Tom, an FBI agent from Washington. "It's beyond anything I ever imagined. It's going to be very hard for me to go back to the office."

Jane Schmidt, a horse packer for the U.S. Forest Service in California, says, "I now realize there is no wilderness in the lower 48 states. Just urban parks."

On the ninth day, the skies that have stayed indelibly blue for us— when poet and Cistercian monk Thomas Merton visited Alaska, he wrote of the "Bardo of pure sky"—darken and drop a deluge as we depart the Walker. Even the best MontBell rain gear, with hood up and cuffs cinched tight, can't prevent a few icy rivulets from making glaciers on my skin.

The big glaciers shoulder down into the river canyon now, and we pass several that loom right above us, their towering seracs streaked with brown dirt and laced with sapphire and emerald light.

At length, we reach the long sand spit separating the river from Alsek Lake, and struggle, in the wind and rain, to set up camp before darkness falls.

But storm clouds unexpectedly part to reveal the distant high peak of Mount Fairweather, with snowclad slopes gilded by sunset. Even the Tlingit Nora seems in awe of the natural beauty she has lived near since her youth. "Isn't that wonderful!" she exclaims, standing with an arm around Richard's waist.

We stay two days at Alsek Lake, then are shocked when our final day on the river approaches. Tomorrow, we'll float between icebergs calved from the Alsek and Grand Plateau Glaciers, heading to Dry Bay. This last afternoon in freedom, in wilderness, we cozy up in our sand-spit camp.

Just before Nora's last tale, *Huhtz,* the huge black grizzly appears, wandering the shore across the river. And I had about given up hope of ever seeing more than his tracks! When Nora is done, yet another bear plunges through the shallows of the far bank, scampering easily over huge logs, tremendous power revealed in rippling grace. It then vanishes into the woods.

Monarchs in their domain. These river canyons, preserved by agreements as strong as humans can make them, have been migratory routes for great brown bears for millennia, linking their coastal populations with those inland. In the words of Stephen Herrero, a professor of environmental science at the University of Calgary and a world authority on arctic bears: "If you had to bet on any world region where there could be a natural brown bear population 1,000 years from now, it would be here, along the Alsek-Tatshenshini river corridors. This unified region of four big parks is finally large enough to ensure the survival of the bears, who are at the absolute top of the food chain. That suggests most of the other species of plant and animal in this ecosystem will make it, too."

It's my final night, deep in this Alaskan wilderness. Before I fall asleep on the sandbar between an iceberg-clogged Alsek Lake and the brown, rushing Tatshenshini, I grow aware of another bear. The one who walks the sky, Ursus Major, brightest star of the Great Bear constellation. In the lower 48, they call that asymmetric cluster the Big Dipper.

Out here, though, it's definitely the Bear that wheels overhead, a spectral and totemic guardian, hovering above his earthly refuge. A vast wildland where life can now continue as it did well before Hammurabi began to conjugate his Code. And well before the first bone of driftwood was whittled into a rib for a walrus-hide Aleut kayak.

These brown bears are of a venerable tribe. It is seemly for them to flourish.

WILD PLACES

TRIP NOTES

A Tatshenshini River run is one of the best and easiest ways to explore the deep wilderness of the Yukon-Alaska border area. Trips that transit the interior of the area are available on both the Tatshenshini and Alsek Rivers. These rivers join and become one after about a week of travel. Multiday excursions on a commercial raft trip offer a chance to let powerful impressions of the arctic wild permeate your senses.

When to go
The best time to reliably plan a river trip is from July through August. However, depending on whether spring is early or fall is late in any given year, these parameters may expand or shrink.

How to go
A score of American and Canadian rafting companies now operate on the Tatshenshini and Alsek. Full-length Tatshenshini trips range from 10 to 14 days. Generally, longer trips provide more time for layover days and side hikes. Costs range from $1,500 to $2,200 per person. Some leading outfitters include:

- **Chilkat Guides.** Box 170, Haines, AK 99827; (907) 766-2491.

- **James Henry River Journeys.** Attention: James Katz, Box 807, Bolinas, CA 94924; (800) 786-1830.

- **Mountain Travel/Sobek.** 6420 Fairmount Avenue, El Cerrito, CA 94530; (800) 227-2384.

- **Nahanni River Adventures.** Box 4869, Whitehorse, Yukon Y1A 4N6, Canada; (403) 668-3180.

- **Yukon Mountain & River Expeditions.** Box 5405, Whitehorse, Yukon Y1A 4Z2, Canada; (403) 668-2513.

To receive a complete listing of outfitters on the river, contact Glacier Bay National Park, at the phone number and address listed below.

Where to go
The four parks in the Tatshenshini-Alsek region offer a wide array of options besides rafting on the main rivers. Here's a summary:

- **Glacier Bay National Park** (United States). This 3.3-million-acre park, established as a national monument in 1925, became a park in 1980. It is only accessible via cruise ships (which bring half its visitors), boat, or airplane. Alaska Airlines flies into Gustavus, a frontier town 10 miles south of the park; from there, shuttle buses will take you to the visitor center and campgrounds at Bartlett Cove, where there are lodges, a restaurant, and 7.5 miles of nature trails. Small boats offer one-day tours of Glacier Bay. For information, contact the Glacier Bay National Park, Pouch E, Juneau, AK 99811; (907) 697-2230.

- **Kluane National Park** (Canada). Founded in 1972, this is one of Canada's largest national parks. Sprawling across

5.4 million acres, it holds that country's tallest mountains, as well as one of the largest nonpolar ice fields in the world. There are 115 miles of trails and 143 miles of marked routes in this Yukon Territory park. Recreation here includes backpacking, hiking, camping, mountaineering (especially on 19,500-foot Mount Logan), Nordic skiing, fishing, rafting, and some horse packing. For information, call (403) 634-2251.

- **Tatshenshini-Alsek Provincial Park** (Canada). Established in 1993, this brand-new park of 2.3 million acres has recreational options that are still being discovered and cataloged. Besides the raft trips on its main rivers, the park to date has been used primarily for winter snowmobiling, Nordic skiing, and dogsledding. There is some climbing and hiking opportunities in the summer. The rugged, alpine terrain holds between 350 and 400 major glaciers. For information, call (800) 663-8843.

- **Wrangell–Saint Elias National Park and Preserve** (United States). The largest park in the United States, this behemoth of 13 million acres was established in 1980. Two unpaved roads, totaling 99 miles in length, provide the only automotive access; the rest is via foot or bush plane. Recreation, as you might imagine, consists primarily of hiking, camping, and watching wildlife. Still, there's also some mountaineering: The park holds 9 of the 16 highest mountains in North America, including the 18,000-foot Mount Saint Elias. There's also rafting on the Copper and Chitna Rivers. For information, contact the Wrangell–Saint Elias National Park and Preserve, P.O. Box 439, Copper Center, AK 99573; (907) 822-5235.

What to bring

High-powered mosquito repellent is a must. Capsicum (pepper) bear spray should be bought on-site in Alaska; it cannot be transported on planes. A top-quality rain- and windproof suit is also essential; even in the summer, the weather can be capricious. Good gum boots or knee-high rubber overboots can prove quite useful, too.

Additional information

For more details on the region from the perspective of the native peoples, write to the Sealaska Heritage Foundation, 1 Sealaska Plaza, Suite 201, Juneau, AK 99801; or the Champagne-Aishihik First Nation, 10137 Jarvis Street, Whitehorse, Yukon Y1A 2H3, Canada.

For an in-depth review of the area, a good source book is "Tatshenshini River Wild," which combines the work of three dozen of North America's finest outdoor photographers and more than a dozen political and environmental leaders. To order a copy, contact Westcliffe Publishers, Box 1261, Englewood, CO 80150; (800) 523-3692.

The Lure
of Hoodoos

by Linda Watanabe McFerrin

Maybe it was the hype—a nacreous veneer of transcendentalism lacquered over the high desert. Maybe it really *was* the call of the vortices, energy points said to exist on the steeples of fire-red rock. I'd like to say it was some mysterious convergence of mystical events that led me to Sedona. Most probably, it was simply the lure of canyon and mesa, geologic wonders haunted by Indian lore and legend, where saguaro cactus and sage share space with coyote and sidewinder.

My friend Samantha, newly pregnant and glad of it, was feeling the call of the arroyos. Call it a craving. We decided to indulge.

Sedona, a small town in Arizona with a very large mystical reputation, lies north of Scottsdale, a straight shot up Highway 179. Arriving at the Scottsdale airport in the late afternoon, we rented a car and set out at once.

Not even our backgrounds in wide, wild expanses of California prepared us for the magic of that scrub-strewn terrain. We saw 12-foot saguaro cacti that looked like lonesome cowboys heading on home to the ranch. Twilight played coyote trickster with shadows and light. In the gathering gloom, squat scrub chaparral—manzanita, mesquite, and shrub live oak—took on the forms of various animals: jackrabbits, prairie dogs, and ringtail cats. The rocks themselves seemed to come alive, twisting and snaking upward. Then darkness fell like a tomahawk, stars opened up like tiny eyes in the sky, and a full moon rose over the desert.

We hurtled down that rattlesnake of a road, halted on a crescent of gravel and dust, and got out to stretch our legs. After a fast, snappy splattering of rain, the air was humid and cool, the moon a glowing smudge behind a halo of moisture.

On both sides of us, the desert rose in fabulous hoodoos, in snaggle-toothed spires. We thought we heard a wolf howl, an owl hoot. We found ourselves speaking in whispers, like kids at a campfire. A spooky feeling swept over us, and we got back into the car.

It wouldn't start. Not even the comforting whir of the ignition greeted our efforts. Only silence. Was this the Twilight Zone?

Since Samantha could not start the car, I tried. It started right up. We turned nervously to one another, eyes as big as saucers, eyebrows jumping to the tops of our foreheads.

"We're almost there," I said encouragingly.

Samantha just nodded.

We almost passed Sedona. At night this little town is easy to miss. Its sprinkling of lights is no match for a big desert sky studded with stars. (Even by day, the soft hues and lines of its Southwestern architecture seem lost in the expanse of a land where 300-million-year-old cliffs of limestone, shale, basalt, and sandstone climb to form sheer walls, towers, and elegant minarets.)

Our hotel, rather inappropriately named L'Auberge de Sedona, was tucked off the main thoroughfare. Our home for the night was an aerie of an apartment perched on the hillside overlooking a canyon. It was 10 o'clock by the time we sat down to eat and midnight by the time we got back to our room. We went out like a couple of well-used candles.

By six the next morning, the sun had already muscled its way into our room. Along with the heat, we were showered in an incredible wraparound sound that seemed to swell mysteriously from the forest below. I couldn't place it. It sounded like cards being shuffled over a PA system. It sounded like a million maracas being shaken at once. But investigation could wait: I substituted the more proximate hiss and splash of my shower.

In our room, a sheaf of newsletters and brochures promised Disneylike adventures, replete with Native American rituals, wildlife encounters, spiritual awakenings, and pink jeeps. We were ready to meet Sedona head-on, but like any good scouts, we first opted to explore our immediate surroundings. We had to walk down the hillside into Oak Creek Canyon and find the source of that sound.

The rattling rose and fell around us on our short descent into the canyon. Fat faces of daisies gazed up at us. June bugs as big as hummingbirds buzzed us. It grew cooler as we closed in on the creek. Irises grew in the small patches of shadow. Oak Creek was so clear we could see flat, gray-green rocks resting like turtles beneath the water on the opposite shore. Ducks cut slow ciphers into the water's glassy surface. I began to feel drowsy.

That's when I met him—my first denizen of the desert. I came face to face with a fat grasshopper with leopard markings and pearl-gray eyes at the top of its head. It was clinging to one of the green rushes at the side of the creek that cut through the canyon.

It stared at me, its thorax heaving. I bent closer, until it was inches away from my cheek. Was this one of those monumental meetings in which creatures from disparate worlds connect spiritually and exchange greetings? It didn't seem frightened.

Suddenly, I was aware of thousands of similarly beadlike eyes. I had not even seen them. They perched on all of the rushes around the creek. They peered out from the short grass at my feet. They were the source of the ocean of sound that rolled in great waves through the canyon. It seemed as if some great truth had just been revealed, but I wasn't sure what. I was overwhelmed with the sense of missing some significant point.

I looked around for Samantha. She was sitting on a red rock some distance away, looking over the creek, still as a sandstone statue, already one with the landscape.

My second encounter with a denizen of the desert occurred after breakfast, when our guide arrived. Samantha and I had selected what seemed the most promising tour. Offered in affiliation with a local bookstore, it guaranteed smudge sticks, cornmeal offerings, and prayer-feather rituals. However, for a guide we did not get a sunburned mercenary or a native mystic. We got Jill, a tiny transplant from Tennessee by way of New York, street-smart, troubled-scarred, and tough as a prairie chicken.

"Look," Sam said to her, trying to explain our slightly cynical point of view, "we're not woo-woos."

"Woo-woo?" Jill asked, raising her eyebrow.

"You know, New Agers," Samantha explained.

Actually, I was beginning to have my doubts, after my brief communion with the grasshopper.

"Yeah," I seconded heartily.

"Well, good," said Jill. "Neither am I. Now that we've got that out of the way, let's get going."

In Jill's minivan, we set out through a landscape whose beauty has made it a pilgrimage destination for generations. Jill explained that the Indians measure time in worlds. The rock that towered around us accurately recorded these incarnations—ocean five times, freshwater lake two times, swamp twice, desert twice—and each incarnation had left another layer of personality.

"So, why did you guys choose a Vortex Tour?" Jill asked with studied carelessness, squinting into the sunlight.

Samantha piped up, "We want to know more about the vortexes."

"Vortices," Jill corrected with a snakelike hiss of the sibilants. I pictured the warning flick of a rattler's tail. "I prefer 'vortices.' Well, you picked the right spot. The vortices are power spots, places where energy collects and swirls. The Bermuda Triangle is a vortex. There are vortices all over the world. You know about them. They're where mysterious events occur. People are naturally attracted to them. We have seen vortices in Sedona. Some are negative, some are positive.

"Let's start right here. See that rock over there?"

Our eyes followed the apocalyptic pointing of Jill's finger to an enormous bluff that rose like a callused red giant from the low plane of the desert.

"That's Apache Leap. It's a powerful negative vortex. I tried to climb it once." Jill frowned. "I couldn't. Fear gripped me. Do you know what happened there? The story goes that when General Crook was rounding up Indians to put them on reservations, the few free remaining Apache got wind of it. The braves, all the men, got on their horses and rode right up to the top of that cliff where it looked as if they had nowhere to go, and then . . . they leapt over. All the braves in the party plunged to their deaths rather than face white man's captivity. Maybe they stayed free.

"And see that beautiful swath of green stretching beneath the leap? You'd like to say it's a well-tended Indian burial ground, a kind of memorial, right? Wrong. It's a golf course. Yep, a golf course. I guess some people are immune to bad vibes."

Our guide was silent for a while. She seemed deep in rumination. Suddenly she stuck a thin arm out the window again, gesturing toward an immense dome-shaped rock up ahead, to the left of us.

"That over there's Bell Rock," she said. "Remember 1989, the Harmonic Convergence, when all of the planets supposedly lined up and big things were supposed to happen? Well, some of the people let on that Bell Rock was a spaceship that was meant to take people away from this planet, which was slated to be destroyed. They even sold tickets. And people bought 'em! But, as you can see, old Bell Rock never took off, and I don't think those ticket holders ever got their money back.

"Yeah," she laughed, "it can get pretty weird here, and if you ever want that kind of action, you just go to the Coffee Pot Restaurant in West Sedona. You'll find them there any day of the week, those woo-woos you're talking about, playing flutes and dangling crystals. Heck, these people have to consult a pendulum before they go to the bathroom."

As Jill kept up her gravelly commentary, Samantha and I slammed up and down in the bucking seats of the minivan, which Jill drove with great disregard for stones and potholes. Every so often she'd fling out a botanical note. "See that manzanita. It's a natural fire retardant. When lightning strikes it, it puts itself out. The Indians call it the Plant of the Gods. You can use the bark for bronchial problems."

We had turned right, off Highway 179, and were bumping along the back road toward an elegant constellation of spires and towers known as Cathedral Rock.

Jill hit the brakes right before the road ended, jumped from the van, slammed the door shut, and lit a cigarette in a series of quick, well-synchronized movements. She fished around in a shabby day pack and, pulling out two bundles of weeds, ignited the tip of each one with her cigarette. The tightly wrapped grass didn't burn, just smoldered, and the air was perfumed with sage.

"Smudge sticks," Jill informed us. "This is Cathedral Rock, your first vortex. Now, I want you to pass the smoke before the different parts of your body and repeat after me:

"I am pure of thought,
I see the truth,
I speak truth,
I am pure of heart,
I walk in peace,
aho."

We repeated the words, waving the sweet-smelling smudge sticks before forehead, eyes, mouth, heart, and feet—the pertinent parts of our bodies.

"Kind of a cleansing," Jill said, grinning. "Now, go." She gave us each a shove in the direction of Cathedral Rock.

The desert was silent and still. We looked back at Jill. She leaned against the minivan, taking long, slow pulls on the rest of her cigarette. Midday sun washed over us, warm and soporific. Lizards blinked up at us. Time seemed to stop. Jill had told us that Cathedral Rock was a feminine vortex. A holy place for Indian women, who had come here for centuries to bear children. Shaped like a coronet, its several turrets encircled a lower, rocky center. I watched Samantha, my dear friend, in the months before motherhood, as she moved ahead, picking her way past walls of rust-colored stone, a solitary figure climbing up into the high lap of that natural sanctuary.

I could feel it—a kind of gentle tug. Sedona was pulling me into another dimension. It was a wordless dimension of feelings and a heightened sensitivity, a sense of inner-connectedness with everything around me. It scared me a little. Perhaps this is a phenomenon similar to what Jill felt on the trail to the summit of Apache Leap.

The terrain I hike through is generally one of physical landmarks, of objective reality. Here, in Sedona, things shifted into a kind of double exposure: the external and internal landscapes seemed to have become superimposed.

I said nothing of this to Samantha. She remained focused, with her own intensity, on an ascent into the rugged saddle of shrub and sandy stone. In fact, we spoke little, if at all, on Cathedral Rock. We climbed about silently, bewitched by our surroundings and the specter of our identities. We descended from those escarpments a quieter and more reverent twosome.

Jill had other adventures in store. At the mouth of Boynton Canyon we stepped carefully into and out of a tangle of wide green leaves and enormous, white funnel-shaped flowers.

"Beautiful, huh?" Jill queried suggestively.

Samantha and I nodded assent.

"Yep," Jill agreed, "very tempting. Datura. You've heard of the deadly nightshade? Well, datura is part of that family. Also called angel's trumpet, jimsonweed. It's an alkaloid hallucinogen. Indians use it. I wouldn't recommend experimenting."

I studied the perfect belled cones, wondering how the hallucinogen was extracted, thinking how easily one could be seduced by these angel-white blossoms.

Jill's voice interrupted me.

"Here we are. This is a perfect spot."

She thrust her hand into the battered day pack again and pulled out a small plastic bag.

"Prayer-feather offering," she announced. "Stand on that little pile of rock over there, close your eyes, and hold out your hands."

We did as our guide instructed. Jill turned our hands so that the palms faced upward. She filled them with weightless down.

"Now make a wish," she said breathlessly. "Wish for something you really want and throw the feathers into the air. The wish will come true. This is a sacred ritual."

I thought about wishing, as I generally do, for vast material wealth, but I couldn't bring myself to do it. The moment seemed to dictate something else. I think I wished for something intangible—world peace, love, happiness for all—I honestly can't remember. At the time, whatever it was, it seemed the unequivocal choice. We opened our eyes and stood for a while, in silence, watching the snow-white turkey feathers drift off in the wind. Across the canyon the Enchantment resort sprawled behind its guarded gates. It seemed to be chiseled in rose and ocher from the stone around it, an elaborate and inaccessible four-star cliff dwelling.

We visited other places with Jill. She pointed out the Vortex of Confusion (home of the U.S. Post Office) and a curtain of rock formations—Cockscomb, Chimney Rock, Capitol Butte, Sugar Loaf, Coffee Pot Rock, and Steamboat Rock—that stand north of Sedona like a movie-set backdrop. At Schnebly Hill, an electrical vortex, we made blue corn offerings and squatted for what seemed like hours, our hands on the earth, struggling to sense an energetic surge. If we felt anything it was the numbness in our legs, spreading upward with an old, familiar tingle.

"Feel anything?" Jill asked.

"No," we shook our heads dumbly.

Jill shrugged. "Oh, well. Not everyone does."

The vortex tour took four hours. We returned to L'Auberge de Sedona under a soft blue sky in which angelic puffs of cotton-white cloud floated.

"Too bad," Jill said. "This is monsoon season. We haven't had enough rain this year."

I puzzled over Sedona, cynical and chastened in turns, still trying to figure out what the place was all about. It's difficult to be arrogant in that towering landscape, difficult to shelter under the puny umbrella of self, that entity full of doubt, cynicism, and fear, and not be edified by the broader context. It's hard to ignore the big picture. That awareness is, in its way, a miracle.

What humans make of their miracles is another matter: In Sedona, as in so many places, the spiritual, inspirational, and miraculous fall prey to capitalism. Everyone's trying to make a buck. Yet there always have been hawkers at pilgrimage sites. They cater to our need to bring back tokens, a long-lasting memento of the ineffable. To stand in the center of honest wonder and its glitzy overlay of hype seems to be an experience of great value. It is highly educational to embrace both sides of a paradox.

We paid Jill and said good-bye in the parking lot of the resort. Money changed hands. The sky opened up, and it started to rain.

"Monsoon," Jill announced, winking at us from the window of the minivan.

"Call me next time you're in Sedona. I'll give you a midnight Medicine Wheel Tour. No charge."

TRIP NOTES

As the center of several "vortices"—great steeples of rock where energy collects, converges, and supposedly generates heightened forms of awareness—Sedona, Arizona, is unquestionably the gateway to some extraordinarily expansive and awe-inspiring terrain. The mystical is intimately connected with the mysterious: Sacred sites, sanctified by centuries of Indian ritual and pilgrimage, cap 200 million years' worth of spectacular geography. This geologically fascinating desert setting produces a natural high and provides the perfect launching pad for an array of adventures in which external and internal landscapes ultimately meet and blend.

When to go

The climate is mild year-round. Changes are dictated largely by geography. The higher you go, the wetter and colder it gets. Lower elevations are dry and hot. Late spring, summer, and fall are particularly beautiful.

How to go

Due north of Phoenix and south of the Grand Canyon, Sedona is right in the heart of central Arizona and easily located on any map. Plan plenty of time for the drive; sight-seeing along the way is a substantial part of the pleasure.

Where to go

Extraordinarily beautiful terrain and a variety of ways to see it are part of the lure of Sedona and the Coconino National Forest, which completely surrounds it. Here is a partial listing of points of interest and tours:

Parks and Monuments:

- **Chapel of the Holy Cross.** Architecturally austere and intriguing, this shrine built in the 1950s vies with the red rock cliff face upon which it hangs. Located on Highway 179, three miles south of the "Y" (the intersection of Highways 179 and 89A); (520) 282-4069.

- **Fort Verde State Historic Park.** This was a major fort for General George Crook during the Indian campaigns in the 1870s and a significant landmark of Arizona history. Located in Camp Verde, southwest of Sedona; (520) 567-3275.

- **Grand Canyon.** The South Rim is only a two-hour drive from Sedona. You can also take a turn-of-the-century steam locomotive to the park; (800) 843-8724.

- **Jerome State Historic Park.** An old mining town perched high in the hills, the site offers views that stretch all the way to Flagstaff's San Francisco Peaks and recalls Arizona's mining history. Located 37 miles south of Sedona on Highway 89A; (520) 634-5381.

- **Montezuma Castle National Monument.** Like a ghost town, this deserted cliff dwelling, one of the oldest and finest in the Southwest, is thought-provoking and hauntingly beautiful. Located 50 miles south of Flagstaff, off Interstate 17; (520) 567-3322.

- **Red Rock Loop Crossing/Cathedral Rock.** The grandeur of these natural spires and turrets creates an exquisite natural monument. Picnic tables are available. No overnight camping. Take West Highway 89 to Upper Red Rock Loop Road.

- **Red Rock State Park.** This 286-acre park is an environmental education center. Located five miles south of Sedona on Lower Red Rock Loop Road, off West Highway 89A; (520) 282-6907.

- **Slide Rock State Park.** As the name implies, this park features a natural water slide. Located six miles north of Sedona in Oak Creek Canyon. Small vehicle-entrance fee; (520) 282-3034.

- **Tuzigoot National Monument.** This Singagua Indian ruin dates back to the thirteenth century. Located between Clarkdale and Cottonwood, west of Sedona; (520) 634-5564.

- **Verde Canyon Railroad.** Try one of a variety of rail excursions that follow the Verde River; trains depart from Clarkdale; (520) 639-0010.

Tours:

- **Dorian Tours.** Offerings include Medicine Wheel Tour, Navajo Tour, Grand Canyon Tour, Jerome Historic Tour, Scenic Tours, Hopi Tours, Verde Valley Indian Ruins Tour, and a Stargazing Tour. P.O. Box 3151, West Sedona, AZ 86340; (520) 282-4562.

- **Earth Wisdom Tours.** Offerings include Earth Wisdom Vortex Tour, Earth Medicine Tour, Earth Ecology Tour, and an Earth Ancestors Pilgrimage. 293 North Highway 89A, Sedona, AZ 86336; (520) 282-4714.

- **Kachina Stables.** Offerings include Indian Sacred Pipe Ceremonial Horse Ride, Full-Moon Ride, Autumn Color Trail Ride, pack trips, and breakfast, lunch, and dinner rides. P.O. Box 3616, Sedona, AZ 86340; (520) 282-7252.

- **Northern Light Balloon Expeditions.** P.O. Box 1695, Sedona, AZ 86336; (520) 282-2274.

- **Pink Jeep Tours.** Offerings include Broken Arrow Tour, Scenic Sedona, Touch the Earth Vortex Experience, Sterling Canyon–Dry Creek Experience, and the Soldier Pass Experience. P.O. Box 1447, Sedona, AZ 86339; (520) 282-5000.

- **Pink Jeep Tours Ancient Expeditions.** Offerings include Warren Cremer's Tour, Sacred Places Tour, Ancient Ruin Expedition, Peak Experience, and the Zane Grey Trail Tour. (520) 282-2137, (800) 999-2137.

- **Red Rock Balloon Adventures.** 295 Lee Mountain Road, Sedona, AZ 86351; (520) 284-0040, (800) 258-3754.

- **Sedona Adventures.** Offerings include Peaceful Warrior Tour, Vortex Adventure, Scenic Adventure, Sunset Tour, Mogollon Rim Tour, Wildlife Safari, and Sedona Wilderness Quest. P.O. Box 1476, Sedona, AZ 86339; (520) 282-3500, (800) 888-9494.

- **Sedona Red Rock Jeep.** Offerings include Cowboy West Tour, Wildlife Tour, Archaeological Adventure, Scenic Points of Interest, Original Vortex Tour, and Medicine Wheel Tour. P.O. Box 10305, Sedona, AZ 86336; (520) 282-6826.

What to bring

Pack a light jacket for winter, shorts and sandals for summer, and long pants and boots for horseback adventures.

Additional information

For more information about Sedona resorts, lodgings, restaurants, arts and crafts, and culture, contact: Sedona–Oak Creek Canyon Chamber of Commerce, P.O. Box 478, Sedona, AZ 86339-0478; (520) 282-7722.

Paddling Off the Edge of the Big Easy

by Bob Marshall

It's midmorning at midweek, and fleets of 18-wheelers growl down Interstate 55 heading for Pass Manchac. Exhaust pipes leave plumes of black smoke above the concrete combat zone leading to New Orleans. Truckers jockey with salesmen, students, and shoppers as the wheels of commerce send a steady rumble into a crystal-clear day.

Chris Brown, Melanie Clary, and I don't notice. A wall of cypress and tupelo blocks the interstate from our view, and what noise filters through—past the curtains of Spanish moss, past their canoe, and past my dugout pirogue (a Cajun trapper's boat)—makes no impression. We're already in the grip of sensory overload: The leaves of swamp maple flutter like red flags in the cool autumn breeze; the crowns of cypress glow deep-rust above flowing moss beards; a family of yellow-crowned night herons perches on a snag; willows rain golden leaves on tea-colored water. Three mallards circle overhead, wondering if the open water amid the hyacinths is a safe landing spot—despite the 10-foot-long alligator who suns on a nearby cypress log.

"It's so pleasant back here," says Brown, a local dentist enjoying a swamp outing with his wife and me. "It's so wild, so beautiful, you'd think you were a thousand miles from the city."

But we aren't.

A mere 20-minute drive from that 10-foot gator, throngs of tourists crowd into the French Quarter. They line up for lunch at Paul Prudhomme's restaurant, attack platters of boiled crayfish and stacks of raw oysters in the seafood houses, and nurse hangovers proudly earned the night before in jazz clubs from Bourbon Street to the Faubourg Marigny. Yet if these same fun-seekers actually thought about traveling more than a half hour in any one direction, they might slip out of the twentieth century and into a world that would be quite recognizable to the French and Spanish explorers who first traveled this landscape some 400 years ago.

That's what my friends Chris and Melanie choose to do with me for recreation, any time the mood strikes. For New Orleans residents like ourselves, the neighboring wetlands form an exotic and sprawling backyard. We don't have to travel very far to launch their canoe or my traditional-style pirogue into an ancient, watery world.

One of the easiest options for a nearby paddle is the one I've just described: Shell Bank Bayou near the Bayou LaBranche Wetlands. Shell Bank runs between Lake Maurepas and Lake Pontchartrain and is accessible from Interstate 55, just 20 minutes from the city. To go for a day paddle is effortless and one of the best ways to experience this landscape like a local—or even like the area's first settlers.

The wondrous irony is that the Big Easy—America's unrepentant citadel of hedonism—may be closer to nature than any metropolis on the continent. You'll find more Birkenstocks and Earth Day T-shirts in one square block of Seattle or San Francisco than in the entire French Quarter, but when it comes to trading concrete, steel, and traffic jams for habitat where fur, scales, and feathers rule, you can't make a faster exchange than in the New Orleans area.

That's because the city was started on a small speck of land deep in the delta of North America's greatest river. It was surrounded by a vast wetland wilderness, the largest of its kind on the continent. The big river flowed through lands dominated by expansive cypress swamps, freshwater marshes with acres of waving cane fields, and salt marshes whose knee-high wire grass ran for distances that reminded explorers of the northern prairies.

Travel was strictly by boat—down winding bayous with water as dark as molasses, across lakes and bays, and along the many fingers of a mighty river reaching across the delta.

New Orleans' growth was naturally limited. No matter which direction the developers turned, they soon ran into water. The result: a modern city with a visible edge between civilization and wilderness.

Cities thriving in America's West swoop up and over the mountains that surround them, or gobble expanses of desert at their feet. Midwestern towns eat at the prairie. But New Orleans kept coming up against insurmountable problems: a lake, rivers, bayous, marshes, swamps. When the concrete no longer floated, city builders constructed a levee to keep the storm tides out, then turned in another direction.

Walk atop one of the levees, and you get to see this edge. On one side your eyes will fall on houses, shopping malls, or jazz clubs. On the other you'll see marsh, swamp, bayou, or lake, all arrayed in scenes that might have greeted René-Robert Cavelier Sieur de La Salle in the 1860s when he paddled his birchbark canoe on his first voyage through this area.

Out here, the roar of Mardi Gras fades into the quiet of finger lakes hidden by deep hardwood wetlands. Traces of ancient waterways once paddled by natives are now graced by sentinel oaks and magnolias. There are countless bayous and trenaises (trapper's ditches) winding through tall green marshes hedged by saw grass and bull tongue that's eight feet high. The 23,000-acre Bayou Sauvage National Wildlife Refuge, located within city limits, is the winter retreat for about 50,000 ducks. It's also the permanent home for deer, mink, otters, alligators, egrets, herons, pelicans, and eagles. And only 20 minutes from Bourbon Street is a national park where thousand-year-old cypress preside in cathedral silence over fields of wild iris. The land remains little changed from the days when pirate Jean Lafitte called it home.

None of this is the result of wise urban planning. The wetlands survived because for generations New Orleans' city fathers didn't have the technology to conquer them. By the time they got the know-how, federal laws protected what was left.

But it has suffered. A tour of the surviving wetlands shows just how hard life has been for delta habitats. In its rabid thirst for oil money, the state allowed the dredging of more than 20,000 miles of canals through priceless coastal marshes and swamps. This opened the door to ruinous saltwater invasions from the Gulf of Mexico. In order to build a city where none should stand, levees were raised that today carry a death sentence for the wetlands outside the mud walls. The result: Louisiana's coast washes away at the rate of 35 square miles a year.

It's a catastrophe of historic proportions for North America, one with abysmal consequences for fish, wildlife resources, and people.

Some scientists even think New Orleans should immediately look for a new site for itself, planning ahead for the day when the Gulf eats the last of the wetlands and pounds on the levees of the French Quarter.

Most citizens of the Big Easy wonder what all the hurry and worry is about. They plan to think about the looming catastrophe right after Mardi Gras. Or perhaps after the Jazz Fest, or the Spring Fiesta, or the French Quarter Fest. In the meantime, the city clings to its anthem: *Laissez les bons temps rouler* (let the good times roll)!

For outdoors people, a good time is as simple as a walk out the front door and across a levee. The edge allows a quick escape. Although the increase in oil and gas exploration left a land littered with abandoned wells, pipe fields, storage tanks, and barges, nature lovers can find daisies among the shrapnel.

Lafitte National Historical Park is a favorite of lifelong residents such as myself. On another voyage, on a spring day, I go paddling with a naturalist, and we stop to have lunch. The spontaneous scene belongs on a calendar photo. Our two canoes rest on a yard-wide ribbon of water dotted with white water lilies. On either side, miles of shoulder-high bull tongue reach to the horizon. That sea of green is shattered only by violet islands of iris. Snakes slither. Alligators sun. Cranes, herons, ibis, and ducks call from countless hidden potholes.

We could be marooned in the emerald depths of the Amazon. Yet one look at the northern horizon dispels that fantasy: The New Orleans skyline, equipped with the great white eggshell of the Superdome, looks down upon us. There's no denying it; we are only in the Barataria Unit of Jean Lafitte National Historical Park, in Marrero, a bedroom suburb of New Orleans that's just seven miles from the city's heart.

"People who live five miles from our gate don't even know this park exists," says ranger Bruce Barnes as he peels an orange. Barnes, like the city, has two personalities. When he's not in a ranger's uniform, he's the star of Sun Pie and the Sun Spots, a top Zydeco band, rocking audiences across Europe and the States.

This park protects 11,000 acres of freshwater wetlands on the north end of the giant Barataria Bay estuary. It also preserves the remnants of a cypress wilderness that was the home of Jean Lafitte, a hero of the battle of New Orleans.

Subdivisions of Marrero push against the park borders, but beyond the levees protecting these homes, the world changes dramatically, peeling back 200 years of history.

Most park visitors just take one of the elevated walkways through the swamps, near the visitor center on State Highway 45. The walkways can offer a glimpse of a bottomland hardwood swamp, but it's like trying to see the Grand Canyon without leaving the rim.

"Seventy-five percent of the park is accessible only by water," says ranger David Muth. "You've really got to get on the water to experience the landscape. You can spend a few hours or a few days on the canoe trails—and you'll never forget it."

The trail system has three components: bayous, trenaises, and canals. Until the levees were built, natural bayous such as Des Familles and Coquille distributed flow from the Mississippi River. Formerly used by Lafitte to ferry contraband from a base in Barataria Bay, they are now quiet old riverbeds, their banks crowded with ancient cypress, live oak, and magnolia. Curtains of moss hang to the water.

Trenaises meander through floating marshes called floatants. They were originally hand-dug ditches that were wide enough for a pirogue, but trenaises today can be five yards wide. Since shallow water quickly collects vegetation during a long, warm growing season, plastic poles mark trenaise routes to help guide modern-day explorers.

Canals are part of the water traffic system in Jean Lafitte. Some, like Kenta, were dug a century ago, when cypress loggers took trees from this area. Others, such as Tarpaper, were dredged in the last 50 years so oil workers could suck petroleum from under the marshes. Their dredged mud was piled beside the canals, forming levees that soon sprouted hardwoods and shrubs.

R anger Barnes has planned a route for us that will reveal each type of habitat and watercourse. Yet the choices of where we can go aren't entirely his. "The water levels affect the route," he says. "Everything we do here is controlled by the tides."

Today the water level is below normal, so old bayous will be too shallow to navigate. Barnes' route combines canals and trenaises, and our put-in is at Twin Canals.

Clouds of green duckweed coat the water. Spoil banks host thick hardwoods. An ichthyologist, Barnes never goes anywhere without a fish-sampling net. He pauses every third or fourth stroke to see what's under the surface.

"You won't find water anywhere that has more life in it," he says. "There's so much in these wetlands, it's hard to imagine."

Soon, we are immersed. Small alligators watch our progress from moss beds; others swim several yards ahead. Turtles sun on logs, bream slap at dragonflies, and a great blue heron swoops across the canal and vanishes into a cypress-tupelo swamp behind the spoil levee.

In one mile, we come to a break in the levee that marks the trenaise system's entrance. The bull tongue covers the open marsh for miles, waving in the stiff breeze like broad-leaved wheat.

"A week ago, the bull tongue was a few inches high," Barnes says. "A month ago, it didn't exist—this marsh was just flat and wide open. One month from now, the bull tongue will be six feet tall."

A floatant is built by bull tongue, hyacinths, and other plants. Each winter the greenery dies, leaving brown husks on the water. After many years, a layer of detritus forms and compacts its own weight into a mat several inches or feet thick. The mat becomes a floating marsh as the delta underneath it slowly subsides.

Stepping onto a floatant is like walking on jelly: The surface rolls in small waves under each footfall. Barnes leads us across, carefully probing with a stick for holes—a swamper's equivalent of a crevasse.

"Make the wrong move, and you can sink up to your hips," he says. "If you fall through, you can sink in over your head."

As the trenaise system snakes across a floatant, a paddler gets an alligator's-eye view of this world. Bull tongue, already shoulder high, crowds in on both sides. Stands of wild iris swim above the green tongues. White water lilies grace ponds. Small waterways cut tunnels through groves of wax myrtle dotted with birds' nests. Small fish scurry ahead, gators slither away, snakes watch from the sidelines.

Sometimes the path is blocked by the "living land." Chunks of floatants, moving like green icebergs, break off and drift down the waterway.

"I'm amazed at how fast things change," Barnes says, as he tries to push a piece of floatant out of the trenaise. On the horizon, the New Orleans skyline catches the glow of the evening sun. The ranger looks at the buildings, and smiles. "It's a short distance from here to downtown. But it's another world away."

At eight o'clock the next morning, my wife Marie and I decide we'd like to be in that other world. Our heads are still buzzing from the throaty roar of blues mama Marva Wright. And the beers that washed down fiery creations at K-Paul's Louisiana Kitchen didn't help. But I need to do some research to write a paddle-of-the-month article for the newspaper, so we drive west from the French Quarter to make another escape.

Creole cottages give way to suburbia, and then we cross the levee guarding the city's western flank. We're over the edge again. Here the metro area is outflanked by a stretch of freshwater marsh and cypress forest called Bayou LaBranche Wetlands. Wedged between Lake Pontchartrain and U.S. Highway 61, this area is bordered on the west by subdivisions of LaPlace, and on the east by the runways of New Orleans International Airport. Other neighbors include the twin spans of Interstate 10, striding on concrete legs down the lake's south shore, and giant oil refineries and chemical plants whose towers and smokestacks line the horizon, spitting vapor (and worse) into the humid southern air. Beneath, between, and around those eyesores rests a slice of heaven for those who like their world tinted by a rainbow of greens.

Bayou LaBranche once flowed between the southwestern shore of Lake Pontchartrain and the Mississippi River. Before the river levees were built they undoubtedly carried spring overflow into the lake, spreading water into the cypress forests and open freshwater marshes. During dry summers, when the river dropped below its banks, bayou currents probably slowed to a crawl, and the deep quiet of the swamp would have been broken only by the cries of herons, the hoot of owls, and the screech of wood ducks.

Levees ended that relationship with the Mississippi. And some years later, U.S. Highway 61 chopped off the bayou's southern third. It, too, got worked over by loggers and oil miners, and for years developers looked for ways to drain the region. Yet today its future looks wet. Conservation groups and sportsmen's clubs consider it a wetland fragment worth saving.

Our put-in is at a parking area off the shoulder of U.S. Highway 61, about 6.7 miles north of Williams Boulevard in Kenner. The first mile is spent paddling the Cross Bayou Canal, a cypress-lined waterway that struggles to be beautiful: As is typical of south Louisiana canals, its allure is obscured for several hundred yards by litter and garbage tossed from the road and a film of engine oil. But within half a mile, the litter and noise taper off. At the end of the first mile, the canal turns west and empties into Bayou LaBranche, and the world becomes 200 years younger.

On the east side, a natural levee holds cypress, gum, and maple, a thin line that gives way to the open floating marshes stretching for miles toward the airport. Bird life is abundant. Depending on the season, waterfowl paddle among wading egrets, ibis, and herons.

The west side is another world. It's a cypress swamp with an understory of palmetto. Old timber canals and trenaises, their surfaces coated in duckweed, wind into the swamp like long green snakes. During high water, they offer excellent side trips, twisting through canyonlike walls of cypress and leading to hidden lakes. A quiet paddler is likely to surprise wood ducks, herons, egrets, and perhaps a deer.

After about two miles, a low wooden weir guards the mouth of a small canal on the east bank, and signals another change in character for the bayou. Saw grass and cane begin to line the east bank, and huge cypress have moss-draped branches reaching over the water. Red maples become more abundant, and cattails sway in the breeze.

This is a good place for a break. Hip boots enable Marie and me to step out of our boats and explore higher ground, following our ears toward some curious sounds. Soon we spot the source: A tangle of maples seems alive with white feathers, a writhing mass of noise that grows more animated as we approach. It's a yellow-crowned night heron rookery. Most of the young are just a few days old, sheltered by parents who noisily demand that we leave. These birds have some reason to be nervous. Known locally as "gros becs" (big beaks), the herons are the object of a cultural tug-of-war between Cajuns and federal wildlife agents. The gros becs suffer from a serious problem: They taste good. But since they are a protected species, federal agents are sworn to save them from the ravages of the gumbo pot. That conflict of interest has produced an endless array of folk yarns over the years.

We're not hungry, just curious, and so the birds are left in peace, and we continue down Bayou LaBranche.

After three miles, a westerly wind brings a murmur of faint noise from Interstate 10; a quarter mile later, we can see the elevated bridge spans. But just beyond is the shoreline of huge Lake Pontchartrain, a reminder that for New Orleanians, there is no escape from nature.

The following day, I yearn for more of the outdoors. This time, it's the voice of Dr. John that rattles between my ears, and some crayfish étouffée that provides energy. I'll need it. Today, I'll be taking the ultimate plunge off the edge—exploring the mouth of the Mississippi River with a group of seven other paddlers.

The Mississippi River delta is farther from town than the previous outings, but it's a voyage that encapsulates the south Louisiana paddling experience. Canoeing the great delta takes you through emotional white water—territory where you can be moved from awe to anger in an instant, where each leap of the spirit carries a tug of guilt, like laughter at a funeral. It's a trip everyone should make.

Just 70 miles from the city, remnants of one of the earth's great wildernesses hang on against all odds. Carved to shreds by oil and gas exploration, condemned to death by a system of levees and jetties that rob it of life-giving silt, littered by the ugly garbage of failed oil and gas projects, the place is literally a skeleton of what it was just 50 years ago.

But what a skeleton.

It has more birds on any one day than most places in this country see in a year. Wide and powerful waterways bear two-thirds of the nation's runoff. Delicate, ribbon-thin bayous flow through vast green prairies of elephant ear splashed with islands of yellowtop, violet iris, and startling white spider lilies. Bloody sunsets and dawns are delivered on a dreamlike carpet of fog.

Wreathed about that skeleton are the detritus of the twentieth century and the terrible insults left on this precious land. For those who love wetlands and wildlife, what's left of the delta offers one challenge: To find the beauty within the beast.

Our group of eight accepts the challenge on a two-day trip. It's an eclectic gathering, including a college professor, a massage therapist, a game warden, and a Coast Guard officer. The plan is to paddle south through the federally managed 48,000-acre Delta National Wildlife Refuge and into the Pass-a-Loutre Wildlife Refuge, a 66,000-acre companion area managed by the state. Both are past the road's end; the only travel within each is by air—or water.

The high waters that come in the spring allow a paddling route off the main river passes and across wide shallow lagoons and natural bayous. We may cover 20 miles in two days—if all goes well. Spring's cooler temperatures provide some relief from mosquitoes and gnats. Bird migrations could be near their peak.

The morning is chilly and windy as the group boards a boat in Venice to reach the put-in, on a canal off Baptiste Collette Pass, about five miles away. This is the last town on State Highway 23, the end of the road. There's no mistaking what rules the morning rush hour. A diesel roar rises as commercial shipping engages in its morning melee: Shrimp boats mix with long liners, oil field crew boats, offshore tugs, tiny bass fishing boats, gillnetters, and oceangoing tankers. By the time we reach Baptiste Collette, our ears are ringing and our eyes have had their fill.

Thankfully, silty brown water quickly grabs the canoes, pulling the party south into the heart of the delta—or what's left of it. Signs of humanity's heavy hand are everywhere: straight canals, spoil banks, abandoned oil tanks, rotting barges.

"It gets better," Mike Guidry, a game warden with the U.S. Fish and Wildlife Service, assures us. "It gets really beautiful."

Once, it was one of the most beautiful spots on the continent. The original delta was formed by the huge load of sediment carried by the Mississippi. As the river nears its mouth at the Gulf of Mexico, its flow gradually slows. Eventually, it is not traveling fast enough to carry the silt, and fine-grained particles start dropping out.

In the old days, when the river ran over its banks in floods, those particles fell on the sides of the passes, building the river's delta. Fresh water from the river was critical to the plant life that held the soil together against the ravages of salty storms from the Gulf.

That building of the delta covered an immense area. If the main river is an arm, the delta is its hand and fingers. Major passes branch from the wrist across the land base, and scores of smaller passes and bayous make river fingers, twisting and turning toward the Gulf across hundreds of square miles of green wilderness. Huge marshes once rose from the gifts of the silt and fresh water. Forests of cypress were interspersed with marshes, ponds, and lagoons. That landscape was constantly being re-shaped as the river changed courses, surging through high and low cycles.

The first European settlers found a staggering array of wildlife on the delta. It was the winter home of 30 percent of the continent's wa-terfowl. Mink, otter, and deer were abundant. And the water writhed with fish, shrimp, crabs, and oysters. It was a paradise for wild things. The few humans hardy enough to try to live here were far from the nearest city and exposed to the ravages of the tropical heat, humidity, insects, and storms.

It all stayed relatively unchanged until the 1930s. Then the nation extended its flood protection levees below New Orleans. Communities south of the city no longer had to worry about the flooding Missis-sippi—but the resources that provided their livelihood had been handed a death sentence. The once-free river was now locked in mud walls. Its load of silt, needed to build and maintain the delta, got shunted right off the continental shelf.

Robbed of its basic building material, the delta is doomed to slowly sink. This process got speeded up dramatically when the canals were dredged for oil, gas, and ship traffic. Thousands of acres of marsh have been destroyed outright. But the canals have had another impact: In low-water years they've provided a direct line for salt water into the interior of the delta. Plants have died, and erosion has increased. Mining for oil and gas has forever affected the wilderness in the delta. Industry is now everywhere.

State and federal wildlife agencies have had some success in slow-ing the destructive tide. Two wildlife areas preserve a large section of the delta's eastern side. Experiments with silt-trapping fences have helped build new land, but the underlying problem remains: Levees continue to squeeze and speed the river. So the delta continues to settle. Huge areas once filled with marsh grass or elephant ear are now open lagoons and bays. Southern edges of the delta, battered by salty waves from the Gulf, collapse at a steady rate.

Everyone on our trip knows this story. That's why they've come.

Within minutes of leaving the put-in, we turn off the main canal into a mile-long lagoon less than six inches deep. Islands of willow grow on the ridges of ancient sloughs, now silted in. Thousands of swallows shuttle overhead, feasting on gnats and other spring insects. Red-winged blackbirds, warblers, and woodpeckers dart between the willow islands. Herons and ibis probe the shallow flats, using long beaks to skewer meals from the muck. Groups of white pelicans float like icebergs across the water's edge.

Soon the roar of diesel engines is forgotten. Eyes are glued to binoculars, and sightings ring out.

"Prothonortary warbler."

"Barn swallow."

"Mottled duck."

"Green heron."

"Blue-winged teal."

The spell is broken as a helicopter lumbers overhead.

"Louisiana wilderness," scoffs Oliver Houck, the college professor. "White pelicans and straight exhaust. What a combination."

Yet soon the chopper is forgotten. Probing the shoreline, we paddle out of the lagoon and find ourselves in a watercourse hardly 10 feet wide, lined with patches of cane. A swift current hustles us past ponds alive with birds. Five minutes later, we are deposited in another large, shallow lagoon.

"We're really going with the flow," says Richard Carriere, the masseur. "This is perfect. No rush, just exploring where the water takes us."

That's the way to spend a day crossing between lagoons and trenaises, and bays and bayous. Each choice is an adventure. Although modern aerial photos show most of the watercourses, they don't show depth. One bayou might lead to a lagoon deep enough to paddle; the next, to a dead end on a mudflat.

Each choice can lead to different emotions. One turn could bring wonder: sighting a peregrine falcon, finding a field of iris, watching an osprey fly off with a meal. Another turn brings disappointment: abandoned oil tanks, a wrecked camp, rotting hulks of boats.

Sometimes we fight the flow.

"The highest ground around is the natural levees," says Robert Martin, a state game warden and avid sea kayaker. "The water coming off those passes runs down into lower ground. I guess by staying off the passes, we have more work, but we're also seeing more."

By five o'clock we push through the Delta National Wildlife Refuge, paddle across the Main Pass, and find a campsite on Raphael Pass, just outside the refuge boundary. It's perfect for the total delta experience: A high spoil bank from a dredging operation is flanked by beautiful, willow-lined sloughs. Mudflats are covered with shorebirds and waterfowl, but the scene is marked by camp lights and the sounds of crew boats from nearby Pilottown. In addition, there's a bedtime lullaby of foghorns blaring through the darkness every 10 seconds.

The next day our group passes into state-owned Pass-a-Loutre, where the scene shifts delicately. Roseau cane islands are more prevalent and the bays are larger, including Sawdust Bend, which stretches for almost two miles. Like others on the delta, this bay is the spawn of hurricanes.

"Storm tides from hurricanes came through here and just rolled up the floatants like carpets," Guidry says. "Before the hurricane, this was all solid marsh."

By five o'clock we reach Pass-a-Loutre's state research camp and begin pulling out. Our two days and 20 miles of paddling the great delta of the continent's largest river has left some grand impressions.

"It's a surreal mix," Carriere offers. "On one hand, you have this feeling of wildness, these great concentrations of birds and a wonderful stillness of isolation. But you're constantly being yanked back to reality by all the signs and sounds of industry. You're going back and forth. The nice thing is, you can always get away in a hurry."

It has that edge.

TRIP NOTES

The Bayou country of Louisiana is an extensive and complex landscape; many skills are required to navigate it successfully. Foremost among these, of course, is the ability to handle a canoe. Before embarking, one should know basic paddle strokes, gear stowage techniques, and how to recover from a capsize. Good map and compass skills are also essential, especially if you travel far from urban landmarks.

When to go

Spring and fall are the best seasons for exploring the wetlands around New

Orleans. Temperatures are cool, bug populations are smaller, colors are optimal, and wildlife is abundant.

On the delta, the spring season is fickle; it could last two months or two days, but in general you'll find springlike conditions from the first week of March through mid-April. Red maples bloom in mid-March, and irises explode in the first part of April, followed closely by lilies. The Jazz Fest always takes place from the last weekend of April through the first weekend of May.

Fall doesn't come to the bayous until mid-November or early December, when much of the nation is already in the early stages of winter. Temperatures on the bayous might dip into the 40s and 50s at night, but usually rise into the 70s by day.

Where to go and what to bring

• **Bayou LaBranche Wetlands.** This sprawling area a few miles away from New Orleans is not managed as a park, and is not under the strict supervision or jurisdiction of a particular agency, so paddlers will be a bit more on their own. However, the water is flat and easy, and suitable for beginners.

Finding a canoe or pirogue rental in New Orleans is difficult. If you can't bring your own, try Canoe and Trail Outings, 6976 General Haig Street, New Orleans, LA 70124; (504) 283-9400.

From New Orleans, take Interstate 10 west and exit on Williams Boulevard. Turn left and travel about five miles to U.S. Highway 61, then turn right and drive for about 6.7 miles.

The put-in is on the right side of the highway.

Maps: All but the first mile of the route is on the USGS Bayou LaBranche quadrangle. The first mile is on the Luling quadrangle. Paddlers also might want to take the LaPlace quadrangle, which shows the course of adjoining Bayou Trepanier.

What to bring: Pack hip boots or waders for exploring beyond the main bayou, along with plenty of water, sunscreen, and insect repellent.

• **Jean Lafitte National Historical Park and Preserve.** This park is divided into four units, and the largest tract of swamp habitat close to New Orleans lies in the 20,000-acre Barataria Preserve. Canoe rentals for self-guided trips are available nearby at the Bayou Barn on Highways 45 and 3134, about three miles from the visitor center. Outfitters will provide a shuttle to and from the put-in. The shop often has a good Cajun "fais-do-do" on weekends, complete with food and Cajun music. Reservations for canoes are recommended; call (504) 689-2663.

The National Park Service offers day and moonlight ranger-guided paddling excursions during the spring and fall. For information, contact the Barataria Preserve at (504) 589-2330. For information about the park's other units, contact the park headquarters at 365 Canal Street, Suite 3080, New Orleans, LA 70130; (504) 589-3882.

From New Orleans, take U.S. Highway 90 West across the Crescent City Connection (the Mississippi River bridge). Turn left on Barataria Boulevard, which becomes State Highway 45. Stay on Highway 45 for about 10 miles until you reach the visitor center, where you'll find maps and information on current paddling conditions.

Maps: USGS Bertrandville and Lake Cataouatche East quadrangles.

What to bring: Pack knee or hip boots so you can leave the canoe to stretch your legs and explore the marshes and swamps. Bring plenty of water, insect repellent, sunscreen, and rain gear.

- **Mississippi River Delta.** This vast region is where the spoils of a river that drains 41 percent of the United States have wound up over the millennia. Only in recent times, with the ill-advised dredging of channels and the breaching of natural barriers by industries, has the great delta begun to shrink; it is now losing about 35 square miles a year. However, the intrepid explorer can still find splendid examples of its original natural beauty.

Paddling is generally easy on the delta and the water is flat, but the logistics of this trip, plus the need to navigate by chart and aerial photographs, make it unsafe for beginners.

Canoe rentals are available in New Orleans through Canoe and Trail Outings, 6976 General Haig Street, New Orleans, LA 70124; (504) 283-9400.

There are no established guides for the delta. However, Canoe and Trail may be able to refer you to experienced delta paddlers available for hire.

Shuttle services from Venice to the delta are available through charter boat operators at Venice Marina, (504) 534-9357, and Cypress Cove Marina, (504) 534-9289. Rates are typically about $150 round-trip. Overnight accommodations are available at both facilities.

Before planning a trip, get up-to-date information on the delta by calling the U.S. Fish and Wildlife Service at (504) 589-4956, and the Louisiana Department of Wildlife and Fisheries at (504) 568-5886. Regulations on touring the delta change yearly, and permits may be required. Also, some areas occasionally are closed to protect wildlife.

Maps: Aerial-photo maps of the delta are the best choice, since they show the most up-to-date conditions. A series of color photo maps is available at most tackle stores in New Orleans. Laminated versions cost about $12 per map, and you'll need two maps to cover the east side of the delta. Contact Standard Mapping Services at (504) 887-0364.

Note: Even aerial-photo maps can be outdated after one high-river year, because sandbars appear, flats fill in, and bayous change course. Go over your intended route with the authorities and the shuttle skipper before departing.

What to bring: Although humanity's handiwork is never far away, this is a true wilderness. Come prepared with enough fresh water, food, and first-aid gear to handle being stranded. Insect repellent, long-sleeved shirts, and long pants might be required at any time, especially after dark. Use extreme caution crossing major passes: High winds can create Class II waves, and navigators of fast-charging commercial marine vehicles often have a hard time seeing canoes and kayaks.

Additional information

The Louisiana Nature Center has a museum with hands-on interpretive displays and a bookstore, and sometimes organizes canoe field trips into the LaBranche Wetlands. For more information, contact the center at P.O. Box 870610, New Orleans, LA 70187-0610; (504) 246-5672.

To find a certified canoe instructor near you, contact the American Canoe Association at (703) 451-0141.

In Pursuit of the Leaper

by Paula J. Del Giudice

The airplane plows through the night, a silver dart circling an obsidian sky. Below, the town of Saint John's, Newfoundland, lies entombed by thick fog. Apparently, this is common for Saint John's. We've been circling in this machine for hours and all passengers are antsy and tired. I can't wait for this droning boredom to end so my fishing and touring adventure can ignite. An ardent fly-fishing angler, I've come primarily on a quest to feel the strike of a legendary Atlantic salmon at the end of my line . . . *Salmo salar,* the leaper.

Just as the pilot says it looks like we'll have to change schedules and land in Halifax, the fog parts and we barrel through it toward our destination.

Not only have I traveled thousands of miles from Reno, Nevada, to visit this outpost on the North Atlantic, but I soon discover I'm about to travel a good distance back in time as well.

At the Saint John's airport, a representative of the provincial government's tourism branch greets me and hands me a packet of information on a tour I'm signed up for. I'm too tired to do more than stuff it into my bag.

It's two o'clock in the morning before I finally mount the three flights of narrow, creaky stairs that lead up to my room at the quaint, Victorian-era Prescott Inn, near the waterfront of Saint John's. Under my arm I carry an aluminum tube that holds a graphite Fenwick rod. This rod will be my cat's whisker, my insect antenna for feeling my way through experiences in this new, maritime world.

As my head hits the pillow, I feel my body try to realign itself with the new time zone. Late the next morning, I go downstairs to find out about the breakfast part of this B&B. The inn's co-owner, Janet Peters, greets me and explains that it's so quiet here because her other guests have already eaten and are long gone. However, she's saved me a good breakfast. While eating, I study the trip itinerary in the packet I was handed at the airport.

As I read, I find to my growing dismay that I'm not booked on a fishing tour, but a general tour of Newfoundland, with just a few angling days tucked in at the end. In fact, Saint John's is on the opposite side of the best Atlantic salmon fishing on the island. What's the problem here? I'd requested fishing; I'd sent them clips of hunting and fishing stories. . . . Did some office bureaucrat make some arbitrary guess that a woman couldn't possibly be seriously interested in angling?

As I mull this over and consider raising heck and throwing out the itinerary, I surprise myself by realizing that I do find something attractive about a general tour. This whole island is unfamiliar, intriguing terrain. Saint John's, despite its location high on the eastern seaboard, enjoys the distinction of being the oldest city in North America. It's rich in a culture and history I know nothing about.

The fact that I've been handed something unexpected doesn't necessarily mean I should reject it out of hand. Think of it as serendipity,

I tell myself. As the writer Kurt Vonnegut says, "Unexpected travel suggestions are dancing lessons from God." This tour does have some good fishing days on the end. And I can always seize any fishing opportunities that may present themselves en route.

So, like any good stream-wader, I decide to move with the flow.

After breakfast, I meet with Regina Mcarthy, the tour guide, and we head for Signal Hill. This hill was originally used by messengers to signal merchants that ships were approaching the harbor. It became famous at the turn of the century when Italian engineer Marchese Marconi received the first transatlantic wireless message here, from a radio transmitter in Cornwall, England, on December 12, 1901. Also on Signal Hill is the imposing brick structure known as Cabot Tower, built in 1897 to commemorate the 400th anniversary of John Cabot's discovery of Newfoundland and to honor Queen Victoria's Diamond Jubilee. The lofty tower is enveloped in a dense bank of fog this morning; standing at its base, I'm enthralled by the ethereal quality of the billowing wreaths of mist. It adds a mystical aspect to my sense of drifting backward through time.

As Regina shuttles me around Saint John's, my time-travel trip takes on a more human tone. She speaks lovingly of her city, her province, and her ancestors. Regina's roots, dating back to the 1700s, are firmly planted in the soil of Saint John's. And her relatives even helped build much of the town. I look up at the stained glass of the Catholic Basilica of Saint John the Baptist. Regina tells me her grandfather is actually depicted in one of its windows, as an altar boy attending the consecration of a bishop in the late 1800s.

It strikes me forcibly how different this place is from my home in the western United States. Newfoundland is a place where people don't scramble around every 10 years chasing a job market. It's a place where many generations of children grow within the security of large extended families, thus gaining a sense of proprietorship about their city, province, and country. When oppression, invasion, drought, hurricane, or fire beset them, Newfoundlanders dig in their heels and weather the storms. They emerge with a fierce loyalty, an incomparable pride and dignity, and an unwavering optimism.

They also must be the friendliest people on earth. They have the highest respect for others—my gosh, they even stop their cars to let pedestrians cross the road. That this practice is considered mandatory was underscored for me in no uncertain terms when I was briefed on the proper way to drive through the province.

A quick tour of this city barely gives you an adequate taste. But two spots definitely worth exploring are the Newfoundland Museum, which provides a fascinating look at the lives of the Beothuck Indians, and Water Street, the oldest business district in North America, where ghosts of rowdy whalers and sailors still seem to linger in the pubs and shops.

Next, Regina takes me north to Quidi Vidi Village, on the shore of Quidi Vidi Lake (naturally), which has access to the sea via a narrow channel into a small bay. My trip back in time is nearly complete as I look at the "established in . . ." dates posted on the small fishermen's shacks, which date back to the 1700s. I'm filled with awe over this truly "newfound land." My 10 days here will not be nearly enough. Our last stop is the harbor, where I meet Charlie Anonsen, captain of the beautiful S.V. *Scademia,* the last grand bank schooner built in eastern Canada. As I board the ship to the strains of saucy accordion tunes, I realize that this is the perfect soundtrack for my trip.

Snoozing on the deck is Bosun, Charlie's enormous black Newfoundland dog. Bosun seems right at home, with good reason. His breed originated on the east coast of Newfoundland near Saint John's. Intelligent, lovable, furry dogs that swim well (they have webbed paws), they were once used to rescue people who were stranded in the water after a boating accident. As the *Scademia* begins to move out of the harbor, I marvel at the array of other vessels all around us, sailing under every flag imaginable.

Fog embraces the lighthouse marking the harbor entrance, granting it an eerie beauty. I don't think we'll do any whale-watching today, since the fog is growing heavier, choking the landscape.

After we've sailed awhile, it's time to try a way of fishing that's foreign to me: jigging for cod. The "jigs," rigged by Captain Anonsen, are mere planks of wood with heavy line encircling them. There's a big, bare hook on the end of the line. You unwind the line all the way, then jig the line up quickly, hoping to find a fish on the other end. Occasionally, there is one. I actually snagged a cod.

I don't realize, just then, how lucky I am: At the time of my visit, the cod-fishing industry along the east coast of Canada is plunging toward a tremendous crash. In 1992, the island's northern cod fishery was closed for two years to let stocks rebuild. Then that moratorium was extended indefinitely. It's estimated that more than 100,000 fishermen and processing workers are out of luck and out of work—25,000 of them from Newfoundland alone.

Everyone lays the blame for this on someone else. Small-time inshore fishermen point to operators of offshore trawlers—big boats with sprawling nets that pick up all the fish they want, along with plenty they don't. Nearly everyone accuses the foreign fishermen of overfishing, because cod stocks migrate back and forth between Canada's 200-mile-wide exclusion zone and international waters.

Actually, the Canadian government may have had the biggest hand in the crash. Officials refused to believe the gloomy predictions of fishery scientists. Instead, they blithely continued to subsidize new boats and processing plants. But it's expensive to manage by hindsight, which the government is now discovering as it pays an average of $260 per week to unemployed fishermen and plant workers.

Bottles of dark beer are offered by the skipper. The brew tastes potent and wonderful, even on a cool, foggy day. I close my eyes and listen to the music as billowing sails drive us back toward the harbor.

If I keep my eyes shut tight, I can imagine the faces of the Viking adventurers peering through the mist as they discovered this region in 1001 A.D. They named it Markland, or "land of forest." I can envision the others who came to this island part of the province, too: the Brits, following Cabot's claim for England; the French, who fought Britain for dominion in North America; and the French colonials, Acadians seeking refuge from persecution. In addition, the Basques traveled here from the Pyrenees, the Portuguese and Irish came to fish, and the Scots came to herd sheep and start a textile industry. I can also dimly perceive the faces of the native people, most of whom disappeared before the European settlers arrived.

The Maritime Archaic Indians—so named by historians because no one knows what they actually called themselves—were the area's earliest known inhabitants. The decline of their culture, which lasted from about 2000 B.C. to 1000 B.C., is not fully understood. It's thought they were driven from the east coast of Canada by environmental problems, or by the southward drift of Eskimo tribes.

The Eskimos moved in from the central Canadian arctic by way of coastal Labrador. Their era is traditionally divided into pre-Dorset and the later Dorset cultures. It was the Dorset culture that persisted on the island of Newfoundland until as late as 700 A.D., enduring until just a few centuries before the first Norse visits.

The Beothucks (or "Red Indians," who were named after their tradition of painting their bodies with red ocher) occupied Newfoundland when the Norse arrived, and may have originally come from the Quebec-Labrador boreal forests. The reasons for their demise are many and complex, traceable in large part to European diseases brought by the Norsemen and conflicts between the two groups. The Beothucks were dependent on coastal resources, such as birds, fish, and mammals; when Europeans began establishing their fishing encampments along the coast, competition and, ultimately, ruin were inevitable.

Like the United States, Newfoundland is a melting pot of those who came seeking a better life. It seems, however, that eventually Newfoundlanders figured out how to get along more peacefully than we Yanks have. Perhaps it will take us another hundred years or so to follow suit.

I am hauled back from such reveries by our ship's captain. "I understand you're a writer," he says. "What kind of writing do you do?"

"I write about fishing," I tell him. I acknowledge that I'm having a great time exploring but am getting damned anxious to angle. (Jigging for cod gave me a taste, but only whetted my appetite for piscatorial pursuits.) I explain how depressing it is that I'm not scheduled to fish for several more days.

"If it's trout you're after," says Charlie, "maybe I can help."

Early the next morning, I bid farewell to my B&B host, Janet. "Too bad you can't stay longer," she says. "You haven't even learned of our local custom of 'screeching in' honorary Newfoundlanders." She tells me about a less-than-solemn ritual for initiating a prospective "Newfie," as the locals are called by other Canadians: The newcomer must learn to swill the strong, black rum called Screech, imported from Jamaica, and survive to tell the tale. As I pull away from Number 19 Military Road to hook up with Charlie on a quest for some trout, I'm glad I don't have a "screeching" headache; I decide to save that particular dram of local culture for another visit—maybe.

It took me only seconds to derive the answer to a popular riddle about Saint John's weather: It isn't always foggy in Saint John's—sometimes it rains. And now it's raining too hard for my windshield wipers, forcing me to strain to see Charlie's car in front of me. Saint John's slips away in my rearview mirror.

B less their hearts, I think. Charlie and his brother are the epitome of Newfoundland's friendly people. However, it is clear, after fishing a pond or two, that they don't know anything about trout fishing in eastern Newfoundland. Then again, neither, apparently, do I. I cast every fishing fly I have in my arsenal and do not win a single rise. After a while, I suspect there are no fish in these ponds, and my effort to break away from the tourist-office schedule for some real fun will prove fruitless.

So I relax and reduce my expectations. I pitch a rock for Bosun to chase, enjoy a brief reprieve from the rain, and admire the ambient countryside. It's time for lunch, and we start looking for a restaurant in the nearby village. Spotting a local cafe, we park nearby and walk over. I'm learning that Newfoundland cuisine isn't fancy, but I'm determined not to let any local gastronomic traditions pass me by. I see cod tongues on the menu and inquire about them, hesitantly. I'm game to eat anything once, so I order a plate. The tongues are tasty, not unlike deep-fried clams, yet not quite as rubbery. They seem to go down best if I swallow fast, not letting them pause very long on the back of my own tongue.

When it's time to say good-bye, I thank Charlie and his brother for showing me a part of the island that wasn't on my itinerary. With a pat on the head for Bosun, I head back to my car to finish the drive to Clarenville.

The next morning I set out to enjoy my first chance to visit a national park in the province. Terra Nova National Park is difficult to miss; the Trans-Canada Highway, which traverses the island of Newfoundland from Saint John's to Channel Port aux Basques, goes right through it. But that topographical incongruity is nothing compared to what's in store: As I enter the preserve, I am stunned to see a manicured nine-hole golf course.

There's plenty of nature, too. Three fingers of the North Atlantic reach deep into the park boundaries: South West Arm, Newman Sound, and Clode Sound. The sea has a definite influence on the temperate park climate, yet rocky headlands provide shelter from the open ocean's awesome power. The warm Gulf Stream flowing past the island delays the onset of winter, while the cold force of the Labrador Current lends a chill to the spring and winter months. And of course, the climate in turn affects the park's plant and animal life. The rolling hills and knobs are covered with black spruce and balsam fir; wetlands are rich in low-lying vegetation.

Because Newfoundland is an island, separate from the Canadian mainland, the wildlife here differs from that of other boreal forests. You won't find porcupines, skunks, or snakes. Nonnative species such as snowshoe hare and moose have adapted well to their new surroundings, coexisting with indigenous species such as lynx, beaver, and bear. The park also protects a remarkably diverse coastal zone, with rugged, rocky cliffs as well as smooth, sandy beaches. Those who like marine creatures are in luck: Sea urchins, starfish, mussels, periwinkles, and rock crabs inhabit the rocky shore. You may also see bald eagles, ospreys, ducks, and shorebirds feeding here.

Watching others enjoy the park is nearly as much fun as taking the time to do it myself. I snap a few pictures of a family hiking with their youngster, who's being carried on his dad's back. I photograph a life-size silhouette of a blazing-orange bull moose posted by the road to warn highway motorists to slow down while cruising through the park. I watch the cars approach; when they see how a life-size moose compares to the size of their compact car, they slow down immediately. I love the looks on their faces.

I arrive in Gander early in the afternoon, in time to meet Marg Kuta, owner of the Cape Cod Inn, a delightful B&B. Marg has remarkable enthusiasm and volunteers to show me around town. Gander is a complete contrast to the old towns I've visited so far. After Newfoundland joined Canada in 1949, it was modernized to replace a shantytown of war-surplus buildings that had sprung up around the big international airport, which was a strategic staging point for movement of Allied aircraft to Europe during World War II. On the way to the airfield, I spot street signs bearing names of famous aviators who wafted over through the decades: Alcock, Brown, Lindbergh, and Earhart.

Marg designates herself as the one who's responsible for making sure I don't miss anything I want to see or do during my last few days in the province. When I tell her I'd like to see some of the island's wildlife, she calls the tourism office in Gander and enlists some help to show me around the Gander River the next day. I pick a local restaurant recommended by Marg for dinner. The hosts bend over backward to make sure I enjoy my meal. All at once, though, I feel awfully homesick, wishing I had someone along—like my husband—to share it all with.

The next day, I feel distress of another kind as I talk with John Curran, regional manager of the Department of Development and Tourism, who meets me for a tour. He tells me the western part of Newfoundland suffers from the worst drought in four years and is desperate for rainfall. As a result, vegetative resources for wildlife such as caribou and moose are severely depleted. And most of the salmon streams are now closed to fishing.

"What about the rain that was falling as I left Saint John's?" I ask.

"It helped and was enough to open a few rivers to fishing, but it was not enough," Curran said.

My heart sinks to my toes. We drive in silence as I watch my dream of catching an Atlantic salmon fade. When we stop by a protected portion of stream to observe some fish, I see them waiting in pools for rain to fall so the rivers will flow again and they can ascend to spawn.

They are stacked up nearly on top of one another. The sight is almost more than I can bear.

I pull out my camera and shoot three rolls. At least I can capture the salmon on film. The fish are exceedingly beautiful. I say a small prayer for them that it rains hard. I say a small prayer for me that it rains soon.

We cap off our trip by spotting several caribou and a beautiful bull moose who pose for my camera. Then I endure a rather long, dark drive to Cornerbrook.

During breakfast the next morning, my guide, George Pike, tells me that Harry's River is still open for fishing. I suddenly feel optimistic. After breakfast, we work one stretch of the river for hours. As I rub the new blisters forming under the casting calluses on my hands, I realize there's only one other place in my entire life where I've cast my fly rod for so long with so few results: at Pyramid Lake, near Reno, Nevada, when I was fishing for trophy cutthroat trout. "We only need one fish," I tell George. "Anyone can catch it. I only need some photos of one fish."

A few other anglers are working the beat. After lunch, George and I walk along the bridge traversing the stream to see how their luck is running. I happen to look down into the shallow river. Right below me is a very big Atlantic salmon. He must weigh 35 or 40 pounds. There are fish in the river, there are! And they're *big!*

This is what I've come to do. I've come to catch *that* salmon, I think, with a sharply renewed sense of mission. I tie on another pattern and head back down to the river. It's a popular gathering spot; before long people are lined up on the bridge to watch. I look up and scan the faces. I am the only woman present.

"It's a girl," I hear. I close my eyes and ears to the other whispers and concentrate on my casting. I raise my line out of the water and false cast a couple of times. *Whoosh, shhwwiiii, whoosh.* "Poetry in motion," I've heard some call a good fly cast, and I remember the words of my casting instructor, Mel Krieger: "If you make a bad cast in public, your Fenwick Fly Casting School patch will disappear."

I let the line carry the iridescent fly out on the water. My breath goes with it, long and smooth. I know this fish has probably never seen this fly pattern before. I let the fly drift downstream past the fish. "Too far over," I hear them, coaching from the bridge. "Cast a little more to the right." So, what is this, fly-fishing by committee? I quickly strip the line in and raise the rod tip to begin again. *Whoosh, shhwiiii, whoosh, shhwiiii, whoosh,* stop.

The fly sails out to the exact spot I'd picked. I look down to see if my patch is still on my vest. It is. I breathe a sigh of relief. "Here it comes! He sees it! He's a moving on it! Here he comes," I hear, as the gallery begins to cheer. My pulse begins to escalate. I hear my heart beating in my ears. My knees are shaking. My palms are sweating. Oh, my God, now what am I going to do?

As it turns out, that doesn't matter. The big salmon doesn't take it.

George Pike feels even worse than I do that I didn't hook that fish. If anyone else wants to see me catch an Atlantic salmon while I am here, it's him. His apologies are profuse. He tells me he knew it was going to be tough. The river is low. Because of the drought, there are few new fish coming into the river, and those that are there (like the old fish under the bridge) have seen most patterns known to man.

I would have felt better about being skunked after spending a full day on the river if I had known then about the angling statistics of some of Newfoundland's best salmon streams, including Harry's River. During the previous year, anglers spent nearly seven rod days there trying to catch a grilse—a salmon measuring between 12 and 24.8 inches. A large salmon measures more than 24.8 inches. On the island of Newfoundland, only grilse may be retained.

As we drive back to George's log-cabin lodge, I realize I have only one more day to fish. Still time to catch one, I think, ever the optimist. While taking a break the next morning, George and I stop to visit a group of college students and their supervisor; they are conducting some studies on salmon. I mention that I am a writer and tell them about the big fish under the bridge. One of the men says, "You know that big fish must have looked up and saw that you were a woman. No wonder he wouldn't take your fly."

I start to shake and can feel myself turning red. My trip back in time is now really complete, I muse, as I try to figure out how to respond. On the one hand, my natural reaction is to tell him what I think of him in no uncertain terms. On the other hand, I am a guest in his country, up until now have enjoyed a wonderful experience, and do not want to embarrass my kind fishing guide. So, I just walk off. No, I stomp off. George comes after me, apologizing. (He wasn't the only one who apologized: Two weeks later, back at home, a letter arrived from the president of the Salmon Preservation Association for the Waters of Newfoundland [SPAWN]. His son was one of the students there that day and was embarrassed by the attack.)

We go back to our fishing, and I'm even more determined now. I look up from my casting and stripping to see an angler next to me holding a bowed rod. He has hooked a salmon! I stumble to shore to grab my camera. All I need is one good photo. I hold the camera up and focus. I snap a few shots. But then I notice something has changed; the bend in his fly rod is gone. So is the fish.

Downhearted, I stow my camera and pick up my fly rod. I cast and cast and cast. My arm is sore, my hand is sore. I have blisters on my blisters. I am ready to go home. Now I surrender, and we leave Harry's River at dusk. Fulfilling my hope of catching an Atlantic salmon will have to wait until my next visit to Newfoundland. My plane departs in the morning.

I came to Newfoundland to touch the elusive *Salmo salar*, the leaper. All I got were some tantalizing glimpses. Yet, to my surprise, I ultimately don't feel that disappointed, because what I found in Newfoundland, almost as a by-product of my quest, was just as precious as what I sought. On many vacations, one travels to a place and participates in it in a relatively shallow, detached way. But I felt I had immersed myself in Newfoundland and experienced the province in many of the same ways its inhabitants do. I had been given a gift of belonging.

TRIP NOTES

Newfoundland is the easternmost province of Canada. Part of it consists of the huge island of Newfoundland—at 42,734 square miles, it's one-third the size of Ireland—separated from the North America mainland by the Strait of Belle Isle, the Gulf of Saint Lawrence, and Cabot Strait. The rest of the province consists of Labrador, a mainland territory of 105,000 square miles.

As much as 45 percent of the island's surface is covered with water—streams, lakes, and ponds. Under normal (i.e., non-drought) weather conditions, the place is a haven for cold-water-loving fish such as trout and salmon, and a heaven on earth for anglers.

When to go

Although Newfoundland benefits from its location at the northern end of the Gulf Stream, winter weather is still hurled ashore from the North Atlantic and can be severe. The best time to enjoy the landscape is between late spring and early fall.

How to go

You have two choices for visiting Newfoundland: Either take a commercial flight to Saint John's, the capital of the province and the island's largest city, or drive to Cape Breton Island and take a ferry to the island's year-round ferry port, Port aux Basques. On the island, highways connect the major towns, but be aware that the winding roads parallel the rugged coastline and take time and care to navigate.

For great trip-planning information, request a copy of the "Newfoundland Travel Guide" from the Department of Development and Tourism, Tourism Branch, P.O. Box 8700, Higgins Line, NF A1B 4K2, Canada; (800) 563-6353.

Commercial tour information is available from Regina Mcarthy at Mcarthy's Party Tours, (709) 781-2244, and from Adventure Tours, P.O. Box 116, Saint John's, NF A1C 5H5, Canada, (800) 779-4253. Adventure Tours arranges voyages on the ship "Scademia," which departs daily from Pier 7 across from the Murray Premises on the Saint John's waterfront.

Where to go

There are 177 named river systems in Newfoundland and Labrador, and each branches into innumerable tributaries. Some of the best streams for Atlantic salmon are the Humber, Gander, Terra Nova, Portland Creek River, and the Great Codroy River.

For a copy of the most recent fishing regulations, contact the Department of Fisheries and Oceans, Communications Division, Newfoundland Region, P.O. Box 8700, Saint John's, NF A1B 4J6, Canada; (709) 772-4423. In general, a salmon and trout license for nonresident anglers costs $50 per person and $75 per family. A trout-only license costs $5 and $10, respectively. Call (709) 729-2630 for information. Season dates vary but are typically between June 4 and September 18. Nonresident anglers must fish with a licensed guide except when fishing from a highway crossing on scheduled (open) salmon streams. A complete list of guides is published in the booklet "Newfoundland and Labrador Hunting & Fishing," available from the Department of Development and Tourism, Tourism Branch, P.O. Box 8700, Higgins Line, NF A1B 4K2, Canada; (800) 563-6353.

Here is one highly recommended guide service:

- **George Pike at Dhoon Lodge.** A six-day fishing excursion costs approximately $1,200. Pike also guides hunts for black bears, caribou, or trophy moose, and will combine hunting and fishing in one package upon request. For trip details, contact George Pike at P.O. Box 41, Black Duck Siding, NF A0N 2C0, Canada; (709) 646-5177 (phone), (709) 646-2552 (fax).

Parks:
Newfoundland boasts numerous provincial parks, national parks, and historic sites, and many have campgrounds; for more details, contact the Department of Development and Tourism, Tourism Branch, P.O. Box 8700, Higgins Line, NF A1B 4K2, Canada; (800) 563-6353.

The following parks are two of Newfoundland's top attractions:

- **Gros Morne National Park.** This 697-square-mile park offers diverse landscapes, from mountains to beaches. Caribou, moose, and snowshoe hares share this habitat. Boat rides take passengers under the cliffs of a glacier-carved fjord. Winter activities include cross-country skiing and snowshoeing, and the big summer attraction is fishing for Atlantic salmon and brook trout. (With conservation measures in place, the salmon fishing is improving.) The park lies on the western end of the province, just 45 miles from Deer Lake. For information, contact the park at P.O. Box 130, Rocky Harbour, NF A0K 4N0, Canada; (709) 458-2066.

- **Terra Nova National Park.** Canada's easternmost national park is on the Trans-Canada Highway, approximately 149 miles north of Saint John's and 50 miles south of Gander. The park is best explored by canoe or on foot. Anglers can catch brook trout or marine fish here; the park also holds one of the nation's most scenic golf courses. For information, contact Terra Nova National Park, General Delivery, Glovertown, NF A0G 2L0, Canada; (709) 533-2801.

Lodgings:
Bed-and-breakfast inns are plentiful, and staying in a B&B is a good way to meet Newfoundland natives. Here are a half-dozen recommendations:

- **Cape Cod Inn.** Rates range from $45 for a single to $55 for a double. There's also a luxury unit with a kitchen for $65 for one person, plus $10 for each additional person. 66 Bennett Drive, Gander, NF A1V 1M9, Canada; (709) 651-2269.

- **Delta Saint John's Hotel.** Rates range from $185 for a single to $200 for a double. 120 New Gower Street, Saint John's, NF A1C 6K4, Canada; (709) 739-6404.

- **The Glynmill Inn.** Rates are $85, plus $5 for each additional person. 1 Cobb Lane, Corner Brook, NF A2H 6E6, Canada; (709) 634-5181.

- **International Plaza Hotel.** Rates for a standard room are $156. 655 Dixon Road (near the Toronto Airport), Rexdale, Ontario M9W 1J4, Canada; (416) 244-1711.

- **Maynard's Motel.** Rates range from $62 for a single to $90 for a deluxe cabin. P.O. Box 59, Hawke's Bay, NF A0K 3B0, Canada; (709) 248-5225.

- **Prescott Inn Bed and Breakfast.** Rates range from $35 to $115. Some accommodations have shared baths, and there are suites with kitchens. A house with a harbor and ocean view is available at the base of Signal Hill. P.O. Box 204, Saint John's, NF A1C 2J5, Canada; (709) 753-7733 (phone), (709) 753-6036 (fax).

What to bring

Fly fishers who are wondering what the heck might draw an Atlantic salmon needn't worry: Local "Newfie" shops carry plenty of tied flies that are proven workers. However, you might want to bring some of your personal favorites, just to show the fish something new. The fly my salmon moved on was an unnamed leech pattern with an iridescent green body, custom-tied by a friend.

Other than that, the gear you'll need for a Newfoundland fishing trip is pretty straightforward. The weather is cool and often wet, even in the summer, so wherever you go, bring light insulating garments that don't absorb much moisture (that means no cotton) and a wind- and waterproof hooded shell. Footgear of the Maine hunting-boot variety is ideal in lowland and riparian areas. And those of you who like to stand in cold rushing streams while flogging the waters should definitely bring neoprene waders. (Nonanglers, too, should carry wind- and rain-resistant clothing.)

Transporting your prize fly rod will be tricky, since some airlines (including Air Canada) won't let you bring it into the cabin. If you have to check your pride and joy, secure it first in a tough PVC rod-carrying tube that has a lock.

Additional information

For additional details on resources and environmental issues, contact the Canadian Wildlife Federation, 2740 Queensview Drive, Ottawa, Ontario K2B 1A2, Canada; (613) 721-2286 (phone), (613) 721-2902 (fax).

Note: All prices listed in this story are in Canadian currency.

On (Not) Climbing the Grand Teton

by Pam Houston

They rise out of the Snake River Valley like a rich, dark promise. Taller than the Grand Canyon is deep, sharper than the blade of a bread knife, the Tetons stand more than 7,000 feet above the Wyoming town of Jackson Hole. Although there are many formidable peaks in the Teton Range, there is no mistaking the Grand Teton, 13,770 feet above sea level, steely gray, deeply fissured, and bent slightly southward—as if after enduring the cataclysm that made it, it wished to rest and turn its face to the sun.

The Grand, as it is known to all who have had the pleasure to live under it, or ski near it, or hike around it, or climb to its summit, is more than the highest peak in what is arguably the continental United States' most spectacular range. It is a magnet, a mother, a kind of home base to a breed of people who have no home. Not just people who ski and climb, but skiers and climbers, the ones who relegate real-life activities like laundry and relationships to a few weeks in the spring and fall when the lifts have closed but it's too slick to climb, or the snow has come but the runs aren't open yet. The Grand calls out to those people, calls them from their lives in Wisconsin or Florida, calls them from their high-paying jobs and their reasonably happy marriages, and says, Come see what it's like to ski Corbett's when the snow's still soft, come see what it's like to have your morning coffee after flashing the Exum Route to the top of the Grand.

There was a time in my life when I was one of those people. When I had to run all the rivers at high water, ski all the hardest runs.

You would think by now I'd know better. That by the age of 33 I'd have some understanding of my own strengths and weaknesses, that I'd know which challenges to take on and which ones to leave behind. I know I don't need to bungee-jump, for example. I don't need to sky-surf. I won't need to run the Selway River at high water ever again. I know the media in which my body performs best, and they are the soft ones: water, snow, the back of a particularly responsive horse. The ones in which my body stumbles are rock, pavement, and any place more than 20 feet off the ground.

I've tried to use this knowledge to stay, in my 30s, out of emergency rooms. To put an end to the most repetitive scenario of my life: i.e., me following someone who is stronger, faster, and better at whatever terrifying sport we are about to try. It is me, girding my loins, holding my breath, and believing—really believing—that if I don't keep up they or she or (most often) he will no longer love me. I did that from the tennis courts of my childhood to the glacial crevasses of my 20s. By the age of 30, I declared myself finished with hard surfaces and with the people—mostly men—who insisted I court adventure on them.

Imagine my surprise, then, when I found myself dangling by a 150-foot length of rope on a rock face called the Open Book, several thousand feet below the summit of the Grand. Dick Dorworth—the fastest man on skis in 1963—was holding fast to the other end.

But there I was.

Dick Dorworth is a climbing guide in the world-renowned Exum Mountaineering School, where a neophyte climber can take an intensive two-day course and, if the guide deems her capable, spend the next two days climbing the Grand.

Perhaps what went wrong in my case is that we tried to do the whole three days of training in one day. Perhaps, as Dick said, I just didn't really want to climb that mountain.

But on the morning of my training session, I thought I did. It was late September, the air as clear and fine and sharp as the big mountain that loomed above. We passed a cow moose on the way to the practice area near Hidden Falls, and I took it as a good omen. It was early when we started, and the trail traffic consisted of big, slow birds. Dick didn't know what they were called, but I found out later they were ruffled grouse.

In spite of all my rock-related, height-related fears, I was excited about the climbing. I'd learned the value of professional instruction only last year, when finally, after seasons of trying to improve my skiing by staying close on the heels of one World Cup–wannabe boyfriend or another, I finally bit the bullet and took a set of lessons from a certified ski instructor. That had improved my skiing the first day by 50 percent.

Dick was both patient and supportive, and I cruised through what would have been the first day's training climbs before we sat down for lunch in the shade of a huge overhanging wall.

When he motioned to the perfectly vertical rock face that adjoined the overhang and said, "That's what we climb after lunch," I was sure he was kidding.

"And if you make it, then we cap the day off with this," he pointed directly overhead, "the advanced rappel."

After one short morning, Dick knew me well enough to know this was the right incentive. Though I'd only done it a few times, I loved rappeling, loved the trust I had to put in the equipment, loved the moment of stepping over the edge, the last contact with the rock before it curved away below an overhang. I loved hanging there, free for a moment, controlling my descent with the rope in my hands, and I loved looking out over all that landscape, which in this case was the sparkling surface of Jackson Lake and clouds making shadows across the Teton Valley floor.

But when I looked at the Open Book, at its sheer, daunting height, I doubted that all that faith and joy and elation would translate to the part where I had to stand on my feet and actually go up.

I got off to a pretty good start, surprising myself by climbing the first 75 feet or so without so much as a hesitation. Then I looked down.

My knees started doing the sewing-machine thing, and I felt fatigue in my joints from the morning. There was a lot more rock above than below me, I noticed, and to continue I would have to move laterally, toward the crease in the "book," and use a hand jam, a technique whose logic my stubborn brain would not quite let me believe.

As any climber will tell you, one moment of faithlessness leads in a straight plumb line to another. The hand jam wouldn't work; the toe-hold was much too small; even the place where I'd been resting, which just moments ago seemed so secure, was suddenly fraught with un-speakable danger. There was no hope for me; the only thing left to do was fling myself upward, sideways, and pray that by some miracle I stuck to the rock.

I didn't. Stick, that is. I fell, 10 feet or so, and clunked hard with my head and my knees and my elbows into the rock, every ounce of my weight hanging from my harness and the rope that Dick held on belay well above me. I couldn't fasten onto a hand jam or a toehold again to save my life.

"Stand on your feet, Pam," came Dick's order from above, and I looked down again, at the 65 feet of wall below me, to the ground that I would kneel down and kiss if only I could get to it, and I said to myself, "Goddammit Pam, how did you get here again?"

"Climb this rock, Pam," Dick said. "Now."

And I tried to do just that. I had faith in my equipment, and more faith still in Dick. My head knew this was only a practice run, for heaven's sake, the bunny hill of climbing. If I needed to I could try again and even fail again, I could hang from that rock all day without getting seriously hurt. But somewhere between my head and the rest of my body I missed a connection, and my heart pounded hard, like I was already cut loose and falling, and my arms and my legs started shaking worse than ever. I clawed and clawed at the wall like a bug on the inside of a water glass, with no result at all.

"Stand on your feet, Pam," came the order, the voice calm, a little bored even. You didn't know the name of that bird this morning, I thought in a completely uncalled-for moment of vindictiveness, you didn't even know that *moose* we saw was a cow.

"Hey Dick," I ventured. "What would you think about letting me down?"

"I can't do that, Pam," he said. "Come on, you can do it."

"Is it that you can't put me down, Dick," I said, "or that you won't?"

"Oh, I can put you down," he said. "But if I do, then you can't do the rappel."

"That may be true according to the laws in your universe," I said. "In my universe I can hike around the back side of this rock and do the rappel anyway."

"We all need challenges in our lives, Pam. It's what keeps us going."

I thought about the top three items on my current list of challenges: a chronically unfinished novel, an impossible relationship with a difficult man, a close friend dying of advanced melanoma. I needed to climb the bunny slope for Exum Mountaineering School like I needed a hole in the head, but I was mad now. I dug my fingernails into the rock and started climbing.

I'm not sure what happened over the next minute or two. I imagine there was a lot of cursing, several ungraceful postures, and judging by the minor abrasions I discovered on nearly every exposed piece of my body when I got to the top, a little pain, though I didn't feel it at the time.

"There," Dick said. "Now, doesn't that feel a lot better?"

But I was shaking too much to tell for sure.

"Okay," Dick said, "one more pitch and we'll call it a day."

I looked up at the rock rising another hundred feet above the ledge we sat on.

"Dick," I said. "I think we both agree that whether or not I make it the rest of the way up this rock, I'm not going to be Grand Teton material."

"I'm afraid that's true," he said.

"I don't know if you will understand this," I said. "But in my life right now, the bigger challenge is to say I'm scared, I don't like this, and I want to go down."

Dick studied my face for a moment, then the rope in his hand. "Okay," he said, and I thought that would be all, but then he said, "Is there anything I could do to make the day better?"

"Yeah," I said, smiling. "You could let me do the advanced rappel."

And he did.

It was wonderful. But I went away sad and disconsolate anyway. The outdoors, the mountains—particularly the Rocky Mountains—have been, since I was old enough to think clearly, my church and my religion. To fail in them, in whatever small or specific way, felt much too much like a failure of my soul.

I needed to make peace with the mountains, peace with the Tetons, peace with myself. I needed to create another challenge, something difficult but not impossible, something that let me be in the mountains in the way that I wanted, with my hands free enough to take pictures and touch tree bark, and my head free enough to do the one thing I do best in the mountains, which is to take them all in.

I decided if I couldn't get to the top of the Grand Teton, I could get to know it some other way, by walking around it, by seeing it from more than one side.

Had I been able to go with Dick, we'd have drawn an arrow up the side of that mountain, but now I'd draw a circle around it instead. The idea appealed to everything female inside me. I'd love the Grand like a satellite, like a spirograph, in all the revolutionary ways only a woman can love.

The ranger I spoke to told me the best views of the Grand were up the north fork of Cascade Canyon, so instead of circling the Grand as planned, I decided to make my circle to the north of it, up Cascade and down Paintbrush Canyon, seeing the Grand from three sides. The views should get better the higher I climbed up Paintbrush Divide.

With the shortening September days and the unpredictable weather, a day hike of 20 miles and an elevation gain of 4,000 feet would be just enough of a challenge. My pack would be a little heavier than a normal day pack, with provisions I'd need if winter came early, extra clothing, and a stove in case I wound up out for the night.

I was up at first light, and the temperature was well below freezing. I tried to ignore the signs at the trailhead about grizzly bear attacks and violent rutting moose in Paintbrush Canyon, about how I should avoid hiking alone or during the low-light, high-predation hours between dusk and dawn. The most fearful thing I saw between the car and Hidden Falls was a muley doe who saw me and didn't startle. The air was softening as the sun climbed higher, and it smelled leafy and loamy, like the ground was ready for winter, waiting for the snow.

By the time I had climbed my first 500 feet into Cascade Canyon I was shedding clothing layers like crazy. The morning fog had lifted and I saw it would be a perfect fall day. The canyon was flat and broad, and I shared the trail with more deer than I could keep track of. Every now and then the Grand winked out at me from above the canyon wall, awash in the morning sun, sterile and alone.

In the north fork of Cascade Canyon on its way to Lake Solitude, the trail climbed up the side of the canyon and rose above tree line. When I looked back I knew why the ranger had recommended this hike. Behind me the walls of the canyon formed a soft cradle of reds and browns and yellows, which held the steely gray Grand perfectly inside it, and I could see every block and fissure, every snowfield, every steep pitch I wouldn't be climbing, backlit and magnificent against a perfect blue sky.

I put my foot in Lake Solitude's icy water. I put my hands on every rock I went by. I played with my camera, shooting patterns I saw in the surface of boulders, the occasional shock of red in the mostly brown tundra, the emerald green siltiness of high and tiny Mica Lake. And I shot the Grand again and again as it rose higher and higher out of its cradle, its shadows lengthening and shifting as the sun tumbled over it. I finally took the last shot when I arrived at the top of Paintbrush Divide, 10,700 feet above sea level. Still 3,000 feet below the Grand's summit, I felt sufficiently reverent, sufficiently awed.

It was four o'clock, and I had 4,000 feet of descent and many miles to make before nightfall. I started down the much steeper Paintbrush Canyon, past Holly Lake and a couple of backpackers, the first people I'd seen since early morning at Hidden Falls.

I was making time like crazy, hoofing it down the trail at top speed, my strong legs pumping, my pack feeling light as a feather, feeling the faith of an outdoorswoman again and sure I was gonna make it back to the truck just within the envelope of visible light, when I heard a noise that made me stop so dead in my tracks the only sound that came next was the echo of my step in the hard-packed dirt of the trail.

It was a loud huff, the unmistakable sound of an animal—a big animal—exhaling. It's a noise they often make when they are threatened, or when they are mating, or in the moment just before they attack. I waited five long seconds of silence before I took two steps forward and dropped my pack. If it was a grizz', I knew he might check out the pack long enough to give me a head start running. If it wasn't a grizz', I wanted to lose the pack and get into position to see what it was.

The huff again, no louder, but this time I could pinpoint its direction. Whatever it was, it was in a stand of ponderosa pine not five feet from where I'd just passed. Whatever it was, it could smell me, and so far it wasn't showing any signs of being scared. The musk of something huge and dark hung like a cloud in the clean evening air. Whatever the animal was, it was making the tops of the ponderosas rattle awfully easily.

I grabbed my camera and a roll of 1,000-speed film from my pack and cut a wide swath around the ponderosas on my way to a glacial boulder I hoped I could climb. It was steep, and smooth as glass, but I dug my toes and fingers in just like I'd practiced and in no time at all made it to the top.

"Thanks, Dick," I said out loud, laughing. But I was silenced by another huff, this one louder, maybe a little angrier than before.

From the top of the rock I could see it was a big bull moose, and I could see the paddles of his antlers, broad and blond and almost glowing in the twilight as he thumped them, again and again against the thick trunk of a tree. His dark head, his huge improbable nose were just a suggestion in the shadows, but I thought I could make out one dark eye gleaming. He was the biggest moose I'd seen in the lower 48, rivaling all but one I saw in Alaska, and that one from a backcountry plane.

I loaded the high-speed film in my camera and started shooting. As if to accommodate me, the moose took a step forward into the remaining light, pausing a minute before finding another tree to bang his head on. Maybe he was mad because I'd invaded his territory, or maybe his antlers were itching and it was getting to be time to knock them off. Maybe there was a lady other than me in the vicinity he was trying to impress. But he wasn't getting anywhere for all his passionate thumping, and I thought of myself scrabbling up there on the Open Book, all the will and rage and desire I'm capable of pumping through my body, and all of it to no avail.

"I know how you feel," I said, softly, but the moose had forgotten all about me.

Until my film rewound, that is, and the camera made a noise he'd never heard before, and he huffed again and made four steps of a mock charge toward me.

"Easy, big boy," I said, and he pawed the ground and fixed me with that gleaming eye. I put my hands in the air and slid down the back side of that rock, gentle as I could, grabbed my pack, and hit the trail at an easy but determined trot. I could hear him coming behind me, the heavy footfalls, not running but walking steadily, the huffing softer now, but regular, in time with his step.

He followed me as far as the next set of switchbacks, but always at a respectful distance, a little like a gentleman, not sure if he wants to make a pass. When I looked back the last time he was nothing more than a dark shape against a darkening sky, but I could tell by the way he held his head that he hadn't taken his eye off me, and he wouldn't until he knew I was gone for good.

It was well past dark when I got to the trailhead, but the harvest moon was bright and full and I had no trouble finding my way. The woods were full of the rumbling of animals, and I could hear the elk bugling their unearthly music in the meadows, a song so full of longing it silenced even the crickets and the owls. Above it all, the summit of the Grand rose to bathe itself in the moonlight: stony, radiant, as good as a million miles away.

TRIP NOTES

Grand Teton National Park in Wyoming is a 310,000-acre kid sister of the huge Yellowstone National Park, which sprawls to the north. Roughly, Grand Teton is divided into three main features: the Snake River plains to the east; the lakes (including Jackson, Leigh, Jenny, and Phelps) through the center; and the magnificent Teton Range, part of the Rocky Mountains, which soar up to form the park's western boundary.

Geologically, the Teton mountains are quite young and extremely interesting. They were formed barely nine million years ago, in a dynamic period of faulting and upthrust from tectonic blocks. Mountain glaciers of the last major ice age then took over the job of sculpting the peaks, leaving a magnificently jagged ridge that includes Nez Perce, Teewinot, Mount Owen, Middle Teton, and the 13,770-foot-high Grand Teton itself. Because of the way these mountains were formed, the view of them is unencumbered by foothills.

When to go

Winter conditions dominate this semi-arid mountain landscape for more than half the year. For rock climbers, the season tends to run from June through mid-September, when the park's mountaineering registration desk is open at the Jenny Lake Ranger Station. Summer is, of course, also the most popular time for hiking and camping.

During winter, cross-country skiing is the popular way to enjoy the park; the park's Moose Visitor Center serves as headquarters for this activity.

How to go

Climbers should avail themselves of either of the two guide services that have permits to operate in the park:

- **Exum Mountain Guides.** The oldest guide service in the park and one of the most famous in the nation, Exum offers a wide array of options, including a two-day school with the goal of summiting on the Grand Teton. Contact Exum at: Box 56, Moose, WY 83012; (307) 733-2297 (phone), (307) 733-9613 (fax).

- **Jackson Hole Mountain Guides.** Based in the nearby town of Jackson Hole, this service has a wide range of year-round options, from ice climbs and ski mountaineering to single and multiday climbs, including a four-day ascent to the peak of the Grand. Contact the guides at: Box 7477, Jackson, WY 83001; (307) 733-4979.

For general reconnoitering and year-round courses on nature in the area, contact the Teton Science School at: Box 68, Kelly, WY 83011; (307) 733-4765.

For information on camping and hiking in the park, contact the superintendent's office at: Grand Teton National Park, P.O. Drawer 170, Moose, WY 83012; (307) 739-3610.

Where to go

About 2,000 climbers a year make the summit of the Grand Teton, following any of more than a dozen routes ranging from easy (for the fit and trained) to difficult, on terrain that varies from vertical rock to steep snow and ice.

The park has entrance stations at Moose and Moran. The most developed visitor centers are at Colter Bay (summer only) and Moose (year-round). Seasonal centers open at Jenny Lake and Flagg Ranch.

Hikers will find upwards of 230 miles of trails in the park. You can get warmed up by taking self-guided nature trails, such as the Colter Bay Nature Trail (two miles), the Taggart Lake Trail (three miles), or the Cascade Canyon Trail to Lake Solitude (nine miles, one-way). After that, options range all the way up to the Teton Crest Trail, which rises from the valley floor at a 6,500-foot elevation to a path above 10,000 feet that circles the range's highest peaks.

Campers will find five fee campgrounds, holding 907 sites, in the park. Jenny Lake allows tents only; the other four (Colter Bay, Lizard Creek, Signal Mountain, and Gros Ventre) can also accommodate trailers or RVs. Colter Bay is the largest, equipped with a restaurant, store, and laundry. In addition, the park concessionaires provide another 287 sites. Backcountry camping requires a permit and is allowed only at designated locations.

Lodging is available inside the park at Colter Bay Village, (307) 543-2811; Jackson Lake Lodge, (307) 543-2811; Jenny Lake Lodge, (307) 733-4647; Signal Mountain Lodge, (307) 543-2831; and Triangle X Ranch, (307) 733-2183. Other options outside the park are at Flagg Ranch Resort to the north, (800) 443-2311; and Jackson Hole to the south, (307) 733-3316 (Chamber of Commerce).

What to bring

Anyone interested in climbing would be well advised to take a few introductory courses before leaving home; that way you can figure out which climbing shoes and harnesses feel most comfortable and safe, and bring them along on the trip.

Other mountain basics include good hiking boots, a sun hat, high-altitude sunglasses, strong sunscreen, moleskin (for blisters), a day pack, a water bottle, a wind-and-rain shell, and a compass.

Additional information

The Grand Teton Natural History Association will mail you a basic information kit including the "Grand Teton Official Guide Book," "Birds of Grand Teton," "Plants of Yellowstone and Grand Teton," "Teton Trails," "Creation of the Teton Landscape," "Origins," and the "Grand Teton Official Guide and Map"—a retail value of $47.65—for $43, plus $5 shipping. They also have a catalog of other useful books available by mail order. Contact the association at: P.O. Box 170, Moose, WY 83012; (307) 739-3403.

Home Is How Many Places

by Gretel Ehrlich

ene' mu. "Resting place." That's what the Chumash Indians called this Southern California harbor, because it was here that they waited in their high-bowed, oceangoing canoes for rough seas to subside before they paddled to their island homes. My destination is *Tuqan,* the Chumash name for San Miguel, the northernmost of the Santa Barbara Channel Islands, about 60 miles away.

In the dark, I step onto the *Peace* and stow my gear. The *Peace* is a 65-foot, diesel-powered boat outfitted for diving expeditions, although tonight it is taking 20 of us on a museum-sponsored tour. Eleven o'clock rolls around. It is usual for the Chumash to wait until at least midnight before heading out, when the seas are calmer. James, the young, dark-haired captain, stumbles into the galley, rubbing sleep from his eyes. He asks for water and glances at the clock. "Not yet," he says to no one in particular, then disappears up a ladder to his bunk because he'll be on watch all night.

The harbor is quiet, only a gentle breeze. The decks have been scrubbed down, but the bolts that hold this iron workhorse together are rusted. By comparison, the Chumash *tomol* (canoe)—used as transportation between the mainland and the islands—was constructed from driftwood shaped with rock tools into planks and sanded smooth with cloths made from sharkskin. Lashed together with milkweed fiber and sealed with black asphaltum—the same tar that seeped up on Santa Barbara beaches not so long ago—the *tomol* was painted ocher, its bow inlaid with several abalone shells that flashed in the moonlight like two eyes.

For 8,000 years or more the Chumash lived in isolation and peace. One of at least 60 tribal groups in California, they once numbered 15,000. They had no neighboring enemies and no warrior cult. Personal vengeance, carried out with poisonings, was the only violence they knew. Climate, the unjust taskmaster of the Plains nations, was a blessing for the Chumash; they enjoyed year-round sun and abundant food from land and sea. Tule elk, deer, and bear were hunted; mussels and abalone were plucked from rocks; acorns, seeds, and berries were gathered. They lived in a 5,000-square-mile paradise. From San Luis Obispo south to Malibu, the Chumash nation included a chain of pristine, habitable islands, a unique, south-facing coastal range, inland valleys, and 300 miles of beach.

Hardly anything would be known about these people had it not been for John Peabody Harrington, a Smithsonian anthropologist and one-time resident of Santa Barbara. In 1912 he returned to his hometown and rented a spartan room in the ivy-covered Riviera Hotel. He was not a young man and had already amassed 800,000 pages of notes on Native American cultures elsewhere, but the Chumash were dear to his heart.

When he sat down with Fernando Librado, Maria Ignacio, and Mary Yee—Chumash descendants—to record every remembered detail of traditional and contemporary Chumash life, Fernando was already 108 years old.

"I remember Mr. Harrington," Paulina, my friend, told me. She had grown up with Mary Yee's daughter. "He wore an old suit, always the same one. He didn't eat, he didn't sleep. He was sick, but he always worked. Every day he came to Mary Yee's house. She had married a Chinese man, but she was Chumash, and she was teaching the language to Harrington. We girls went out because she didn't want us to hear. She was ashamed to speak that way in front of us. But she told Mr. Harrington everything she knew."

Those notes were kept uncataloged in 800 cardboard cartons in the basement of the Smithsonian until recently, when the Museum of Natural History in Santa Barbara brought them home piecemeal. The resident anthropologist had to order the notes by the inch ("that's all we could afford," Paulina said). Now the museum is a workshop of Chumash culture: Recordings of Mary Yee are being transcribed by her daughter, notes written in longhand are being typed and archivally stored, and Harrington's one-of-a-kind typewriter, fitted with Chumash-language keys, is on display.

Sometime after midnight, James, the young captain, reappears, hair slicked back De Niro style: "Get ready to go under way," he yells down to the two galley cooks, Ventura women along for the ride. "This isn't going to be an easy night," he whispers, passing me. Then the diesel engines rev, and we move slowly to sea.

The moment we pass beyond the harbor's protective breakwater, heavy winds hit. Nothing has prepared me for the swell outside: Ten-foot waves slam against us as James heads the *Peace* up into the wind, the heavy bow dropping down into troughs as new swells rise.

Long after the museum people have gone below to sleep, I sit alone on the deck, holding the rail. There's no place else I'd rather be than under way at night in a small boat. Once, on a sailboat, I was lashed to the tiller in a sea this rough and felt the wind send shocks up through the keel and down the mast into my hands. Now the coastline lights of Oxnard, Ventura, and Santa Barbara recede and those of a drilling platform loom ahead. We seem to move forward only by going up and down—as if a giant were playing ball with an elevator.

I was raised not far from here, in a house in Montecito with a view of the sea, and never understood how the steel legs of an offshore drilling platform could stand so straight in the water, and why, at Christmastime, the rig was made to look like a Christmas tree. Now the *Peace* chugs under the platform's city-sized deck, stacked with metal containers for living and sleeping, its cold immensity mocking us as we lunge away into the dark curvaceous violence of the sea.

The wind strengthens. I think of Saint John of the Cross's "dark night of the soul." At least he had decent footing. I feel sudden happiness. Who cares where water stops and wind begins, or if night ever ends, or what the difference is between dream and hope and doubt and reality? There's a sameness to it all, which I relish, even as the boat stands upright on swells, walking the ladder of night, and then—kabam—belly flops again. Matsuo Bashō's friend Saigyo wrote:

"Since I no longer think
   of reality
   as reality,
   what reason would I have
   to think of dreams as dreams?"

I lick salt water from my face. Spray blots out stars. Above, the boat's running lights are the only constellation. No celestial navigation tonight, unless it is possible to take a fix on oneself, which would mean I'd have to know where I was while still lost.

Now, instead of salt, I lick darkness from my mouth. It's said that at the bottom of the gravest doubt there is satori, and mention is made of fireflies lit up inside a grave. Light can come into being anywhere. The boat shudders, and the captain's face, illuminated by chart lights, is a torch.

The Chumash thought the cosmos was made of three flattened disks floating in the ocean, and that the middle one, where they lived, was the biggest island of them all. Two giant serpents held it up, the story went; when they grew tired, their tails moved, and that is what caused earthquakes. The lower world was inhabited by *nunasis*—creatures who came out after dark. Some could swallow whole trees, while others had faces with loose, putrefying skin. The upper world was presided over by *Slo'w,* an eagle whose flapping wings—like bellows—caused the moon to grow full, and after, the wings were knives, cutting the moon to a sliver. The water in streams and rivers was the urine of frogs.

I lay my bedroll between the hatch and rail on the deck behind the wheelhouse. Neither the wind nor the storm swells have diminished, but I can see stars. The Chumash called the Milky Way *suyapo'osh*, after the white insides of pinyon nuts and the long trail they walked to gather them. Lying on my back, I see the Milky Way as a rope, one I try to grab in order to steady myself but, at the boat's highest pitch, keep missing. How was it possible to survive these seas in a *tomol*?

Every once in a while James sticks his head out the wheelhouse door to check on me. I've climbed into my bag with shoes, clothes, and glasses on, because anything loose will be tossed overboard. The entire boat is wet. With both hands I hold on to scuppers and hatch covers. The bow of the boat is like a hand feeling the weight and shape of each swell, how and when the wind shifts, from which side we are being ambushed by water. Every now and then I catch glimpses of what looks like a cozy bachelor pad behind the wheelhouse's red curtains: James enthroned in a pilot's seat covered with sheepskins; his three helpers playing cards at a table bolted to the floor; sexy music playing on a tape deck . . . then the curtains swing closed again.

The boat tips up and down, and fins of salt water spray my face. Old Fernando Librado said that at night the sun goes to rest in the hole of a sand dollar, leaving its rays outside while the sun rests within. I stick my head under my canvas bedroll cover and smile in delight.

Toward dawn—I must have dozed off—I wake with a start because the boat has stopped shaking. The water is smooth and gray; the sky is gray. Beads of moisture drip from my hair. Then I see blue cliffs: Santa Cruz Island. As the sun rose from its hiding place, the fog melted away.

There are four northern Channel Islands: Anacapa, Santa Cruz, Santa Rosa, and, most remote, San Miguel. Geologically, they are part of the continental borderland—what geologists call "fringing islands," as opposed to archipelagoes made and cut away by rising and dropping seas, the lateral shear of tectonic plates, and volcanism. Controversy still rages over whether there was ever a land bridge to the mainland. Regardless, early-human sites have been found on Santa Rosa dating back 40,000 years, linking these early islanders with dwarf elephants that, land bridge or not, swam over from the mainland and flourished in isolation.

The word *chumash* means "islander." The First People were thought to have been born on Santa Cruz and radiated out from there. Islanders spoke a different dialect from mainlanders and danced different dances. They paddled their *tomols* to the mainland to buy and sell goods, using tiny shells as currency. On both island and mainland they lived in villages, whose male or female leader was called a *wot*. A council of officials called a *siliyik* took care of village ceremonies and problems. The word *siliyik* also means "whole world."

An old man called an *alchuklash* named the children and took care of the sick. These men were also astronomers and astrologers. As soon as a newborn child moved, these *alchuklash* gave it a name based on celestial temperament. For example, those born in January were considered self-willed and virtuous and named accordingly; the ones born in April, "when the flowers are already in bloom," were cheerful and worked for the community; and December's children were ecstatic, then lethargic, then like gods in the world.

Fernando knew an old man whose star maps were embedded with shells—one for the fall sky, one for the winter, and so on—and the Chumash 12-month lunar calendar was adjusted with the solstices, when feather poles were stuck into the earth, an umbilical connecting the human to the natural world.

In 1542 João Cabrilho—whose Portuguese name was changed to the Spanish Cabrillo—took command of the exploratory voyage along the California coast after his captain died. When Cabrillo's two ships, *La Victoria* and *San Salvador,* paused in the channel, the Chumash paddled out to the strangers. They had never seen a European. Bartholome Ferrel, Cabrillo's diarist, wrote: "All the way there were many canoes, for the whole coast was very densely populated and many Indians kept boarding the ships. They pointed out their pueblos and told us their names."

Unbeknownst to the Chumash, their "biggest island in the universe" was being reduced to a mere point on a much larger, imponderable map.

In 1769 more Europeans came to stay. Dispatched by King Carlos III to protect the area from Russian seal hunters, a priest and some Mexican soldiers arrived on a hot August afternoon. They had been told to build four military forts, or *presidios,* as well as a chain of missions along the California coast like "beads on a rosary." Again, the Chumash displayed extravagant hospitality. They entertained the men with singing and dancing that was so continuous the travel-weary conquerors moved to another camp to sleep. The Chumash didn't understand that their conviviality had been interpreted as acquiescence. Already they had been betrayed.

Fernando Librado said: "Civilization conquered the world at the point of a bayonet. There was also much money at the point of that bayonet." Chumash were lured to mission settlements out of curiosity. Horses, livestock, blacksmithing, gardening, tools—so much they hadn't seen before. Some resisted contact with the whites; others let themselves be baptized, then dexterously juggled two sets of beliefs for the rest of their lives.

The Chumash were taught to be masons, carpenters, cooks, gardeners, vaqueros. Intermarriage was encouraged. Those who resisted "missionization" were often punished. Librado describes how: "There were two kinds of stocks. One was shaped of wood to cover the foot like a shoe. . . . These pieces of wood were joined to a ring which went about the knee, and from this ring straps were attached to a belt that went around the waist of the person. Weights were fastened to the straps. As punishment, the priests would work men and women in the fields with those weighted shoes. The priests also sometimes shackled the feet of the Indians or shackled two together at the same time."

The "civilizing" presence of the Spaniards included many violations, including the use of Indian women for sex by "celibate" priests. "They took all the best-looking Indian girls," Librado said, "and put them in a nunnery. The priest had an appointed hour to go there. When he got to the nunnery, all were in a big dormitory. The priest would pass by the bed of the superior and tap her on the shoulder. She would commence singing. All the girls would join in, which, in the dormitory, had the effect of drowning out other sounds. While the singing was going on, the priest would have time to select the girl he wanted, carry out his desires, and come back to where the superior was. In this way the priest had sex with all of them, from the superior on down."

Though a good deal of Chumash culture was tolerated—Bear and Blackbird dances were performed on the completion of each mission building, for which the men had carried pine timbers on their backs all the way from the mountains—the elastic present of their tribal society had been transfixed. What had formerly been marked by tides, seasons, solstices, and eclipses was now splintered into hourly work schedules, ringing bells, whippings, and rapes. Food gathering, feasting, canoe building, and ceremony—the staples of Chumash life—were crimped into the leanest corners of existence.

When Mexico declared independence from Spain in 1835 and the missions were secularized, the Chumash were to inherit half the land and livestock. They didn't. The newly appointed Mexican governor meted out large ranchos to friends. The Indians worked as cooks, sheepherders, servants, and vaqueros. They lived a double life: *alchuklash* by night, Catholic ranch hand by day. One of them said: "Yes, much from the outside has been forced on us. But inside we change more slowly. We may wear the European's clothes, but we do not wear all his thinking."

Midmorning on the *Peace,* and it has taken 10 hours to go 60 miles. "Kind of a long night," James says, handing me a cup of coffee. "I cheated and took Dramamine," I tell him. "So did I," he says. The boat glides on calm waters, with the copilot at the helm. The islands' sandstone cliffs move past, each island generating its own private weather of marine mist and inland valley fog, and its own unique, endemic species of animals, plants, and eccentric human islanders.

When I was a child, I lay in bed at night and looked out at these islands. "There's no sense sailing to San Miguel," my father always said. "There's nothing out there." Sometimes when the wind shifted and blew in from the southwest, however, I could hear seals barking and a sound like women singing, and I wanted to swim to San Miguel. It stood for the separateness I felt from my family, for the mystery of how identity is formed. Now I find I can't say I am one thing without saying I am another: As these islands are defined by their relationship to the coast, so is my sense of aloneness rooted in the context of family, existing because of it. I knew the ways in which I was different, and how the water between us could be bridged by what we shared. . . .

Islands are reminders of arrivals and departures. In 1835 the last American Indians were removed from the Channel Islands by Franciscan mission fathers on a chartered schooner inauspiciously named *Peor es Nada,* which translates to "Worse is Nothing." By the time they reached San Nicholas Island, about 30 miles south of San Miguel, winter was coming. The islanders were hastily gathered. When one woman discovered her child had been left behind, she jumped overboard and swam to shore. Because the storm was closing in, the captain sailed without her, intending to return in a few weeks, but the schooner, living up to its name, sank, and so no one returned for her.

Eighteen years later, George Nidever, a fur trapper who had explored California with the Walker expedition and later became an early owner of San Miguel Island, set out to find "the lost woman of San Nicholas." He found fresh footprints, which led him to her shelter, made of whale ribs covered with sea grass and brush. The woman was roasting wild onions over a fire. No child was present, but she had dogs and two pet ravens. She wore a dress made from the skins of pelagic cormorants with the feathers still attached, sewn together with bone needles.

It is said she went willingly with Nidever. It was an easy passage that day, and she was welcomed at the Santa Barbara Mission, baptized, and given a Spanish name, Juana María. But like other "wild people" who have been brought into the so-called civilized world, she did not thrive, and six weeks after her arrival, she died.

The three-mile passage between Santa Rosa and San Miguel is rough. During the night, the swells are obsidian boulders, not cut by the keel's knife from the sea but carved from the blackness above our heads. Now, in early light, San Miguel is cut from day, a blue muscle dropped and floating on water.

We pass Caldwell's Point, Nichols Point, Challenge Point, Bay Point, Hoffman Point, then cruise past Prince Island, blackened by pelagic cormorants and dotted with western gulls, and finally turn into the turquoise calm of Cuyler's Harbor. Small, and the most remote and inaccessible of the Channel Islands, San Miguel is only 14 square miles (about 10,000 acres) and is hit hard by prevailing northwesterly winds, which have made the western end the site of many shipwrecks. The fractured shores—part volcanic, part sedimentary—split the California current, some of the water curling clockwise toward the mainland in cyclonic eddies, the other part breaking out into open seas.

A piece of dead whale floats by, perched upon by two gulls, and sea lions bask on an island of undulating kelp, acknowledging our arrival with a blink of the eye. James drops anchor, and groups of us are rowed to shore. Who planted the three palm trees that greet us? They are not native to the island. A swallow's nest hangs from a hunk of conglomerate rock: best view in the world of this white sandy beach and natural harbor.

As I walk, the palm fronds behind me come alive with finches. I kick blue mussel shells, red abalone, purple-hinged scallops, and thick slabs of jingle shells. There are spiny sand crabs, cancer crabs, and sand dollars. In which one does the sun find its resting place? Above a sandy shelf of plovers' nests is an ancient Chumash house site, much like the lone woman's—a curved depression where a whale rib house once stood.

Was this the shelter occupied when Cabrillo was here in 1542, the year he wintered on San Miguel? Where did he live? Did he befriend the Chumash islanders, eat with them, sleep with them, fall in love? Sometime near Christmas he broke an arm or a leg and suffered gangrene; he died in January of the new year. A monument to him stands above Cuyler's Harbor.

This is the island my family wouldn't sail to because it was barren, they said, but walking up a steep trail from the beach, the one used by sheepmen who lived here long after Cabrillo's demise, I find that flowers and grasses abound. Ice plant frosts the cliffs, and there is native buckwheat, bromegrass, lupine, morning glory, and coreopsis. Halfway up, I come upon sea rocket, a strange flowering plant ingeniously adapted to island life because its seedpods break into two parts: one has a corky outer coating and drifts on water, enabling it to migrate to other islands, while the second pod drops close to the mother plant in order to colonize the ground nearby.

Islands are evolutionary laboratories. How did plants and animals get here? How did they fare in isolation? Did they mutate or stay the same? Get smaller or bigger? Flourish or go extinct? Now conservationists are looking at all kinds of islands, not just the ones surrounded by water but islands of vegetation in desert seas, and deserts surrounded by tundra. The biologist Paul Ehrlich warns that "the earth is rapidly becoming a system of habitat islands surrounded by a sea of human disturbance," and that as fragmentation increases, so will extinction rates. The same could be said for the islands of the psyche and the soul.

Up top, blow-out channels cut in the sand by the wind rib the northern end of the island, and to the south, gentle, treeless grasslands slope down to the sea. There is an eerie forest of caliche, the calcium carbonate encasing tree trunks, broken remnants of 200 years of continuous unmanaged grazing that stripped the island of vegetation—vegetation that is now returning. Out across a grassy plain, island foxes bound, then leap in place, pouncing down on prey; in the Chumash islanders' Fox Dance, performers painted their faces and bodies in white bands, their necks vermilion, and wore headdresses made of junco feathers twined with flowers and a long, braided tail weighted by a rock tied into the end. Dancers shook rattles made of mussel shells and sang about their crossings to the mainland: "I make a big step. I am always going over to the other side. I always jump to the other side as if jumping over a stream of water. . . . I make a big step."

There were Swordfish, Barracuda, Arrow, and Skunk dances, and the Seaweed Dance, performed by men and women dressed in feather skirts with their faces painted red with white dots. Mimicking the movement of kelp, they slithered and undulated and sang: "Behold me! I walk moving in brilliance and feathers. I will always endure in the future. *Ailwawila hilele*."

Near the site of the Lester home we stop to eat lunch. Herbert Lester was hired by the island's owner in 1930 to live there and run sheep. He had suffered shell shock in World War I, and the owner thought island life would be soothing for his friend and his Yankee bride, Elizabeth. For 12 years they reigned as "the King and Queen of San Miguel," lived in a rambling house, Rancho Ramboullet, made of planks salvaged from wrecked ships, had two daughters, and produced a decent sheep crop despite dry years and a deteriorating soil surface. But in June of 1942, Lester, in ill health, killed himself, and the happy island days ended.

Was it really ill health that prompted Lester to take his own life, or geographical and emotional isolation? And just why did the lost woman of San Nicholas die after being brought to the mainland? Did "civilization" represent another kind of prison, which she had never encountered before?

As we row back to the *Peace,* I see James leaning against the wheelhouse, mirrored sunglasses reflecting our slow progress, and I reflect on how islands are emblematic not only of solitude but of refuge and sanctuary, the way a small boat is an island in rough seas.

On deck, a stocky young surgeon hands me a glass of wine. "I love these islands, but I could spend days just on the color of the sea. It's so hard to hold in my mind; sometimes it's jade that's been cut, sometimes turquoise," he said. Dinnertime. Twenty of us crowd into the galley and eat greasy chicken and limp coleslaw. A boat pulls up alongside and I hear yelling, then James falls past the porthole window. He has jumped from the wheelhouse to the deck. "You do not have permission to board," he yells. Too late. The men with the badges are already roaming around. Hatches and lockers are searched, then the dining room. "It's the Game and Fish guys," someone whispers. "They're looking for illegal lobster." Relieved, I hold up a drumstick. "Would we be eating this if we had lobster?" I ask. Finally the men depart. When their boat is gone, James appears, with a devilish grin on his face. "Okay, bring out the lobster!" Then he disappears.

Dark. The sea air is velvet against my face, a perfect temperature of 72 degrees. I sit on the hatch behind the wheelhouse and look across the water toward the California mainland, toward the house where I grew up, but can see nothing. No land, no lights, no eucalyptus or lemon trees. *Home is how many places*? Chumash history was not taught in California schools when I was growing up, but recently a friend with Chumash ancestry said, "If you want to know who you are and where you are, you have to know who lived here first."

Up on a rock outcrop above my parents' house, he gave me a geography lesson, naming names up and down the coast: *Humaliwo, Muwu, Mitsqanaqa'n, Shisholop, Kosho, Shuku, Q'olog, Lephew, Lisil, Mikiw*—names of Chumash villages. *Humaliwo*—meaning "the surf sounds loudly"—is now Malibu. *Tinik* was near the Reagan ranch. At Montecito's Hammond estate, on whose rolling lawns I once attended all-night formal dances, condos have been built on top of a Chumash burial ground. To the north, Point Conception—where oil companies have tried to lay pipeline—is the Chumash gateway to the Land of the Dead. Nearby, *Upop,* a village whose name means "shelter," is now Vandenberg Air Force Base, with its new launching pad for missiles. And *Shalawa*—Montecito, where I was born—is a haven to Hollywood's new rich. Just above the fancy houses, a hot spring was once a village called *Alish'i'l*. Its warm waters are now piped through my parents' house.

From the decks of the *Peace* I look down on kelp beds but see only the top of a great watery forest home. Under the golden canopy, opal-eyes, snails, and red abalone dine on drift kelp—fronds that have broken off and are making their way to shore. Kelp fish, camouflaged to resemble kelp blades, advance on their prey in wavelike movements, and blood sea stars tiptoe across the seafloor, shedding sperm and eggs from holes between their many arms. On summer evenings like this one, schools of bat rays mate: The male swims under the female, rubbing against her stomach until she accepts him, and then they mate in an all-night physical feast, resting during the day. Harbor seals, sea lions, mako, and sand sharks all find refuge in these 150-foot underwater trees, and the rarely seen giant pelagic jellyfish, with its 15-foot-long tentacles, bobs up like the sea's penis, exposing its head to the female envelope of air.

Three hundred thousand million years ago, bits of microcosmic plant life—single cells—began clinging together, then took purchase on rock. Single-celled plants evolved into multicelled plants, developing holdfasts, leaves, and bobbing, gas-filled floats. Finally the migration from hydrosphere to lithosphere began, and horsetails, fungus, and ferns gave way to orchids, grasses, flowering shrubs, and majestic stands of trees that produced fruit, nuts, needles, syrup, and leaves.

Midnight. I lay out my bedroll on the wheelhouse deck. Behind red curtains, James, Brendan, Ivan, and Scott play cards. While we traipsed across the island all day, they went diving. Their wet suits and spears hang from hooks at my feet. When the moon rises, James emerges and walks around to the bow of the boat. He doesn't have to ask if I'm all right—he can see me smiling. I watch the moon throw his shadow up; he stands with arms akimbo and one leg bent back as the *Peace* swings on its anchor.

The Chumash say the moon is a single woman with a house near the sun. She is called *alahtin,* and Fernando says she has cleansing powers, that her "forces move the sea, extend all the way to the stars, and control the menses of women and all creatures, even the oak tree."

Lying on my back, I feel the tide change. Waves travel as swells, giant ripples that glide toward shore, where they demolish themselves. If islands have to do with boundaries—or the loss of them—here the rind of earth rubs itself down into water, and water and air become the same thing, always exchanging chemical and physical balances, like trading clothes, so that sea and atmosphere are one caldron from which weather is brewed.

Geophysicists tell me Earth is an island that has two oceans: the one we are floating on, that thin film clinging to the rocky surface of the planet; the other interior, a molten ball of iron the size of Mars, which forms the earth's core. It is in this hot ocean that inverted mountains of mantle material intrude like upside-down cones.

Now waves roll under the *Peace,* pulled by a Chumash moon. The lights in the wheelhouse have gone out, and the boat rocks from side to side. I can't sleep. The channel's cyclonic eddies spin me, half awake, my feet turning like a clock's second hand. A seal barks. In Wyoming, when a single coyote yips, he is trying to locate himself, to find home. On the water, floating continents of vegetation undulate, and red threads hang down: kelp bed, water home, holdfast deeper than I can see. . . . Will I be cut loose during the night? Will I drift free?

Morning. The engines rev, and we pull out of the harbor. Glancing homeward across the channel, I look for signs of the drought that has embraced California for five years. The Chumash knew periods of drought, too. During one, all the streams dried up, the grasses and the animals died. Even in this abundant paradise, malnutrition prevailed. One day a whale beached and died on shore. Runners were sent all over the Chumash nation to tell people that there was food. The people came, carrying the sick and elderly on their backs.

The great whale was carved, meat was distributed, and everyone was fed. During the ceremony held immediately after to thank the gods, it started to rain. Rain continued for weeks and the drought was over.

In unusually calm waters, the *Peace* glides around the western end of San Miguel. We pass Harris Point, where the Lesters are buried, Wilson's Rock, Richardson's Rock, Castle Rock, and we come to Point Bennet, where three major shipwrecks have occurred. Moving slowly, James eases the *Peace* shoreward. A wonderfully pungent guano smell fills the air, and the beach is covered with sea lions, harbor seals, fur seals, elephant seals—perhaps 10,000 of them—back to back, nose to nose, flipper to flipper, packed together Coney Island style.

During the 1976 bicentennial, a group of mixed-blood Chumash descendants who called themselves the Brotherhood of the Tomol made a canoe trip among the islands. A waterman and friend of the tribe, Pete Howorth, helped them build a *tomol* called the *Helek*. "We're urban Indians. We don't know how to do these things," Frank Gutierrez told me. Pete taught them to paddle, then hauled their *tomol* to San Miguel, where the trip would begin. They offered traditional songs: "Give room. Do not get discouraged. Help me reach the place. Hurrah."

Paddling was difficult. In the choppy passage between San Miguel and Santa Rosa, they almost gave up, then found a way to paddle that worked. "A spirit lifted us up, and we flew across the top of the water," another member named Sespe said. "Five miles went by before we knew it, then the cliffs of the island were above us. When we passed an old Chumash village site, we felt the People watching us."

They suffered sunburn and blisters, ran out of cigarettes, and had a shark scare. "But all the time we were out there, the women at home, our wives, told us they could hear us singing. At night they heard our voices. We may not have looked like traditional Chumash, but something was happening, something we can still feel."

Calm seas, clear skies, hot sun. We back out between rocks and shoals and begin our trip home. With wind and current behind us, the *Peace* surfs forward, almost planing from the top of one wave to the next. We slide by San Miguel and Santa Rosa. A Navy listening station erected after World War II to protect the coast from enemy submarines is a white ear on top of Santa Cruz. I stand in front of the wheelhouse and cup my ears. Diesel engines roar; I listen for singing.

TRIP NOTES

The Channel Islands, off the coast of Santa Barbara, have been called California's Galapagos. Starting just 11 miles offshore from the mainland town of Oxnard, there are eight islands in the chain. Running east to west, the four largest are Anacapa (consisting of a west, east, and middle island), Santa Cruz, Santa Rosa, and San Miguel. The islands are home to many endemic and diverse species of fauna and flora. Once used as cattle and sheep ranches, the land is now protected by the Nature Conservancy and the National Park Service. Rough and mountainous, and saved from further extensive human impact, they remain sanctuaries of primeval America. Access is possible, but restricted.

Ninety percent of Santa Cruz Island belongs to the Nature Conservancy, and the other 10 percent belongs to private owners and the National Park Service. In 1980 the U.S. Congress declared five of the islands, plus 125,000 acres of submerged territory, a national park. The southernmost island in this park, Santa Barbara Island, lies far to the south of the other four and is actually nearer to Catalina Island.

When to go

A Mediterranean climate prevails: cool and rainy winters, warm and breezy summers. However, during El Niño years (when warm currents dominate the mid-Pacific), winter rains can be torrential and dangerous, so summer and fall are the best bets. And at any time, a crossing from the mainland can prove rough, even hazardous.

How to go

Each island has its own set of access rules. The official park concessionaire is Island Packers; (805) 642-7688 or (805) 642-1393. The company runs commercial boats to all the large islands out of Ventura Harbor and Oxnard; departure schedules and length of stay vary. Day trips to Anacapa and Santa Cruz are also available. Santa Rosa and San Miguel trips occur more sporadically, because of the long distance and the possibility of rough seas. Here are some other options:

• Very experienced sailors may charter sailboats out of Santa Barbara Harbor from the Sailing Center; (805) 962-2826. The islands' natural harbors are well marked on charts; however, advance permission is required to disembark for hiking, camping, lodging, and other activities. To visit Santa Cruz Island, contact the Nature Conservancy; for trips to Santa Rosa and San Miguel, contact the National Park Service.

• In summer, chartered helicopter flights to Santa Cruz are available from Heli-Tours; (805) 964-0684. There are also flights and voyages to the Scorpion Ranch and Smuggler's Ranch on Santa Cruz (see "Additional information" below).

• Perhaps the best way to visit is on a tour arranged by the Santa Barbara Museum of Natural History. The museum brings small groups on two- to three-day trips, guided by marine biologists, botanists, and anthropologists; (805) 682-4711.

Where to go

For those in good condition, hiking possibilities include an eight-mile-long (round-trip) route on Santa Cruz that begins at Scorpion Anchorage and climbs over the central mountains to Smuggler's Cove. Anacapa offers a 1.5-mile self-guided nature trail. On San Miguel there's a 3.5-mile hike to the caliche "forest"—a formation of upright mineral sand deposits. For the adventurous, there's a 15-mile hike on San Miguel that begins and ends at Cuyler's Harbor.

What to bring

Whatever gear you would ordinarily pack for a good hike makes sense here, including a day pack, water bottle, sunscreen, hat, sturdy boots, and a layer of clothing that will serve as a wind-and-rain shell.

Additional information

For more details on the islands, contact the Superintendent at: Channel Islands National Park, 1901 Spinnaker Drive, Ventura, CA 93001; (805) 658-5700. Another good contact is the Nature Conservancy; (415) 777-0487 or (805) 962-9111.

The privately owned Scorpion Ranch on the east end of Santa Cruz Island is a 6,300-acre site where mountain biking, kayaking, scuba diving (with guides only), and hunting for feral rams and hogs are allowed; (800) 430-2544. Also on Santa Cruz Island's east end is the 6,000-acre Smuggler's Ranch, which offers lodgings, hiking, snorkeling, and kayaking; contact Horizons West at (800) 430-2544.

THE GREAT SALT LAKE

The Year of Living Curiously

by Tom Wharton

As both a day and a year ended in December 1992, a beach on Utah's Great Salt Lake was cold and empty. Gulls keened in the distance. A pale sun set over the corrugated shadows of the distant Stansbury Mountains. Air that swirled around me tasted and smelled like salt.

I dusted snow off a picnic bench at the deserted Great Salt Lake State Park and sat down in silence, letting my spirit become absorbed by the surreal view.

In the cold stillness of the afternoon, I remembered my year of discovery.

While researching stories for the newspaper where I work, I'd spent 12 months gaining new feeling and fresh appreciation for the Great Salt Lake. I found I'd lived all my life beside it, without ever really understanding it. But my year of focused exploration revealed many fresh delights in a place that most view as desolate.

The Great Salt Lake is a dead sea crammed with life, a wild place next to a bustling city. Trucks zoom past on the nearby interstate while avocets and stilts play in the briny water pools that separate freeway lanes. A gaudy tourist palace is situated near untamed settings few visitors take time to explore. To the west and the north lies an all-but-undiscovered wilderness of marshes, salt deserts, rocky hills, bird refuges, and ancient cave homes. But there are also bombing ranges and gambling casinos. Barren, uninhabited islands can be seen from a site where engineers build rockets to power space shuttles. Men drive buffalo into corrals, using helicopters and horses.

The lake's most entertaining dimensions are created by its indelible contrasts. These days, the Great Salt Lake is shallow. But its predecessor, freshwater Lake Bonneville, was 1,000 feet deep. In the present, if the lake level rises even a few inches, it magically covers up several feet of shoreline. In sheer acreage, it is still the largest body of land-locked water in the Western Hemisphere.

Yet the Great Salt Lake we know is only a remnant of Lake Bonneville, which once covered huge portions of Utah, Nevada, and Idaho. As this ancient sea began receding about 14,500 years ago, it left sprawling salt flats and alkali deserts behind. The historical shores of Bonneville ring the valleys of the Wasatch Front. They serve scientists as a sort of concentric target for focusing on geologic lore.

My personal, yearlong quest to rediscover the Great Salt Lake began on a cold, foggy, gray Saturday afternoon in January. By way of introducing my family to my project, I went walking for 10 miles along the dikes at Ogden Bay with my wife, Gayen, and son, Jacob. Except for the occasional plane flying overhead, we had the place to ourselves.

At least in human terms.

Bald eagles were perched in the branches of dead cottonwood trees, searching for a carp dinner in the cold, open waters that hadn't frozen.

Nearby, a duck with a broken wing struggled for survival. We knew the colorful, desperate little bird wouldn't last long, especially with hungry eagles nearby.

Across the white expanse of mudflats leading toward the lake, a red fox appeared out of the fog like a ghost. It was getting late; distances had proven deceptive out here, and our walk took longer than we had anticipated. After the sun set, we hurried back toward the car, fondly looking forward to a warm fire and hot drinks. Suddenly a pheasant exploded out of a bush, frightening us all thoroughly, shocking us back into the moment.

Later, I realized I'd been jolted in more ways than one. There was life out here, considerable amounts of it, revolving in its own drama. I began to consider that my previous mental images of a barren wasteland just might not reflect reality. Like most Wasatch Front residents, I knew little about the Great Salt Lake. And, what I knew, I mostly disliked.

It smelled.

Millions of brine flies buzzed me when I walked along its shores.

It was hot.

The marshes along the lake's east sides might hold ducks and pheasants, but they also served as the home for thousands of mosquitoes that liked nothing better than tapping my blood for a meal. Because there were no fish in the lake, the water seemed useless.

Its recreational beaches were dirty, foul-smelling places. When I had tried to swim in the lake as an adult, salt stung my mosquito bites and turned my hair into a white, crusty mess.

But I was wrong. The more time I spent wandering its shores, the more valuable Utah's strangest natural resource became. As Utah writer Terry Tempest Williams observes: "We live alongside the Great Salt Lake, one of the most extraordinary natural features in North America. I do not believe we, as a community, have honored its rarity. Our lack of intimacy toward this inland sea is not out of neglect, but ignorance. We do not know the nature of this vast body of water that sparkles and sings. If we did, the shores of the Great Salt Lake would look different."

As the year progressed, her words took on new meaning.

In February, I drove to the most remote corner of Antelope Island with geologists Genevieve Atwood and Don Mabey. There, on a wind-swept beach, I stood next to the oldest and youngest rocks found in Utah. I looked across the lake to the Oquirrh Mountains, near the

Kennecott Copper Company's smokestacks, and saw traces of many of the lake's different shorelines, throughout its multilevel history.

About 14 million years ago, a natural dam in southern Idaho collapsed. That sent Lake Bonneville water cascading at 35 million cubic feet per second through Idaho's Snake River Valley. During a four- to six-week period, the amount of water that poured into the world's seas nearly doubled.

"That is one of my favorite cataclysms," University of Utah geologist Frank DeCourten told me. It also marked the beginning of the end of Lake Bonneville. As the Ice Age ended and the weather warmed, the lake slowly shrank to what we now call the Great Salt Lake, its remnant and legacy.

But the natural forces that shaped it remain potent. March took me to Cache County and a tour of the Bear River, one of the lake's main tributaries. There, Audubon Society members and water experts told me that modern society might try to control but will never master this fickle place. As Utahans learned to their great displeasure when the water level rose in the early 1980s after record snowfall, all their dams, desert pumps, and engineering skills still can't control the lake's capricious whims.

So this was the bedrock of my growth in understanding; this was how the shape and the mineral layer of this landscape was created. I went on to discover how life learned to inhabit its fertile crevices, as well as the vast expanse of its harsher elements.

In April, some brine shrimp collectors used their boat to take me, two other journalists, and some wildlife biologists on a trip across the lake's rarely visited northern arm to Gunnison Island. There, I enjoyed one of my prime experiences in 25 years as a writer. Looking at red and milky-colored strands of brine shrimp in the murky blue lake, we headed out to an island where more than 10 percent of the world's American white pelicans come to breed each year. The air was filled with the sound of screaming gulls, the only natural predator of pelican eggs. Flocks of pelicans looked like giant aircraft on the horizon, creating enormous shadows as they flew overhead.

Because of its importance to pelicans, the Utah Division of Wildlife Resources closes Gunnison Island to the public. One of the lake's eight islands, this tiny 155-acre outcropping of rock is located in the lake's northern arm, 17 miles off Promontory Point. A railroad causeway separates it fom the lake's southern arm. Because there are no boat-launching sites and not many places to access the lake on this arm, few boaters venture here.

Walking on this craggy spit of land teeming with birds gave me the feeling of what it must be like to visit the Galapagos Islands off of South America. Gunnison Island is home to some 10,000 pelicans and their chicks, and thousands of seagulls. The birds—graceful fliers yet ungainly divers—must like the remoteness and lack of predators here: They have to fly some 30 to 75 miles to pluck carp from the Salt Lake's freshwater marshes and the shallow waters of Utah Lake.

"That seems like a long distance to us," said Pat White, a former Utah Division of Wildlife Resources biologist. "But they're birds. Flying to Utah Lake for them must be like a drive to the corner grocery store for us."

The most outstanding thing about high desert country is the sweeping view it gives you of the hard, dry geologic bones of the land. Now, I was learning to see those bones swathed with life. I had thought the land harsh, desiccated, and barren. Now, hearing the screeching choir of the birds and the whistle of wingbeats through the air, and treading carefully lest we mash a nest underfoot, I was forced to admit I really had no idea what went on beyond the edge of the obvious.

The biologists told me that other nesting birds such as egrets, cormorants, terns, ibis, and herons once joined the gulls and the pelicans on Gunnison Island. But nowadays those species have found the lake's eastern manmade marshes more to their liking.

So the species who naturally make their home on the lake have been joined by growing numbers of others, their presence caused and stimulated by human presence. In May, I traveled to the freshwater marshes with Westminster College professor Ty Harrison and Utah bird expert Ella Sorensen. They showed me the main differences between a natural salt marsh such as the one at the Nature Conservancy's Layton site and the manmade, freshwater variety seen at Farmington and Ogden Bays.

Humans tend to think of fresh water as more benign. But some intriguingly bizarre plant life flourishes throughout the lake's salt marshes. There are bushes with microscopic salt glands that burst like balloons, and grasses that secrete salt crystals on their leaves. Greasewood, pickleweed, iodine bush, inkweed, and salt grass have evolved to live in an environment where lake level fluctuations, coupled with frequent "flushing" actions by fresh water, combine in an odd ecology. The marshes form a complex food web that serves millions of migrating Western Hemisphere birds. Brine shrimp and two kinds of brine flies feed on the lake's blue-green algae. Shorebirds and waterfowl eat the shrimp and flies. Pelicans consume carp in the freshwater marshes. Birds of prey swoop down on ducks, mice, and voles. Mammals such as skunks and foxes search for the same prey on the ground. Humans consume ducks, geese, and swans.

Of course, hunting isn't the only way for people to insert themselves into the life of the lake.

One June afternoon, I took a sailboat ride on the lake with two friends, Dee and John Rowland. On another day, we played in the sand at a beach near the old Saltair resort, flying kites and building sand castles. That effectively opened the gates to a flood of childhood memories. I realized I'd conducted some research into recreation out here before. . . .

So I spoke to my mom, dad, uncles, and aunts about the Saltair resort, trying to vividly reconstruct what it must have been like for me to get stranded on its legendary roller coaster. The great resort had been built here at the turn of the century, and as a lad of eight or nine, I'd arrived on an old Garfield train to play in the twilight of its grand era. Probably my most outstanding memory was getting my body completely coated during mud fights with my brother. Back then, I guess, I'd seen the lake's goo as having considerably more charm.

By the time of that visit, in the late 1950s, the resort was only a ghost of its storied past.

The most colorful and dynamic period in the Great Salt Lake's history began in 1870, a year after the Transcontinental Railroad was completed. Resorts with bathing beaches, boat docks, dance halls, and hotels popped up along the shores, offering Utahans unusual swimming and entertainment options.

Bathers who got past the smells and gooey black mud could have an interesting time. Because the lake is so shallow, swimmers must walk hundreds of yards before reaching waist-deep water. Once out there, though, you discover the legend is true: The thick, buoyant, salt-laden waters cradle your body and offer it up to the sky like a great blue hand. It's extremely difficult to sink.

John W. Young, the third son of Mormon leader Brigham Young, opened the first resort here in 1870. When the tricky lake started to recede two decades later, he moved it to the base of the Wasatch Mountains near the Davis County town of Farmington. That amusement park is now called Lagoon and is the second-oldest theme park in the United States.

The Saltair resort—constructed in 1893 by the Salt Lake & Los Angeles Railroad Company at a cost of more than $350,000—was once the lake's crown jewel. During the Roaring Twenties, Intermountain residents rode trains to this combination dance hall and amusement park. A Moorish-style pavilion burned to its foundations in 1925 but was rebuilt on the same spot. Retreating waters left it high and dry in the 1930s. After being closed for more than a decade, the building burned again in 1970, probably as the result of arson.

A new Saltair opened south of the original in the spring of 1983. A year later, the fickle lake struck again. This time, floodwaters destroyed the building's interior. Yet the resort has arisen, phoenixlike, from the ash and mud and is now open once again. Keeping the dance-hall tradition of the lake's south shore alive, Saltair serves as a performance site for rock bands and New Age musicians, with souvenir shops, snack bars, and a visitor center.

But these days, a new philosophy and social attitude has taken hold. People have begun to appreciate the lake for itself and admire its complex ecology. So now, recreation also comes in forms that are more educational and attuned.

In the summer of 1993, six months after my year of research ended, Antelope Island was opened to the public. The lake's largest island, it's fast becoming one of Utah's prime tourist destinations. Until Antelope Island became accessible, getting to the lake's wild areas was difficult, though not impossible. These days, horseback riders, mountain bikers, and hikers enjoy new vistas as they walk and ride the trails. Accessible by paved causeway, the island offers pristine beaches, wandering bison, and touches of pioneer history. Most important, it allows visitors to witness the beauty of the original lake. Sailors can depart the South Shore Marina for Antelope Island's smaller marina and return the next day, often spending a quiet night on the waters.

In July of my year of research, I went to Farmington Bay, and there a sense of the richness of the area's wild biology swept over me again. The lake was dedicated as one of 19 sites of hemispheric importance for shorebirds. People from all over the world came to celebrate the lake's uniqueness. At the ceremony, I learned that about 30 million shorebirds are drawn here annually. And between 2 million and 5 million of them, from 36 different species, visit the Great Salt Lake each spring.

My naturalist friend Ella Sorensen talked about watching birds on a Great Salt Lake marsh. "There are waves," she told me. "There is foam. There is a cacophony of all the different sounds. You hear avocets weep, and calls from the terns. The yellow-headed blackbirds sound like a strangled cat. You've got the quacks of ducks. Then, the sky broadens out and you get a feeling of space. People who call it a disgrace and say it stinks haven't really been there."

Most folks have never heard of a Wilson's phalarope. But these are truly fascinating birds. They fly here from the Arctic in late June and early July. About 95 percent of the world's population of the breed sit there for much of the summer, feasting on brine shrimp, the only living creature in the lake. They triple in weight and become so heavy they can barely fly. But eventually, they manage it. They migrate over 5,000 miles to a similar salt lake system in Argentina, where they do it all over again.

"The birds get so fat that at times they can't fly," Joseph Jehl, director of the Hubbs–Sea World research Institute in California, told me.

"You can catch them by hand. Some can barely get off the water. They look like they'd have difficulty flying 100 yards."

Without the Great Salt Lake, there would probably be few Wilson's phalaropes in the world.

When you visit a waterfowl management area on the lake, you touch history. The world's first public shooting area—the Public Shooting Grounds—was built on its shores. The world's first wildlife project financed by a federal excise tax on sporting arms and ammunition—Ogden Bay—was built next to it. The Bear River Bird Refuge was the third such project and remains one of the largest federal wildlife refuges. The Civilian Conservation Corps built Ogden and Farmington Bays and Locomotive Springs during the Great Depression. These days, the Great Salt Lake system now consists of 40,000 acres of marsh, producing between 500,000 and 700,000 ducks annually.

In August, I studied and wrote about the strange creatures of the lake, which include brine shrimp and brine flies. Brine shrimp eggs are so small that 150 could be put on the head of a straight pin. Brine flies, in addition to feeding phalaropes, rid the lake of organic material such as sewage from cities and farms. The algae eaten by these insects would turn the lake into a vast slime pond if left to grow unchecked.

In late fall, brilliant streaks of red, two to three miles long, stipple the broad blue waters. This is no mere reflection of light; it's the abundance of life itself. The streaks are created by billions of bloodred brine shrimp eggs floating on the cobalt water. Commercial shrimpers scoop up the eggs by the million, package them in airtight cans, and ship them to Asia, where prawn farmers hatch them as feed for the larger shrimp that people like to eat.

The brine flies can seem more than an annoyance to the uninformed visitor. At any given time during the summer, there could be 110 billion of them along the lake's 300 miles of beaches. But the flies don't bite; they merely swarm. Summer tourists at a beach often feel like Moses parting the Red Sea as they walk through a cluster of millions of the insects near the shore. Brine flies seldom even land on people; instead, they simply move about in waves, displacing themselves to let a visitor reach the water's edge.

WILD PLACES

Remote areas surrounding the lake offer rugged adventures. Dirt bikers, four-wheelers, and mountain bikers can ride across the old Transcontinental Railroad grade next to long-abandoned ghost towns and graveyards marked by weathered wooden tombstones. Many stop at the Golden Spike National Historic Site to watch restored steam trains chug down the tracks. In this spot, on May 10, 1869, the railroad's completion marked the joining of the east and west coasts of the United States.

These wide-open spaces have been exploited for many forms of human transit. I also visited the Bonneville Salt Flats for Speed Week, usually held mid-August, when hundreds of car enthusiasts from all across the globe attempt to set world land-speed records on the level expanse. The salt flats, located about 120 miles west of Salt Lake City, are one of the most famous parts of the Great Salt Lake legacy. Britain's Sir Malcolm Campbell began the record-setting tradition in 1935 when he raced across the crusty salt at 301.13 miles an hour. Craig Breedlove, driving the *Spirit of America,* gained international fame in the 1960s when he became the first to break the 400- , 500- , and 600-mile-per-hour barriers. Gary Gabelich drove a rocket-powered wheeled vehicle 622.407 miles per hour on October 23, 1970, becoming the fastest man on the salt.

The race cars create a colorful contrast with the sea of white crust. But the show doesn't end there. Try visiting the flats on an August night during a meteor shower. As stars shoot across the clear sky, the lifeless, flat terrain takes on an eerie glow. Even on a moonless night, the mountains loom like strange pieces of abstract art.

Yet this picture may not endure forever. Some drivers, environmentalists, and geologists worry that the flats may soon disappear. Highway development and mining have reduced the thickness of the salt by about 1 percent annually for the past 38 years.

In September, I tried to go on an overview journey with some relatives and friends. We ventured around the entire Great Salt Lake shore, stopping to visit pumps on the west desert that were built at great expense in the mid-1980s in an effort to control serious flooding. At Hogup Cave, the site of what is believed to be the first human habitation in Utah, a barn owl flew out, frightening my youngest son. That night, camped on Crocodile Mountain, we felt as if we were in the most remote place in the world.

"Remoteness," said a companion, "is when you get two flat tires and have only one spare."

The next day, my ancient orange van got two flat tires. We had only one spare. A friend drove me 120 miles one way to get our tire fixed. Though inconvenienced, we had to laugh and savor the sight of an amazing sunset as we returned to replace the tires.

Then, during that last week of December 1992, my journey of discovery drew to a close, and I took that moment to sit alone on a bench near Saltair. It was a time of recollection, and reflection.

The newspaper series had been a lot of work, but very rewarding. It got nominated for a Pulitzer, won an Associated Press award for the best series in Utah and Idaho, and the paper created a 45,000-reprint edition to distribute the entire series in tabloid form. People really wanted to know the secrets of this place, more than my editors or I had ever imagined.

Those external rewards were all important, but, I realized, so were some other entirely personal benefits. Perhaps the biggest of these was that I had been reminded not to take my quick, surface perceptions for granted, particularly regarding nature and the landscape. I had relearned how important it is to see like a child, to stop, examine, and appreciate a leaf, a spider, a rock.

I remembered one day when we went out to look for the globe-trotting Wilson's phalarope. I had to wade in mud and water up to my knees, and my adult mind began to harrumph that I was ruining my shoes. Luckily, the kid in me reawakened and took over, and I thought, "The hell with it! I'm going to have fun." And I did.

Sitting on that bench, looking north toward Farmington Bay, I thought back to my October morning of hunting with Tom Aldrich. I had gotten up at three o'clock in the morning to join Tom for a hunting trip on that bay. He took his shotgun; I took my camera. We lay in an enclosed, coffinlike contraption under the water, and because we were concealed, ducks and birds zoomed overhead and swam all around us. Lights of the city flickered in the distance like the Gotham of a Tim

Burton movie set. Calls of ducks, geese, and shorebirds came from distant shores. In the predawn twilight, shadows of waterfowl drifted across the moonlit bay.

A cold chill gripped the early-morning darkness. Lying there in that contraption, I had simply watched and listened, feeling like an intimate part of the whole scene.

Thousands of ducks lifted off the water. A falcon flew overhead, no doubt worrying the birds as it attempted to single out a stray for an easy breakfast.

The dark sky grew pink. Airplanes roared to and from nearby Salt Lake International Airport, breaking the idyllic silence. I savored the sights, smells, and sounds of the ancient Great Salt Lake river delta. Thousands of commuters headed to work just five miles away.

Sitting on my south shore bench now, at the end of my year of giving myself over to in-depth curiosity, I recalled the payoff of that dawn moment in Aldrich's blind. In that moment, I had been supremely glad to be alive, quietly treasuring the beauty of this place.

TRIP NOTES

The Great Salt Lake is about 70 miles long and 30 miles wide, with an elevation of 4,200 feet above sea level. The salt content averages 20 percent on the north arm and 10 percent on the south. Until parts of Antelope Island were opened to the public, tourist facilities were relatively scant. Even now, commercial facilities are limited to the Saltair resort, next to the Saltair Marina and the Great Salt Lake State Park, and a visitor center at Antelope Island State Park.

When to go

The most popular time to visit is May through October. On clear, still days in winter, however, the desolate beauty is also phenomenal.

How to go

The best and most basic way to see most of the lake is by boat. The Saltair Marina, which has boat-launching facilities, is located in the Great Salt Lake State Park. Sailing is the most popular form of boating, though powerboats are occasionally seen on the lake (and all boats should be thoroughly cleaned and their motors flushed with fresh water after an excursion on this lake).

Another option is to drive to Antelope Island State Park. To reach its paved causeway, take Interstate 15 to Layton, turn onto Exit 335, and follow Highway 108 west for about seven miles. The park's entry fee is $5 per vehicle. Also, the seven-mile causeway is wide enough for bicyclists and in-line skaters to enjoy making the trip via the road's shoulder. A parking area for cyclists and skaters is located next to the tollbooth.

Where to go

The Great Salt Lake State Park (where the marina is located) charges no day-use fee and allows camping on the beach in the summer for $8 a day. Park facilities include a sandy beach, open showers, modern rest rooms, and picnic tables. For information, call (801) 250-1898.

A replica of the old Saltair resort, a large structure complete with Moorish towers, has been built south of the park, and offers souvenir shops, snack bars, a visitor center, and a venue for dances and concerts. For more details, call (801) 250-4400.

Just north of Salt Lake City is 28,000-acre Antelope Island State Park, the lake's largest island, which was opened to the public in 1993. Most of the development is on the northern 2,000 acres; facilities include a visitor center, campgrounds, picnic pavilions, showers, interpretive signs, beaches, and buffalo corrals. There are tour-boat cruises of the lake, boat-launch facilities, a small marina, and in the summer, a small snack bar is open. Antelope Island's beaches are preferred to those on the south shore. The Division of State Parks is developing trails for mountain bikers, horseback riders, and hikers, and about 14 miles of trails are now available; for more information, call (801) 773-2941.

State and federal wildlife refuges surrounding the lake offer some great bird-watching. To find out when foot traffic is allowed on the dikes, contact the Salt Lake office of the state Division of Wildlife Resources at (801) 538-4700.

The federal Bear River Bird Refuge, west of Brigham City, offers a 12-mile auto tour across its 65,000 acres, open year-round. The road also provides access to catfish anglers. Mountain bikers and hikers can get permission to walk or ride on other dikes within the refuge from the headquarters in nearby Brigham City. To reach the Bear River refuge, turn west off U.S. 89 in Brigham City onto Forest Street, just north of the refuge sign. Go about 15 miles to reach the auto tour loop.

State-operated wildlife refuges on the south, east, and north ends of the lake include Locomotive Springs, Salt Creek, the Public Shooting Grounds, Howard Slough, Ogden Bay, Farmington Bay, Harold Crane, Layton Marsh, and Timpie Springs. Farmington Bay offers the best interpretive resources, and Ogden Bay is the largest. To reach Farmington, drive to the Centerville exit on Interstate 15 (Exit 322); go east and then immediately north onto the frontage road that parallels the freeway on the east side. Drive for just a little more than four miles to Glover Lane, and head west over the freeway. After one mile, turn left on a dirt road to a sign marking the entrance.

Ogden Bay's headquarters can be reached by taking the Roy exit (Exit 341) and turning west on Utah Highway 97. Drive two miles to the end, then head north on U-108 for one-tenth of a mile. Go west to Hooper on U-98. Continue west to 7500 West, turn north, and drive for another mile.

What to bring

First of all, you don't need to bring salt. There's plenty, and with a certain amount of refinement, it can be used to season food. However, this is high desert country, and you will need to gear up for all the predictable elements. To combat solar exposure, wear a wide-brimmed hat, sunscreen gel, and a good pair of sunglasses offering total UV protection. You should bring light cotton clothing in the summer, and denser insulating garments (such as Polarfleece) in the winter. At all times, you'll need a nylon windbreaker or weather shell in case the wind kicks up. And carrying a bandanna or two to make a dust mask is not a bad idea.

The marshy areas of the Salt Lake are a breeding ground for a surprising number of mosquitoes, so bring a squeeze bottle of high-quality insect repellent containing about 30 percent DEET. The brine flies won't land on you or bite, so you needn't bother looking for products to cope with them.

Modern sport sandals are the best footgear for hiking on the shoreline, but choose a brand that has secure straps so the muck doesn't pull them off. For up-land areas, conventional, over-the-ankle hiking boots or high-top sneakers work just fine.

And remember: Always carry plenty of fresh water, wherever you go. The Salt Lake is saltier than the sea, and its waters are not potable, even when filtered.

Additional information

The Golden Spike National Historic Site, located west of Brigham City off Interstate 15, is a fascinating spot, especially in summer when its two historic trains operate. The Transcontinental Railroad was completed in this remote place on May 10, 1869. Run by the National Park Service, the facility holds a small museum and auditorium where visitors will find films and exhibits commemorating the event. For information, call (801) 471-2209.

The Bonneville Salt Flats, primarily owned by the federal Bureau of Land Management (BLM), are located off Interstate 80, about 120 miles west of Salt Lake City. Because they are often flooded, they can be inaccessible once the pavement ends at a historical marker; before you venture here, call the BLM's Salt Lake office for road conditions at (801) 977-4300. Speed Week is usually held here (conditions permitting) in August, and there are other speed events in September. For exact dates, as well as other information about resorts and tours, contact the Utah Travel Council office in Salt Lake City at (801) 538-1030.

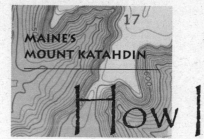

How I Learned to Hate Thoreau

by W. Hodding Carter

It began innocently enough. My feet rested in front of a crackling, compact fire in my cozy Brooklyn apartment. My black Labrador dozed beside me, occasionally driving me from the warmest spot with her cold, wet snout. All was bliss.

I held Henry David Thoreau's *The Maine Woods* before me, reading the chapter "Ktaadn"—a charming account of his 1846 expedition up Maine's craggy Mount Katahdin. This is good stuff, I thought, nothing like *Walden*. A person can believe in this experience. "Instead of water, we got here a draught of beer, which, it was allowed, would be better, clear and thin, but strong and stringent as the cedar-sap," he wrote, detailing a roadside stop during his journey. "It was as if we sucked the very teats of Nature's pine-clad bosom. . . ."

By the time I reached this passage, my future was set. I would follow in Thoreau's wake and embrace the very land he so revered. I would leave civilization and venture into our country's woodlands to suck at the teats of a life without VCRs, Rollerblades, or Senate judiciary hearings. It would be my first step in becoming an American adventurer. "Honey," I called out to my dog, "I'm going to Maine."

But that was then.

I have since returned and now know Henry David Thoreau for the oily charlatan that he was. His accounts of the places and adventures were not honest. Hell, I've learned he was not even born Henry David but David Henry, changing the order simply for effect. Above all, though, Thoreau led me astray. Thanks to him, I confronted the real me without the artifice of civilization—and it was not a pretty sight.

I and my fellow adventurer, Will Blythe, a New York magazine editor, drove nonstop from New York and pulled into Judy's Restaurant on the edge of Bangor for a $1.99 special: eggs, home fries, bacon, toast, and endless cups of good coffee. Half the guests appeared to be eating breakfast, while the other half were tossing down huge mugs of beer and shots of whiskey. It was 9:30 in the morning.

The Penobscot River flowed wide and intimidating through Bangor's downtown hills. "Only experienced paddlers should try to canoe or kayak the Penobscot River West Branch," Maine Geographic's *Canoeing* handbook explained. "The river's severe rapids and precipitous falls require finesse in places where clumsiness invites trouble." Will and I would be canoeing in the West Branch and some adjoining lakes for three days before ascending Katahdin by foot.

But when we arrived in Millinocket, about 80 miles north of Bangor and our point of embarkation, we couldn't find the river. While simultaneously driving and studying the map, I accidentally played chicken with a passing police car. After the patrolman realized we were dumb out-of-staters, he called a game warden, who provided directions—to the western edge of Quakish Lake. (I later learned we couldn't embark from Thoreau's original launch site because Stone Dam had cut the water on the West Branch of the Penobscot to less than a trickle.)

We were soon in the smooth water of the Quakish Lake. . . . It is a small, irregular, but handsome lake, shut in on all sides by the forest, and showing no traces of man. . . .

—*The Maine Woods*

Light gray clouds drifted across the sky as we finally shoved off a few hours later. We easily navigated around tree stumps and knobby boulders rising above the lake's calm surface. Will, stunned by the surrounding beauty, kept repeating, "Look at these leaves." Birches were yellowy brown; sugar maples burned a deep red; and orange sumacs helped keep some light on the fading day. This was bucolic Nature, our ally.

We rounded a bend into a narrow inlet. Suddenly, our boat rushed backward and twisted broadside into a torrent of flowing water. We paddled harder. The boat stood still. I yelled at Will, asking what the hell he was doing, not quite grasping how difficult paddling against a current might be.

"Paddling," he answered and then shot back. "What about you?" We dug in a little harder, and a half hour later, we'd progressed about a quarter mile.

. . . We found . . . men who talked rapidly, with subdued voice, and a sort of facetious earnestness you could not help believing, hardly waiting for an introduction, one on each side of your buggy, endeavoring to say much in little, for they see you hold the whip impatiently, but always saying little in much. . . .

Thoreau said he found earnest and willing Maine citizens in the towns, as he traveled through with his party of five. Two of his fellows had been locals and could guide him past many obstacles.

We found a portly, gray-haired man who sat in his red 1970s station wagon. He stared at us, I imagined, like we were Lewis and Clark forcing our way up the muddy Missouri.

Just as I was about to call out a greeting, we came to another standstill. This did not look good. "Dig, dig," I stage-whispered to Will. We started to make slanted headway.

The old geezer leaned out then, lifting his entire body so he was halfway out the car. We looked over, still paddling but anticipating his praise. "You know," he screamed out, nearly choking on his own mirth, his face turning as red as his car, "you'd make a lot more progress if you'd go downstream!" He wiggled back into the car, his laughter echoing off the far bank.

The truth was, we could have made a lot of progress quite a number of other ways. These days, getting to Katahdin is as simple as driving a car to Baxter State Park, paying the entrance fee, and driving to a campsite or trailhead.

Clearly, however, our quest was more quixotic. Thoreau himself had climbed Katahdin in early September. Will and I waited even later, choosing October so we could duplicate the solitude of his expedition as well as follow his route. Most people go to the park in the summer, by car. Will and I were in the process of finding out why.

For the next half hour we suffered in silence, inching our way up the river. Will did not comment on the foliage and I left all daydreams behind. Then we both saw a concrete monstrosity looming on the horizon. "Ugh!" Will called out for both of us. It was an old dam. We had been forcing our way up the narrow end of a funnel for the headwaters of the Penobscot.

Once we had portaged the dam, which required an abundance of cursing, cuts, and bruises, we paddled for two hours through Elbow Lake, heading due west by our compass reading. This was the first time either of us had used a compass since Cub Scouts. We were exhausted, but a light wind from the southeast blew away our lingering doubts and eased us along.

Soon enough, Elbow Lake expanded into the Twin Lakes. We crossed North Twin, fighting swells that rose above our gunwale. I looked back at Will. His short black hair, soaked with sweat, was plastered against his skull, and he appeared to be working as hard as he could. The wind had simply tightened its grip upon us.

"I don't know about this Thoreau," Will said as we reached the shore beneath North Twin Ridge. "He was a dilettante, if you ask me. And he certainly didn't have to paddle up a dam-made current." Well,

Will had not yet read *The Maine Woods* and so he didn't know that Thoreau and his friends had actually portaged the same dam. I thought it best to keep quiet and agree.

Our camp that night was on a wooded, sandy peninsula four miles south of Thoreau's campsite. Our feet etched shallow impressions in the sand alongside three-inch-deep prints left by wandering moose and bear. Large moose pellets lay clumped beside our tent. Moose, Will read aloud from our guidebook, have a tendency to trample people when startled. And they weigh more than half a ton. Despite a shared bottle of cheap Cabernet Sauvignon, it was a sleepless evening for me. I listened for bear and moose all night. Countless times I rose up on my elbows, cocking my head to raise one ear higher for better hearing, just in case a bull moose charged. The charge never came, but the wind grew stronger and the water lapped louder and louder against the shore.

A thin mist blew off the water as we rose at dawn. It was a sad, spooky morning—the kind of day made to be spent inside, lounging before a fire. The heavy scent of fallen leaves and dried evergreen needles conspired to make me listless. I did not want to go on from here. We knew where we were on the map. And even more important, we knew how to get back.

After a filling breakfast of hot oatmeal, I can't say a fire returned to my belly, but I thought I detected a healthy ember or two. We shoved off around nine o'clock, intending to go north for three and a half miles, northwest for three miles, then north again for three more. Using the map and compass, we figured it would be a cinch. Out from behind our peninsula, a strong wind took hold of the boat, speeding us along as if we were headed downstream.

Far off in the distance, we saw Katahdin for the first time, between darkening clouds. It was a forbidding sight—all craggy, black, and haunted. According to legend, three Native American gods rule Katahdin: Bumole, the evil, winged being with murderous claws and beak and a head the size of four horses; Wucowen, the neutral spirit; and Katahdin, the humanoid, who at some point in his career took a human as his wife. Bumole's favorite activities are conjuring up storms and killing anyone who journeys up the mountain. As I looked across the roiling lake and up at the mountain, it appeared that Bumole was currently in charge.

Around noon, we pulled into a rocky cove to eat lunch, barely protected from the wind and waves. A field of cattails swayed and rustled around us. We studied our map the entire time, trying to convince ourselves we knew where we were. We had passed various islands shown on the map. We had also passed islands not shown on the map.

We pulled out the compass. A compass tells you which way is northwest, but what good does that do if you're not where you think you are? We, however, pretended to know our location and used the compass to set our next heading. We shoved off.

. . . A lake is the landscape's most beautiful and expressive feature. It is the earth's eye, looking into which the beholder measures the depth of his own nature. . . .

The lake turned uglier. Swells were now curling into our boat. The sky had gone from gray to black. The landmarks were not where they were supposed to be.

"I think we're lost," I said. "I don't know where we are." This was a critical point in our navigation of this inland archipelago. Somewhere near where we were, three large lakes and the Penobscot should have been meeting—a huge confluence that I had figured would be a can't-miss proposition. If we took the wrong turn, we would end up paddling into the abyss of lost souls: northwestern Maine. No one lives in northwestern Maine. We only had enough food for four more days. And my feet were cold.

All too quickly, Will replied, "Yeah, I know."

We let the lake toss and turn the canoe as, one more time, we pulled out the map and compass to decipher a new route. Eventually, we convinced ourselves that some hill off to the left—we'd given up on such lofty terms as "port" and "west"—was our awaited landmark. We canoed just past it to a spit of land that looked correct on our road map. We quickly pitched camp in the middle of a dense pine and birch forest to hide from the wind. As Will rushed to build a fire, I raised our tent. The slightest drizzle drifted through the trees.

Whoosh!

I spun around to see a solid flame stretching from Will's lowered hand to his face. He instantly spun onto all fours to escape. Little trees of fire danced around him. Before I could move, he frantically tossed leaves over himself and the gas can he'd been using to hurry the fire along. It seemed as if the entire forest might go up in the blaze, but soon enough the dampened leaves extinguished it. Oddly, Will did not have a single burn.

Something inside his head seemed to have been singed, though. A few minutes later, he stood in the middle of our forest, holding the compass in one hand and our map in the other. He looked at one, the other, and then peered north into the thick woods. It was impossible for him to see farther than 30 yards; nevertheless, he said, "We're not lost. We're where we think we are." He did this for each point on the compass, repeating, "We're where we think we are," over and over.

I did not feel comforted.

> *. . . Not far from midnight we were one after another awakened by rain falling on our extremities; and as each was made aware of the fact by cold or wet, he drew a long sigh and then drew up his legs. . . . When next we awoke, the moon and stars were shining again, and there were signs of dawn in the east. I have been thus particular in order to convey some idea of a night in the woods. . . .*

Once the thunder and lightning erupted, the rain dropped upon us as through an open spigot. We cooked and ate in the downpour like starved wild boars, battling to slurp up gruel before it became lost in a watery pool. Soon there was no wind at all, just rain, thunder, and lightning. Neither of us spoke, and in that silence I knew we both believed this weather would last for days. My new waterproof boots were soaked, inside and out, reminding me of a classic Thoreauvian warning: "Beware of all enterprises that require new clothing."

Before tucking into my sleeping bag, I peed around the perimeter of our tent to ward off unwanted critters—figuring that if it worked for my dog, it would work for us. Nevertheless, around two o'clock in the morning, a black bear began munching on our packs. Since the packs were closest to me, I wasn't too thrilled. I woke Will.

"Really?" he asked, after I apprised him of the situation. "Let me listen." A long silence followed. I asked him if he'd heard it. "Huh?" he asked and immediately began snoring.

A minute or so passed. "Will, what should we do?" I whispered, poking him hard in the ribs. I could still hear the bear munching away, despite the heavy downpour and my pounding heart.

Will rolled back toward me and drew the line that separated our two souls, the line between a Zenlike master and a confirmed worrywart.

"Well, what do you want to do?" he asked sagely. "We can go out there and scare the bear away, but then how are we going to keep it away? Huh?"

He was snoring again within minutes, but I stayed awake, pondering the differences between us and reassuring myself that the bear was content with our packs. The way I figured it, I was entrenched in the Judeo-Christian anxiety ethic while Will had transcended to a higher plane. He was Peter Matthiessen and I was Barney Fife.

> *. . . . Think of our life in nature—daily to be shown matter, to come in contact with it—rocks, trees, winds on our cheeks! the solid earth! the actual world! the common sense! Contact! Contact! . . .*

It hadn't been a bear, of course. The plastic green trash bags stretched over our packs remained untouched. Noticing the water lying on top of the plastic, I figured the munching sound had been the rain hitting the plastic. Such things are hard to distinguish in the middle of the night.

The sky had cleared to a purplish blue, and we decided to launch our boat before breakfast to take advantage of the calm water, just as Thoreau had done 150 years earlier. Since it was so clean and crisp in the Great Outdoors, I attempted to reconcile myself with nature. I consciously took note of a thin mist rising off the driftwood scattered along the shore. The same driftwood had kept us warm the night before, burning even when wet. It was good.

A long day awaited, so this was all the reconciliation we had time for, but I did notice that the ground had been softened by a fresh coat of fallen needles and leaves as we packed up the canoe.

I took the stern. Given the high winds, steering consisted mostly of using the paddle as a rudder, jamming it at a 45-degree angle by the side of the boat. As we slid smoothly around the bend leading to what we thought would be Lake Ambajejus, a lone loon trilled out before diving beneath the surface.

Rocks and boulders replaced what had been an open waterway. Gray mud and silty sand began to fill the gaps between the boulders. Where we were supposed to be, according to our map, was a wide-open lake, but we were stuck in a swamp. We were, in spite of Will's orienteering, hopelessly lost.

For two and a half days, we had seen few buildings, and those we did see had been boarded up for the winter. We now saw one through our binoculars, about an hour and a half's paddle to the northeast. We headed straight for it.

A flag waved in the wind near the shore's edge, and several wooden buildings crouched behind. As we drifted in closer, a man rushed from one building to another and our hearts rose. A wooden sign, leaning against an open boathouse, read, "Whitehouse Lodge. Pemadumcook Lake."

We trudged up the grassy hill to meet our fate head-on. A young man met us outside the main building. "I thought you were a moose cutting through those swells," he said. "But then I realized a moose wouldn't be as crazy as to go out on a day like this." (Later, Will told me he believed this was Maine humor.) About then, Frank Rowan, owner of the lodge, appeared. Frank had a full head of gray hair and a most artfully waxed handlebar mustache.

"No," he said, twirling his mustache into an even greater point, "you're certainly not at Lake Ambajejus."

Inside his warm, homey kitchen, Frank pointed out just how far off course we had strayed. Back at the juncture of the three lakes and the Penobscot, we had made the worst choice possible. We had gone too far west and were now at the very end of Pemadumcook Lake—14 miles from our desired course.

It was getting late in the morning, and since the wind had shifted, bearing down hard now from the northwest, we left Frank, retracing our direction from the day before. Although the sky had cleared, the water had turned wilder than ever, with whitecaps and swells that were as tall as a man. While paddling the past few days we'd babbled about having kids, getting drunk, quitting our jobs, whatever, but now Will was silent. The only time he spoke was when I would yell, "Dig! Dig!" as the wind and waves labored to blow us in the wrong direction. He would mutter back, "I am digging," but his paddle merely slipped through the water.

For the first time, I worried about capsizing. Waves broke over the gunwale too many times for me to remain blasé. I began rocking the boat intentionally, lifting one side of the canoe as a swell threatened to roll us over and then counterbalancing the entire thing as we slipped down the backside of the wave.

The water was cold enough for hypothermia.

Our canoe rode the wind like a possessed sailboat after that. I felt thrilled for sinister reasons. Nature was taking her best shot, but my body was flourishing. And we were riding these waves as if we were some immortal children of Poseidon. I very nearly beat my chest.

We made camp late that afternoon on a protected point within a cove, spreading the tent over a thick bed of feathery pine needles. Now a day and a half behind our (and Thoreau's) schedule, we decided to cut overland to meet up with Thoreau's trail on the mountain. Not incidentally, this would save us from a monstrous portage up an uncanoeable section of the Penobscot.

A moose bellowed throughout the night. Its high-pitched call shook us awake, echoing across the lake. I, of course, worried that it might head straight for us and trample our tent, but its cry was so plaintive and forlorn that even *my* concerns eventually faded away. I wanted to answer it, to show this massive creature that at least one human understood its sad lament. I learned later, though, that the moose was in rut. His call was a mating cry.

... Our breakfast consisted of tea, with hardbread and pork, and fried salmon, which we ate with forks neatly whittled from alder-twigs, which grew there, off strips of birch bark for plates. The tea was black tea, without milk to color or sweeten it. ...

There certainly wasn't any salmon on our plates the next morning, but we ate a good breakfast of oatmeal, granola bars, and hot chocolate. We ate out of metal bowls and drank from metal mugs. Our spoons were late twentieth century, machine-made. The hot chocolate was bloated with sugar and milk. The strips of birch bark that we found crumpled like a weathered bird's nest.

We reached the end of our canoeing leg—Spencer's Cove—in little more than an hour. Summer homes and wilderness camps dotted the shore and islands, and a seaplane service stood at the juncture of the cove and the road to Baxter State Park.

After we pulled the canoe onto the sandy beach, I started unloading equipment that would stay behind with it from our packs. Will, hands in his back pockets, his wool cap pushed to the top of his forehead, sauntered over to the seaplane pilot. Two older men, wearing catalog-issue jackets, leather boots, crisp corduroy pants, and new chamois shirts, had just driven up in a squeaky-clean jeep and were talking with the pilot. All three men inched away from Will as he approached. In that instant, I saw him (and myself) for the first time: His face was grizzled, black with dirt and stubble; three days' worth of food bits clung to his jeans; and his breath could be identified from a few feet away. Those men looked scared. Hell, I was scared. Finally, Will spoke.

"Good morning," he said with a huge grin. The men visibly loosened. One of them even laughed.

The pilot promised to watch our canoe for the next two days. We then disposed of some garbage and began our 15-mile hike. It would be a slow ascent up 2,000 feet to the night's campsite; each of our packs weighed 60 pounds.

... It was the fresh and natural surface of the planet Earth, as it was made forever and ever—so Nature made it. ...

The rumble of timber trucks blasted our way from a parallel road owned by the Georgia Pacific Paper Company. The trees around us, while beautiful in their changing colors, were not very tall. The tallest topped 80 feet at the most. The entire area had been logged in one single whack about 100 years ago. Although the government has since put a stop to that, strips of scarred and stump-stubbled land periodically stretched out behind the living wall lining the road. We spotted an exquisite red fox and a little garter snake. Both animals lay squashed dead beside the road.

After signing in at the ranger's gate, we started our last six miles. The road grew steeper. As we passed Abol Pond on our left, an old man motioned me to the opposite side of the road. A garbled noise reached my ears when he spoke. "What?" I asked. More garble, and then I heard ". . . moose." I followed his finger. Not more than 150 feet away, an enormous, antlerless creature stood right in the middle of a marsh.

I sat down to watch. It was a most ridiculous-looking animal. Its huge daffy ears stood straight out, and its body was a jumble of muscle, joints, and bones. To forage for food, it stuck its head underwater for 30 seconds at a time, chomping on the vegetation beneath. Then it raised its head, shook its floppy ears, and ground away. Next, the moose climbed awkwardly up the bank, folding and unfolding its body like an accordion. We continued on our way.

I collapsed about an hour later. It was a beautiful spot, with young birch trees forming a canopy over the road, but I didn't care. Utter exhaustion struck me down. I was empty. A few minutes later, Will came whistling to a stop beside me. By then I had our camp stove out and was boiling water for the instant rice. Two opened cans of refried beans sat waiting their turn.

> . . . *She does not smile on him as in the plains. She seems to say sternly, Why came ye here before your time. This ground is not prepared for you. . . . The tops of mountains are among the unfinished parts of the globe. . . . Only daring and insolent men, perchance, go there. . . .*

Whether out of meanness or sheer scholarly concern, Will and I devised a theory during our evening meal: Thoreau didn't really make it to the top of Katahdin. The day he and his group chose to ascend Katahdin was extremely cloudy, and a careful reading of his account, we told ourselves, clearly shows him only reaching the plateau just beneath the peak. Not only had we guided (or misguided) our own selves to this mountain—unlike Thoreau—now we would even out-climb him.

The next morning, we roughly followed Thoreau's route up what is now called Abol Trail, since it was the shortest and fastest trail to the top. I didn't bother to tell Will that it was also one of the most difficult.

After an initial stroll through a soft glade of spruce, fir, and abbreviated birch, our walk suddenly steepened to a 70-degree assault. The trail, marked by faded blue strips of paint, had become a succession of boulders. Some we could climb around, pulling on roots and smaller boulders, while others had to be scrambled over. "This is no hike," Will complained for us both. "It's a climb up a damn rock slide!"

Although the temperature barely rose above freezing, we worked up a considerable sweat and shed layer after layer of clothing, hiding them beside the trail. Having started out with a car, a canoe, a tent, and backpacks, we were nearing our goal with only a pair of long johns, pants, and one knapsack. Thoreau would have been proud. Will even took off his wool cap for the first time in four days. He looked like a greased rat. Luckily, I could not see myself.

According to our trail guide, the ascent should have taken at least three and a half hours, but we did it in two hours in our hurry to outdo Nature's scribe. The higher we reached, though, the harder the climb became. I landed on my behind countless times. At one point, Will glanced down at Pemadumcook and Ambajejus Lakes and was struck with vertigo. (The night before, as we sat around slandering Thoreau, Will admitted to suffering from acrophobia.) But he persevered, vanquishing his very real fear.

When we crawled over the lip of the slide on our hands and knees, a frosty tundra was spread out before us. It seemed as if we'd crossed into the subarctic. Down behind us stretched the Maine woods, dark and seemingly everlasting. After contemplating nature from this point, Thoreau wrote, "I stand in awe of my body; this matter to which I am bound has become so strange to me. I fear not spirits, ghosts, of which I am one . . . but I fear bodies. I tremble to meet them. What is this Titan that has possession of me? Talk of mysteries!"

After an easy mile-long hike across the tundra and up a rocky slope, we reached Mount Katahdin's Baxter Peak—5,268 feet high.

For the first time since our arrival in Maine, not a single cloud hovered around Katahdin. Contrary to Thoreau's warnings, the mountain welcomed us. Although the wind gusted at 35 miles per hour and our eyes watered from the cold air, neither of us thought to complain. Our souls lifted beyond the moment. We had made it. Henry David Thoreau had not.

TRIP NOTES

Mount Katahdin, site of Henry David Thoreau's excellent adventure, is the centerpiece of Maine's Baxter State Park and the northern terminus of the famed Appalachian Trail.

When to go
The weather is typically clement from late spring to early fall. However, late spring is blackfly season, which normally hits from mid-May to late June. In July and August, the area is swarming primarily with humans.

How to go
You can either set up your own canoe trip (as we and Thoreau did), hire an outfitter to take you, or drive to Baxter State Park and set out from one of the three main trailheads (Roaring Brook, Katahdin Stream, or Abol). A list of the two-dozen outfitters who operate in the area is available upon request at Baxter State Park (for the park's address and phone number, see "Where to go" below). Two local companies are:

- **Katahdin Outfitter.** Canoe rentals cost about $20 per day or $99 a week; vehicle shuttle service is available for a negotiable fee. Contact Eddie Raymond at P.O. Box 34, Millinocket, ME 04462; (800) 862-2663.

- **Katahdin Shadows Campground.** Canoe rentals are approximately $18 per day or $95 a week; vehicle shuttle service is available for a negotiable fee. Contact Rick LeVasseur at Route 157, P.O. Box H, Medway, ME 04460; (207) 746-9349.

Of course, you could also skip the canoe trip and simply hike the 5,268-foot granite massif. For more information on Mount Katahdin, contact Baxter State Park (see below).

Where to go

To mimic Thoreau's route as closely as possible, start your journey in Millinocket, Maine. The town has a small municipal airport, although it's an easy drive from Bangor, Portland, or Augusta. To reach the put-in, go two miles south of Millinocket on Highway 11. When you cross a small bridge over Quakish Lake, take your first left down a dirt road and park by the water.

Your canoe route will pass through Quakish Lake, Elbow Lake, North Twin Lake, the butt of Pemadumcook, a bit of Lake Ambajejus, and into Spencer's Cove, where Will and I locked up our canoe for the two days we spent climbing Katahdin. It's a 16-mile hike from Spencer's Cove to the Abol Campgrounds in Baxter State Park, if you go through the Togue Pond Gate entrance.

Baxter State Park was created in 1931, when former governor Percival Baxter donated the first 6,000 acres. He continued to acquire and donate land for the next 37 years, and today the park encompasses 202,064 acres, which includes about 165 miles of hiking trails. The park is home to moose, white-tailed deer, and black bears, and has more than 60 lakes, ponds, and streams. It's a managed wilderness area, and is open for the summer season from May 15 to October 15, and for winter snowshoeing and backcountry skiing from December 1 to March 31.

The park offers 10 primitive (i.e., no electricity or running water) campgrounds, including eight drive-up and two walk-in campgrounds. To reserve a site in advance (always recommended), contact the reservations clerk at Baxter State Park Headquarters, 64 Balsam Drive, Millinocket, ME 04462; (207) 723-5140.

What to bring

The right gear for a river trip varies widely, depending on the temperature of the air and water and such factors as the current and windchill. Unless the air temperature exceeds 90 degrees Fahrenheit and the water exceeds 80 degrees, do not wear cotton. Generally, you'll want fabrics that don't absorb water, such as polypropylene, nylon, and polyester. Wear these garments in layers to add warmth, and, if necessary, add waterproof pants and a waterproof jacket. If temperatures sink below 65 degrees Fahrenheit, it's time to start thinking about wearing neoprene garments (they're made of wet suit material), and at temperatures below 55 degrees, consider a dry suit. No matter what you wear, it should always be topped off with a Coast Guard–approved life jacket (flotation becomes very desirable when you've been separated from your watercraft). In rapids rated above Class III, wear a helmet, too.

Other items to pack include water-resistant sunscreen gel, sunglasses (you may not wear them while paddling, but at the end of a bright day they can bring welcome relief), and a bottle of fresh drinking water (just because a river runs clear and cool doesn't mean it's free of microbes). And don't forget your emergency kit, packed with fire-starter gear stored in a waterproof bag, a portable water filter, a flashlight, a space blanket, and a small first-aid kit.

Additional information

A recommended guidebook to the area is "Guide to Katahdin," by Steve Clark ($16.95, North Country Press, Unity, Maine); for information on this book, call (207) 948-2208. Also helpful is the commercially produced Baxter State Park map, and the "Maine Atlas and Gazeteer" map book, which is essential for anyone trying to navigate the 3,600 miles of unsigned dirt roads that web the north woods of Maine. The map and atlas are published by DeLorme Maps, P.O. Box 298, Freeport, ME 04032; (207) 865-4171.

CALIFORNIA'S
REDWOOD COAST

17

The Long-Life Trees

by Paul McHugh

Who can impress the forest, bid the tree
Unfix his earthbound root?
                    —Shakespeare

I have seen Bigfoot.

This occurred in pearly predawn light, not far from a grove of the tallest trees, near Redwood Creek on California's north coast. I'd spent the day gawking at the immense, shaggy pillars of *Sequoia sempervirens* as they soared to arc branches over heaven's brow like dolmens for sun-domed temples.

Then, I had hiked back down a forested gulch that V'd down to the silken bolt of Redwood Creek as it unspooled and rippled, blue and shimmering, out toward the coast.

Light faded fast that evening. Fog from the sea, five miles away, billowed and wisped up the canyon. My gear was minimal, so I sought shelter in a logjam, one that had been stacked helter-skelter by last winter's spate on a gravel bar in the creek bottom. Insulated from the damp breeze by these giant, flood-peeled logs, I slept well. But near dawn I woke with a start.

Ancient, primal senses are a birthright. Yet only in wilderness can many such feelings again erupt unfettered.

Without a sound—instincts kept me quite still—my body suddenly came to full alertness. A large, wild animal was approaching. My "lizard brain," my simpler ganglia, somehow grasped this with a certainty that felt absolute. As my cognate, logical mind scurried to catch up, my nostrils involuntarily sniffed up cool morning air, heavy with mist, searching for evidence.

A stick snapped like a muffled gunshot.

Cautiously, I raised my head to peer over the huge, peeled trunk at my side. A long, lean shape, coated with black hair, made its way down to the creek water, scarcely 80 yards from my campsite.

Holy smokes, I thought. This critter may be moving on all fours, but it's too long and skinny to be a bear. What if it is . . . naw, it couldn't be! But . . . ?

The mythic environment of a grove of virgin redwoods is beyond human imagining. It's a perfect setting for a visit from a mythic creature. These trees are relics from an incredibly ancient time—more than 100 million years ago. As a species, redwoods were contemporaries of the dinosaurs. That they survive here today on the California coast is due to geologic whim, the trees' inspired genetic rejoinders to the moil of time, and some ardent, prolonged labor by human preservationists.

That black, hairy shape ambled toward the creek, making eerie, reachy, graceful steps unlike those of any moving animal I'd ever seen. It splashed quickly across the flowing water. Then it scrambled up the steep bank on the opposite side, looking for all the world like some prank-playing human in a gorilla suit.

The beast vanished between shaggy columns of forest.

Screwing up my courage—which took considerable screwing, I must admit—I extracted myself from my safe and cosy logjam nest, and walked over to the spot where the thing had crossed damp sand.

I fully expected to gaze down upon those famous, human-but-bloated tracks associated with Bigfoot. After all, I was in the sort of deep forest country where this legend lives most vibrantly. I'd been walking through the belly of Redwood National Park, an elongated, 105,516-acre preserve stretching from Crescent City to Orick. The park cradles in its gerrymandered boundary three state parks that are being managed cooperatively with the feds: Jedediah Smith Redwoods State Park, Del Norte Coast Redwoods State Park, and Prairie Creek Redwoods State Park.

A mere 20 miles inland from this spot—as the raven chortles and flies—is the town of Weitchpec, on the Hoopa Indian Reservation. Out on Bluff Creek, near Weitchpec, in October 1967, rancher Roger Patterson vaulted from the saddle on a plunging, rearing horse, and yanked a rented 16-mm movie camera from his saddlebag.

While a partner, Emory Gimlin, fought to control his own horse, and drew a Remington 30.06 rifle from its scabbard for backup, and while their packhorse panicked and broke off the lead rope to run away down the creek, Patterson pressed his camera trigger and caught about one minute of the life of an exceptionally large, apelike female creature.

Covering five feet of ground with each step, she moved with a regal, rhythmic grace, turned her head and shoulders once to face the camera, then vanished into the deep woods.

To Bigfoot enthusiasts, the 952-frame segment of Patterson film takes on the same import as that Zapruder home movie does for those who obsessively contemplate the JFK assassination.

Each frame has been studied and analyzed by scientists of many persuasions and levels of qualification. One can observe that the furry creature's stride is graceful, not forced or awkward, and that her dimensions would be difficult for a human in any sort of costume to achieve. One can see full breasts bouncing, slabs of muscle moving smoothly under black fur. Although various theories have been offered, no hoax has ever been proved. The film holds a tantalizing hint that some sort of reality may lie behind the legend.

Imagine yourself alone in a misty, ancient forest of towering redwoods at dawn, and that prospect becomes gripping. I walked toward the tracks in the damp sand on the bank of Redwood Creek.

I looked at them, then laughed aloud. My eyes beheld California black bear tracks, plain and simple. What I had seen was just a skinny, young bear, hustling quickly through the gloaming, perhaps to keep a major appointment with some huckleberry bushes just over the next ridge.

My point: a forest of virgin *Sequoia sempervirens* is a field for dreams. That's why visiting these groves for any length of time can be so compelling.

The only scientific possibility ever advanced to explain Bigfoot is that somehow, a scion of the presumed-extinct giant anthropoid ape *Gigantopithecus blacki* somehow made it over the Bering Strait land bridge to North America between ice ages, and today survives in isolated colonies in deep forest nooks of the Northwest.

Physically, *Gigantopithecus* could fill the bill. Fossilized skulls from Southeast Asia make a modern gorilla look small. A *Gigantopithecus* descendant might be a close match for the seven- to eight-foot-tall, 700-pound creature supposedly captured in the Patterson film.

So, here's my other point: unlikely as it may be that *Gigantopithecus* survived over the multitudinous millennia, and that today a hairy, breathing unit might make itself available for the viewing pleasure of campers in the Northwest, it is just as unlikely that the ancient coastal *Sequoia sempervirens* could survive and be present for all of us in modern times.

It's notably hard to see a Bigfoot. Yet anyone can drive up to a redwood tree.

Even more astounding, you can hike deep into a remote grove of virgin trees and experience a small slice of the life of dinosaurs. Redwoods once formed the forest cover of Gondwanaland, the ancient supercontinent—that Mesozoic, tectonic jigsaw wherein Africa and Latin America got to be kissin' cousins. In those halcyon days, swaying forests of redwood made a plush carpet covering thousands of square miles of the available landscape.

In contrast to their former grandeur as forest cover for half the globe, redwoods now get to exist solely on a narrow strip of coast approximately 300 miles long and 30 wide, extending from the hamlet of Gorda, on the central California coast just south of Big Sur, north to the Oregon town of Brookings. They survive where the mild, moist clime most resembles the meteorology of ancient times.

That would be where cool fogs from off the Pacific billow up the river canyons, where the temperature averages a low of 45 degrees Fahrenheit and a high of 61, and where, during a typical winter, 80 inches of downpour soak into the oxblood-hued, dense subfloor of redwood forest duff.

My hike from the Tall Trees Grove down Redwood Creek took place in 1986, and it was just one of my pilgrimages to try to fully perceive these forests. Redwood country, like the individual trees, is both elongated and sprawling. It takes many looks to see it all.

When trekking Spanish friar Juan Crespi first saw redwoods on a trip north from Mexico in 1769, he was taken enough with the shaggy giants to christen them *palos colorados,* or the red trees. Crespi's first views were probably of some of the smaller groves, between Big Sur, Monterey Bay, and the then-total frontier of San Francisco.

But when Jedediah Strong Smith, a famed mountain man, explored much of the trackless Northwest (not bad for a New York boy), he probably just called redwood trees a bunch of frontier cusswords. In 1828, he was in an area much farther north, near Oregon, where redwoods are biggest. Here, their virgin groves once sprawled wide to dominate the coast. Trying to trek with pack animals through that endless jumble of logs and calf-deep moss was damn arduous.

Interesting that we modern folks should wind up calling the tree *Sequoia sempervirens.* In the redwood country, plenty of native locals were on hand who could've supplied more appropriate language for their huge botanical buddy. The Tolowa lived up along the Smith River; the Karok and Yurok down lower, along the immense Klamath River corridor; and the Chilula on the flats along Redwood Creek. The tribes built, traded, and used houses made of slabs of redwood bark, and canoes dug out from giant redwood logs. They occupied a sacred landscape, and the canoe was honored as a living being. During the carving process, a special lump was left near the bow as the *keelth,* or "heart," where the spirit of the live tree could dwell and enjoy the ride, for as long as a canoe was paddled.

Laboriously crafted over a period of several months using hot coals, sharpened seashells, and stone adzes, the canoe was a valuable possession, a tool in its own right, for working the lagoons and estuaries and nearshore waters. A large dugout redwood canoe was worth 10 large woodpecker scalps, or two strings of dentalia shells—a heap of currency equal to the same high fine invoked for daring to utter the name of a dead person, one of the strongest taboos. (Seems silly at first—until you consider how long spirits might seem to hover in the shadows of virgin redwood groves. . . .)

Back then, virgin redwood forests still carpeted some two million acres of coastal hillsides in California and Oregon. Chinook, cohos, and huge steelhead trout jammed crystal streams to reach their spawning beds from fall through spring. The tall swaying trees, bugling elk, silver-sided fish, croaking ravens, tawny grizzlies, and the humans all knit their motions together in a vast, sacred dance that lasted for millennia without major perturbation.

The natives believed that sacred power kept this in existence. The whole wheel of life was spiritual, yet a few unique power spots were still defined.

Oregos is the name of a spirit from the beginning of time, when only spirits existed. Her name means "the helpful one." Oregos chose to inhabit a rock at the mouth of the Klamath River, so she could guard the varieties of salmon that people needed for food and summon them in from the sea to swim upstream.

Today, Oregos' job has grown more difficult.

Of the two million acres of virgin redwood forest—swaying there slowly and ponderously in the coastal breeze when Fray Juan Crespi first tilted his hat back to gaze up at them in astonishment in 1769—fewer than 4 percent still existed in 1995. The rest have been cut down, and silt and slash from the logging has filled and degraded many portions of once-pristine streams. Most of that remnant of virgin tree life, some 30,000 acres of it, has been preserved within the boundaries of 35 California redwood state parks and in Redwood National Park.

Declaring an area a protected park is one of the few ways a modern society has of making a place sacred. California's newest sacred spot, as of this writing, is Lime Kiln State Park, at the southern end of Big Sur, below Monterey.

Dedicated in May 1995, the Lime Kiln's 663 acres are located up a narrow canyon, just off the dramatic coastal highway, about 55 miles south of Carmel. The kilns in question are tall cylinders of bolted steel plate. Pioneer entrepreneurs built them to cure blocks of limestone quarried nearby, with scorching heat fueled by chunks from redwoods logged nearby. (Of all the bonehead uses of these magnificent old trees, firewood surely is the most benighted.)

Although the Big Sur region is relatively warm and dry, here at the southern end of their range, the hardy redwood groves—now protected—have struggled back. When I visited in 1995, just before the park opening, I was thrilled to see two young trees thrusting their way back to sunlight and the sky, right up through the center of rusting kilns that had reduced their ancestors to coals.

It's an interesting process, to feel yourself acquiring inspiration and motivation from a plant.

I've had other educational experiences in the mid-range of sequoia country. Take the redwood grove in San Francisco's Golden Gate Park. Once a region of shifting, windswept sand dunes—called the Outlands in the Gold Rush days—this coastal barren fell under the wizardly spell of two master gardeners, William Hammond Hall and John McLaren.

Nowadays, one portion of their legacy is a swale of carefully tended vegetation near the Ninth Avenue and Lincoln Boulevard park gateway that's called the Strybing Arboretum. In 1993, I discovered the Redwood Trail inside Strybing that wends through a grove of planted sequoias. It's a tough spot: these trees are stunted by the sandy soil and their crowns are blasted by ocean winds. Nonetheless, the trees and their gardener-partners are allied in trying to further a microclimate that mimics conditions of real redwood habitat. Some of the trees, planted in 1889, are among the park's oldest specimens.

The advantage herein to the wannabe redwood fancier is that besides the sequoias, the gardeners have planted and labeled nearly 100 associated species from the redwood region, including horsetail reeds, California nutmegs, oxalis, huckleberry, and fairy lantern. A relatively short stroll can introduce you to most of the vegetative fellow travelers of the biome—information that will stand you in good stead on any trek farther north, into the redwood heartland.

Another payoff for the Arboretum visit can be found on the way out. Jog a little to the south as you pass the east end of the Arthur L. Menzies Garden of California, and you'll find three stout metasequoia, or dawn redwoods. A separate subspecies once thought extinct but rediscovered in remote valleys in China, these charming, short, multibranched trees with feathery needles seem like redwoods designed by and for elves. Together with *Sequoia sempervirens* and *Sequoia gigantea* (the giant mountain redwoods of the south-central Sierra Nevada), such trees helped produce the redwood's global forest cover during ancient times.

A major emotional nexus for me in this redwood region was created in 1977 about 200 miles farther north, right in a triangle formed by a confluence of the south fork and main stem of the Eel River. Here, a spot called the Founder's Grove lies an incredibly short distance from Highway 101. What makes it incredible is that—despite the faint roar of nearby traffic—this grove still manages to communicate much of the potent serenity of redwoods as a species.

Some of that phenomenon undoubtedly stems from the fact that this grove contains huge virgin trees, saved from the ax. Some of it stems from the fantasy that any place where two largely wild rivers run together will be a power spot. But I believe much of the feeling derives from the fact that this particular grove was dedicated to the founders of the Save the Redwoods League.

This league, launched in 1918, pioneered the work of modern success stories such as the Nature Conservancy and the Trust for Public Land by engaging in cooperative rather than stricly combative efforts to protect groves of virgin sequoias.

It was here, meditating on the virtues and motivations of the founders of the League (Dr. John Merriam, Professor Henry Osborn, and Dr. Madison Grant), that I first achieved a sort of redwood satori. Present time and present troubles fell away from my mind, and I felt at one with the long reach of the species back into the dawn of time, as well as with that ponderous span of the centuries of the trees all around.

At the very second I felt this most deeply, a raven gave a coarse squawk from high above, and I opened my eyes and gazed up to see those broad, black wings spread over my head, caught in an aureole of sunbeams.

To help mark the moment, I reached down and plucked a leaf of oxalis, or redwood sorrel, and took it between my lips like communion, savoring the crisp, lemony tang as I crunched it between my teeth. You don't want to eat very much oxalis; the tannin content is rather high. But the taste of this humble forb—scattered around the ankles of these giants yet very much an associated species—will always summon the experience of being among them, in my mind.

It's hard to say exactly what transpired, what alchemy changed me during my virgin visit to this virgin grove. But I believe I emerged from it possessing a greater sense of spiritual solidarity with these trees, and with that genteel crew of old-time preservationists who had braved the political unknown at a time when achieving a way to save mere trees was an uncharted adventure.

For what it's worth, I know of one more spot, one more island of verdure in the scalped forests of California's north coast, where the redwoods still literally hold sway. That is up at the north end of their range in Jedediah Smith Redwoods State Park, located on the Smith River by the Oregon border, and pretty close to the trail Jedediah Strong Smith took when he hewed his way through in 1828, searching for a better route to blaze between the Rockies and the Pacific.

Get through Smith park and its campgrounds, and take the unpaved Howland Hill Road down toward Crescent City. After three miles, you'll pass the pathway to the Stout Grove, which holds the Stout Tree. This item has a trunk 22 feet in diameter, and stretches upward to 340 feet. If you've ever hankered to meet a living being that dwarfs a blue whale, here's your chance.

Like the shark and the cockroach, the species *Sequoia sempervirens* is one of evolution's greatest hits. The coast redwood embodies strong, simple answers to survival quandaries posed by the slings and arrows of evolution on planet Earth. Anything that can take a licking from a brontosaurus and keep on ticking has got its act together.

The earliest fossil of the genus *Taxodiaceae* dates back 175 million years. The coast redwood species first appeared abundantly in coal deposits of the Cretaceous period of the Mesozoic era, more than 110 million years ago.

According to one redwood specialist, Dr. Rudolf Becking of Humboldt State University in Arcata, "Since that time they have remained virtually unchanged in their botanical features. Miraculously, they survived not only the ordinary, day-to-day battering of the physical elements but all the more dramatic upheavals of the past as well: ice ages and other drastic climatic changes, volcanic eruptions, geologic uplift of massive mountain ranges, and the forces associated with continental drift."

The scientific opinion has been voiced that redwoods and their associated vegetation became the major contributor to crude oil and hard and soft coal deposits throughout the globe. Considering how much biomass accrues in a redwood forest—they are the most productive forests we know of in tonnage of growth per acre—and how resistant much of that biomass is to rapid decay, this is a possibility worth entertaining. It's especially entertaining if you consider that it means when filling up your car, you're not putting "a tiger in your tank" (as the old Exxon ad would have it), but stuffing in a tree.

What is the biological magic that permitted coast redwoods to prosper and then endure?

First, the high tannin content. That gives the wood its rich, rosy color, which fades to deep gold when oiled, waxed, or sheathed in polyurethane or turns to dark chocolate when exposed, unpainted, to the elements. The tannin makes the tree very resistant to attacks by fungus or insects. In fact, fewer than a dozen insect species try to dine on redwood in its native habitat, and they only attack trees already sick or dying due to other impacts.

Bugs still haven't learned how to pick the redwood lock. "This is extraordinary for a tree species with such a long evolutionary history," Becking says.

Another line of defense is the thick, shaggy slabs of bark, measuring up to a foot thick on a mature tree. The bark not only doesn't burn, it also has a spongy quality, with marvelous insulating properties; in fact, earlier in the twentieth century, shredded redwood bark was used as insulation in building walls and even refrigerators. Such bark helps mature redwoods to survive forest fires, should any ever get seriously ignited in the damp environs of coastal groves.

In addition, the coastal redwood has several means of propagation. Oddly, it's lousy at the most common form of plant sex. The redwood does disperse its seed profligately every fall, from cones the size of a raven's egg, but the pinhead-sized seeds that shower down have a low viability rate: about 2 percent.

Redwoods flower and pollinate in December and January, during the height of the rainy season on California's north coast. Pollen exposed to rain explodes and loses fertility. That's one drawback to being an ancient species: The trees' biological clock is set for some ancient clime, when winter downpours were not a problem. But if you're 100 million years old, maybe you can't be bothered to reset your watch to a weather pattern lasting a mere thousand years. Such a pattern is a mere temporal hiccup.

Luckily, the redwoods have a few more tricks up their genetic sleeves. They can also reproduce asexually, resprouting fresh growth from almost any portion of their bole or burl tissue (that dense mass of undifferentiated tissue near their base). If struck by lightning or "crowned" by a forest fire, they can regrow new branches and a top. In fact, the world's tallest tree, a 367.8-foot-high specimen on Redwood Creek, has a forked crown, indicating that it suffered some sort of insult in its youth, yet recovered handily.

Redwoods can also sprout from portions of their roots. It's by this ability alone that they've survived the constant logging inflicted on them in unprotected habitats. When timber companies indulge in redwood harvest today, they're pretty much cutting second or third growth off of stump sprouts—though some are also eager to log any last, isolated clumps of virgin forest within their holdings. In so doing, the corporations combat two other survival strategies of redwoods as a whole, and no one can predict the ultimate outcome for the species.

First, redwood groves make their own weather, creating a damp and cool microclimate in their valleys. The trees' feathery crowns comb the moisture from the air, and the thick duff of cast-off needles retains it on the ground. Rainfall in a redwood region averages 50 to 100 inches per year. It's estimated that fog dripping off the living needles adds another 14 to 20 inches.

Second, redwood trees hold hands with their root systems. The individual trees have no taproot—no central underground core that digs deep to grapple with cracks in the rock and provide a footing to counter the shove of storm winds. Instead, redwoods extend their roots laterally, in a tangled mat that spreads throughout the grove, intertwining a few yards below the surface with the roots of other trees. Stability becomes a collective phenomenon. (There may be a lesson in this somewhere.)

Selective logging of a few trees here and there out of a redwood grove is probably OK. In fact, I'd like that to happen, because I've worked as a carpenter, and nothing curls up more smoothly from a plane than fragrant redwood, and there is no trim more pleasant to shape and to nail around windows and doors than its clear, vertically grained flesh. But first and foremost, the trees must be permitted to prosper as a species. Otherwise, you don't wind up with wood of this fine quality and grain. That comes from older trees only.

Anything beyond selective logging, especially clear-cutting, is anathema, because a barren area stops creation of the microclimate and destroys the collective foundation. As Becking observes in his *Pocket Flora of the Redwood Forest,* "Isolated trees gradually lose branches, foliage; crowns and root systems begin to decay." And such trees die within 10 to 15 years.

I remember hiking with an official of the Jackson State Forest, near the town of Mendocino. He admitted that most of the second- and third-growth redwood forest being harvested was not made of actual young trees, but of young sprouts off the burls of old virgin trees. He also admitted that no one knew what would happen to the health of these groves if the ancient burls continued to age while the young growth continually got lopped off. "If they ever fail to resprout, we'll just come in and plant some seedlings," he said.

Very optimistic. Disrespectful, too. The maximum age the sprouts would be permitted to reach in a managed forest is 150 years. The prevailing average would be more like 60 to 80 years. Yet the age of a sequoia that's permitted to live out its natural life cycle is 2,200 years or more. To say a redwood has made the maximum contribution to its species at the age of 150 is like saying the same thing of a human who has reached the age of six. Redwoods begin to reach sexual maturity at the century mark. If humans cut off broad swatches of growth earlier than that, we are preventing sexual combination, and actually stopping their evolution.

Come to think of it, that's pretty damned arrogant, too.

When you walk in a redwood grove, it's important to recognize that the trees' roots all around you are linked in an ancient clasp in the soil below your feet. To be aware that those lofty branches across the sun are what produce the cool, moist breeze on your face.

You should also be aware that you are, after all, encountering the genuine Bigfoot. These giants may be vegetative rather than mammalian, but their ponderous footprints have crossed the continent. You may find this concept as preposterous as MacBeth found the idea of Birnam Wood marching to Dunsinane Hill. It's worth pointing out that his inability to entertain the prospect did not prevent it from occurring.

These trees, with 20-foot diameters, have marched many leagues to where they are today. Each step the groves took was made by each new generation, freshly propagated, moving steadily toward a temperate, moist environment where they could feel at home.

Consider that *Sequoia sempervirens* are far older, as a species, than the 40-million-year-old soil where they survive today. That is because they have walked, in the only way that forests can walk—through seed dispersal—to get where they are.

Think it over. Like the symbol for Sherwin-Williams paint, redwoods once covered this earth. Other than a few pockets of metasequoias (or dawn redwoods) in China, the only place they naturally thrive now is on the west coast of California. Why? Because in most other places on earth, the mountain ranges (for instance, the Alps and the Himalaya) run east to west. In North America, they run north to south: the Appalachians, Rockies, Sierra Nevada, Coast Range, and Cascades.

So on other continents, redwoods were crushed against the new, barrier mountain ranges by the south-advancing glaciers of the ice ages. Only in North America were the woods able to walk, seed by seed, away from the hideous cold ... and then, once the ice sheets retreated, to move once more north, to a place where the upwelling currents of the North Pacific produce a moist fog that billows inland to nurture an ancient evergreen in a way in which it delights. To such a scene, over the millennia, these redwoods have grown accustomed.

Long may they wave.

To conclude, it's worth remembering one other tribute to the inspirational power of these plants. Harold Ickes, U.S. Secretary of the Interior in 1945, wrote to President Roosevelt on the occasion of the founding of the United Nations in San Francisco: "When the peace conference takes place in San Francisco in April, one of the sessions might be held among the giant redwoods in Muir Woods National Monument. . . . Here, in such a 'temple of peace,' the delegates would gain a perspective and sense of time that could be obtained nowhere in America better than in such a forest."

On May 19, 1945, they made it so.

TRIP NOTES

Redwood country, stomping grounds of the Sequoia sempervirens, is a strip of California's Pacific coast that extends about 310 miles, from the boundary between Monterey and San Luis Obispo Counties to the town of Brookings in southern Oregon. Generally, the most lush stands exist in a narrow band three to six miles wide, although some native pockets of the trees extend inland 30 miles from the sea. This range of the coast redwoods includes many large state and federal parks and preserves, a few smaller virgin groves in unlikely places, a couple of delights such as the grove in San Francisco's Golden Gate Park, and an assortment of oddball tourist attractions.

When to go
The best time to get around in the redwood region is from late spring through early fall, when most of the parks are open, warm, sunlit, and geared up to handle visitors.

You can also see them in winter, but strolling cold, soggy trails to watch rain drip off needles is an acquired taste.

How to go
Study a road map of California and figure out which venue attracts you most. One

of the great pluses of redwood country is its elongated geography, which offers many other options for recreation and exploration to enjoy along the way. There are nature trails and naturalist-led hikes in places such as the popular Muir Woods in Marin County. But by and large, your redwood trek will need to be self-guided.

Where to go

Here's a selection of excellent parks in California with substantial redwood groves. This list by no means exhausts the possibilities; consult with park staff for additional suggestions. From south to north, some highlights include:

- **Lime Kiln State Park.** About 55 miles south of Carmel on the Big Sur coast. The park's 663 acres include second-growth redwoods down low in narrow canyons, and some virgins up high. There are 42 campsites. (408) 667-2403.

- **Big Basin Redwoods State Park.** On On Highway 236, 20 miles north of Santa Cruz off Highway 9. Its 18,000 acres are about 75 percent redwoods, laced with 75 miles of trails. There are 147 campsites. (408) 338-8860.

- **Strybing Arboretum's Redwood Trail.** In San Francisco's Golden Gate Park, near the entrance at Lincoln Boulevard and Ninth Avenue.

- **Muir Woods.** On the south slope of Mount Tamalpais in Marin County, this 559-acre preserve was set aside in 1908 and dedicated to the bard of the Sierra, John Muir. He, in delight, pronounced the new reserve the "most notable service to God and man I've heard of since my forest wandering began." This small grove recently received 1.6 million visitors in one year—three to four times the number at the much larger Redwood National Park. (415) 388-2596.

- **Hendy Woods State Park.** This 850-acre preserve is on the banks of the Navarro River, eight miles west of Boonville on Highway 128, and half a mile to the south. It has 92 campsites. (707) 937-5804.

- **Montgomery Woods State Reserve.** Thirteen miles west of Ukiah on Comptche (or Orr Springs) Road. An isolated, 1,142-acre grove, it is an adventure to locate, let alone hike. (707) 937-5804.

- **Founder's Grove.** Located just south of the Humboldt Redwoods State Park (see below), this grove is also managed by the state. It's dedicated to the three visionary founders of the Save the Redwoods League, instituted in 1918.

- **Humboldt Redwoods State Park.** Approximately 45 miles south of Eureka on Highway 101; also accessible via Highway 254 (Avenue of the Giants). One of the largest state parks, at 51,143 acres, it has 250 campsites in three campgrounds. (707) 445-6547.

- **Redwood National Park.** This elongated, 105,516-acre park stretches from Crescent City to Orick, and embraces three sizable, cooperatively managed state parks. After founding it in 1968, the U.S. Congress expanded the park in 1978 to protect a grove of the world's tallest living trees. The state and federal parks as a unit constitute a United Nations World Heritage Site and International Biosphere Reserve.

Buyout of the private timberlands was expensive and would be hard to envision today. A big chunk of the $60 million went to compensate and retrain lumber industry workers. The locals were promised that tourism would make up industry shortfalls. However, although 495,000 visited in 1979 and 500,000 in 1984, only 370,000 came in 1991. So this is a fine place to come and spend your tourist dollars, to help make good on the promise of the American people.

Although Redwood National Park has no campgrounds (the state properties have those), it does boast three visitor centers: in Orick, Crescent City, and Hiouchi. It also has the tallest tree grove, and various trails offer a few primitive backpacker camps en route, particularly the 50-mile Coast Trail that transects the park. (707) 464-6101.

• **Prairie Creek Redwoods State Park.** A 12,544-acre preserve that's 50 miles north of Eureka on Highway 101. Besides its famed herds of Roosevelt elk, it features Fern Canyon, which takes its name from the dense tapestries of many leafy species. There are two campgrounds: Elk Prairie, with 75 sites, and Gold Bluffs Beach, with 25 sites. (707) 488-2171.

• **Del Norte Coast Redwoods State Park.** This 6,375-acre park, like Prairie Creek and Smith, is joined at the hip with the national park. It's open year-round (except when too icy) and has 145 campsites. (707) 445-6547.

• **Jedediah Smith Redwoods State Park.** Five miles east of Crescent City on Highway 199. It has 9,560 acres with 106 campsites. (707) 458-3310.

Tourist attractions:
The Ripley's Believe-It-or-Not quality of the towering trees has attracted the sort of hucksterism for which America is renowned worldwide. In Ukiah, there's a gas station made from a single redwood stump. In Leggett, there's a drive-through living tree with a tunnel chainsawed in its base. Here are two of the more notable emporia:

• **Roaring Camp.** Just north of Santa Cruz, this site re-creates an old-time logging village, complete with vintage narrow-gauge steam trains that run daily on a five-mile loop through redwood groves. Cost is $13 for adults, $10 for children, plus a $5 parking fee. (408) 423-1111 or (408) 335-4484.

• **Trees of Mystery.** P. T. Barnum would have loved this place. It sports a lot of hilarious hype, kitsch, crummy folklore statuary, and hokey recorded messages. That said, there's some interesting botanical phenomena, including a "fairy ring" (a circle of grown-up stump sprouts) and a candelabra tree (a fallen tree with sprouts growing from the side). Located 65 miles north of Eureka on Highway 101. (800) 638-3389.

What to bring

Redwood country is fog country, so bring a sweater, even in summer. Comfortable walking or hiking shoes are a must.

Additional information

For details on accommodations, restaurants, fishing charter boats for offshore adventures, horseback rides, and the like, call the Redwood Empire Association (a local Chamber of Commerce) at (415) 394-5991.

The area's native and settler history is interpreted at the Clarke Museum, located at Third and E Streets in Eureka; (707) 443-1947.

An excellent resource on the region's natural history is "Pocket Flora of the Redwood Forest," by Dr. Rudolf W. Becking (Island Press, Covelo, California), which costs about $15.

17

THE POTOMAC RIVER

Following Huck

by Richard Bangs

The navigation of this river is equal,
if not superior, to any in the Union.
　　　　　　　—George Washington

It's a singularly American rite of passage, reading Mark Twain's masterpiece, *The Adventures of Huckleberry Finn*. I was a junior at Walt Whitman High School in Bethesda, Maryland, and the story of Huck and Jim and their rafting adventure down the Mississippi affected me in a way that Jay Gatsby and his silk shirts, or John Marcher and his figurative beast, or George Babbitt's conformity, or even Natty Bumppo's "noble savage" never could. Huck discovered adventure, beauty, self-reliance, peace, and true human values by rafting down a river.

"It's lovely to live on a raft," Huck said, and I believed him. I wanted to raft a river.

I lived just a few miles from the Potomac, the River of the Traders, as the seventeenth-century Indians who bartered tobacco and catfish near my house called it. One Sunday my family took a hike on the towpath of the Chesapeake and Ohio (C&O) Canal up near Great Falls, 15 miles above Washington, where the broad river squeezes through an obstacle course of massive boulders and, in just a half mile, roars downward some 75 feet.

Juno, our golden retriever, saw a squirrel and made a beeline down a tight path through a welter of vegetation. I followed, and found myself on the edge of a 200-foot-high cliff overlooking the Potomac as it swirled through Mather Gorge, a granite defile described at the turn of the century as the Grand Canyon of the East. The sight was dazzling. The fast currents spun reflecting light as though thousands of silver pinwheels were washing downstream. I was hypnotized, drawn toward the shimmering water. I knew I had to get on that river.

Monday morning I announced to Miss Hammond, my English teacher, that I wanted to build a raft and journey down the Potomac just like Huckleberry Finn. She said fine, as long as I didn't miss any school. The three-day Memorial Day weekend was coming up, so I thought that would be my chance. I recruited my camping friends John Yost, Ricky Vierbuchen, Dave Nurney, Fred Higgins, and Steve Hatleberg, and together we started to gather the equipment we'd need to build our raft and float the Potomac. We picked out an eight-mile run through Mather Gorge, one that expert kayakers had been running for years.

But as we talked to the experts—including a scuba rescue team who routinely retrieved drowned bodies from the river—the prognosis was we wouldn't make it through on a log raft. The rapids were too treacherous.

Word of our expedition spread through the student body, and the editor of the school newspaper, Dan Reifsnyder, approached me for the exclusive story. At age 17, Dan was already hard-boiled, and he smelled disaster in my little plan. He made no pretense of concealing his search for blood or a spectacular failure that would fill column space in an upcoming issue. I said I was happy to give him the story, but I was certain he'd be disappointed: We planned to make it down the river on time, and intact.

On Friday afternoon, we all set up camp not far below Great Falls, and started cutting the timber we needed with axes. We rolled the logs to our assembly spot down by the river and began binding them with cross pieces and eight-inch gutter nails.

Our raft was about half finished when a stentorian voice echoed across the canyon. "Have you ever messed with a German shepherd?" It was a park ranger, calling from atop a palisade of gneiss (foliated rock) on the Virginia side, with a huge dog next to him. "You're on National Park land. You can't cut down trees, you can't build a raft, and you can't camp. Now get outta there before I come get ya."

It was the end of our dream trip. We slowly packed up and trudged back to the parking lot. On the drive out we passed a ranger vehicle coming in, and guessed it was our friend with the German shepherd.

We still had two days of vacation left, and couldn't go back home—not with everyone expecting us to have at least attempted our raft expedition. So we headed for Bear Island, a popular camping spot below Mather Gorge, and holed up there for the rest of the long weekend, swimming, fishing, and trying to forget our failure.

Monday night we were all back at my house cleaning the camping gear when the phone rang. It was Dan Reifsnyder, pompous editor of the school *Black and White*, wanting the scoop on our expedition. I put my hand over the receiver and talked to our team. "Let's tell him we did it," I proposed with a grin. "We can't," Steve Hatleberg countered. "It's not the Christian thing to do."

In *The Adventures of Huckleberry Finn*, Huck had to battle with his conscience continuously, because according to the morality of society and the church, he should have tattled on the runaway slave Jim, whom he'd come to love as a brother. His final decision in Jim's favor concluded with his famous reflection, "All right, then. I'll go to hell!" I looked around at our group, then back at Steve, and said, "All right, then, I'll go to hell!" I put the receiver to my mouth and started to tell Dan about our raft trip.

On June 9, the article appeared, entitled "Rapids Capsize Craft; Raftsmen Score First." It went on to say, "The raft had to be scrapped in the middle of Yellow Rapids. 'We scrambled for the inner tubes and kept going,' boasted junior Richard Bangs. . . . 'You wondered if you were going to live.' 'Man, was I scared.' 'It was out of sight, like an LSD trip.' These were just a few of the emotions described by the group, all of whom made the entire passage alive."

The article gave us some notoriety and inspired us to form the Raft Club, which would later become Sobek. Steve Hatleberg couldn't live with our secret, though, and one day told Dan the full and true story. To Dan's credit, he never pursued it in print, but whenever I passed him in the hall he gave me that drop-dead stare that editors around the world have mastered. And it made me want to make good on the Potomac.

It was still early summer when I saw an ad on the bulletin board at the grocery store for a 17.5-foot fiberglass Old Town canoe for $150. I called all the members of the Raft Club and asked if anyone would split the cost with me. Ricky Vierbuchen had the $75, so we bought the canoe, painted R&R on the stern, and toted our new toy down to Bear Island. We launched and headed upstream, toward the crystalline mouth of Mather Gorge.

We were awkward paddlers, and the canoe zigzagged through the water as if we were drunk. We bobbed and weaved and slowly picked up some proficiency as we angled upstream toward Difficult Run Rapids, marking the end of some white water. The white-breasted current got faster as we neared the tail of the rapids. My blood accelerated correspondingly. This was exciting. Then we were in the rooster tails of the rapids, being flung up and down on a dizzy aquatic seesaw, paddling with all our strength. "Let's go higher," I screamed over the rapids' roar, and we sunk our blades deeper and lunged forward. Then the bow snapped to its side, abruptly capsizing the canoe and precipitating us into the spume.

We'd been christened as river runners.

Rick and I spent all our free time that summer in our blue canoe, exploring new routes, refining techniques, scoring the bottom of our boat with a matrix of scratches and dents. We made many of the classic runs, including the coup de grâce run of the Potomac that begins at the base of Great Falls. Here, the Potomac drops spectacularly over the edge of the continental bedrock onto the sedimentary soil of the coastal plain. Above Great Falls the river stretches to a half mile in width; below, it pinches into the 60-foot-wide Mather Gorge, where we would negotiate through S-Turn Rapids, Rocky Island Rapids, Wet Bottom Chute, and pass the ancient rocks that formed the exit gate from the canyon. We would continue downstream on a wider but no less magnificent stretch, through Yellow Rapids and Stubblefield Falls, underneath the Cabin John Bridge, which carries the Capital Beltway (I-495) past the Carderock Picnic Area (where climbers crawled like flies on impossible faces), down to Sycamore Island and the Brookmont dam.

Constructed in the 1950s for the city water supply with no thought for the safety of boaters, this deceptively innocuous dam is a death trap for capsized paddlers. It has a perpetual hydraulic that, like a black hole, sucks in boats and bodies, never to let them go. A sign adjacent to the pumping station says an average of seven people a year drown in this area; its nickname, accordingly, is the Drowning Machine.

Below Brookmont is the most exciting mile of navigable white water along the entire 383-mile course of the Potomac, culminating in the explosive Little Falls. Here, the entire river is funneled from parking-lot width to that of a Grand Prix raceway, then it's spectacularly split in two by a sharp granite-slab island. It was here that Captain John Smith, in his search for the elusive Northwest Passage, was stopped in an upriver journey in 1608. In the massive flood of 1936, the velocity of the water here was recorded as the fastest ever measured in nature.

Just below is Chain Bridge. A short way beyond, the river becomes tidewater, and the nation's capital begins to spread concrete tentacles along the banks.

Rick and I never canoed the Little Falls section; it was beyond our abilities. But that didn't mean we couldn't run it. With the money I'd saved working as a carhop at the local Kentucky Fried Chicken, I purchased a yellow Taiwanese-made four-man raft from Sunny's Surplus. And with it we paddled out to Snake Island, across from the Brookmont pumping station, and slipped over the killer weir where we thought the one clear passage (down a fish ladder) was supposed to be.

But we missed. Suddenly, we were in the backwashing hydraulic, capsized, bouncing about in the aerated water along with beach balls, chunks of Styrofoam, rubber sandals, branches, and other debris stuck in this eternal infernal washing machine. I remembered reading that the only way to escape a strong recirculating hydraulic was to abandon one's life jacket and dive beneath the surface, where water makes a deeper exit. But I couldn't bring myself to take off my flotation, which was propping my mouth just above the terrible froth. I looked over to Rick, who was choking on water splashed into his throat. "Let's swim toward the island," I yelled to Ricky above the weir's gargling. Although it was slow going, we found it possible to dog-paddle perpendicular to the current, along the hydraulic line, back toward Snake Island. I towed our little yellow raft, and after several scary minutes we reached the edge of the island, where a chute emptied water in a straight shot downstream.

Suddenly, we were out, and into the next section, where water accelerated as the river narrowed, and the waves grew thicker with every few strokes. Then the final stretch presented itself, with the river piling up onto the anvil-shaped island, spilling off either side into huge, complex rapids. We blasted straight down the middle, plowed into the saber-toothed island, spun backwards, then collapsed over the falls on the Virginia side, the worst side.

The first drop catapulted Ricky into the air. When he fell back into the bilge, the floor of the raft peeled back like a sardine can, depositing him into the depths. I continued to paddle alone, my feet dragging in the current where the floor had been, my neck spinning, looking for signs of Ricky. The roar of the rapids muffled Ricky's cry as I strained to hear it. Hours later, or so the seconds seemed, he resurfaced 50 yards downstream, all smiles. Climbing back on board, we paddled to our takeout at Chain Bridge on the Virginia side, where my mother was waiting with the Oldsmobile and a prayer.

I discovered the lack of a floor didn't make much difference in the tiny Taiwanese boat, and continued to use it for runs down the Little Falls in the following weeks with the various members of the Raft Club—even Steve Hatleberg, who thought he saw God during one capsize. For us it was the ultimate thrill of a suburban existence.

I fell in love with the Potomac that summer, wanted to know everything about it, every dimple, every curve, where it came from, and where it was going. I began to study its serpentine mysteries in my free time.

The river trickles forth at an altitude of 3,140 feet just downhill from the crest of Backbone Mountain, in a deep fold of the Allegheny Mountains in West Virginia. There it seeps from a spring beneath a chunk of rock, called the Fairfax Stone after the colonial landowner Lord Fairfax. The fledgling river soon becomes the Maryland–West Virginia border, loops back and forth around Appalachian ridges in the region of the Paw Paw bends, and then bursts through the Blue Ridge Mountains at Harper's Ferry, where it is joined by the Shenandoah. Here the plunging slopes and roiling rapids make "perhaps one of the most stupendous scenes in nature," Thomas Jefferson wrote, "worth a voyage across the Atlantic."

Continuing its journey, the Potomac levels off, now alive with geese, eagles, oysters, and shad. Eventually the river becomes a seven-mile-wide tidal giant, easing majestically into Chesapeake Bay, its threshold to the sea, as it broadens between the Maryland and Virginia shores.

As summer faded to fall, the frequency of our trips on the Potomac decreased, because of the cooler weather, school commitment, and a new diversion: women. Ricky and I were both quite taken with tall, blonde Arlene Wergen. The air surged with the dull clacking sound of soft young antlers in nervous ritual combat. Since he shared homeroom and some classes with her, Ricky had the advantage, and he exploited it. He took Arlene caving and camping and bought her an expensive friendship ring. I had an ace up my sleeve, however: the river. I only had to wait for the right moment.

It came in mid-December. We were in the midst of an unseasonable heat wave. The weatherman said the weekend would be warm enough for outdoor activities. I asked Arlene if she'd like to go canoeing.

I picked out a run I had always wanted to do: a stretch beginning at Bloomery, West Virginia, on the Shenandoah, running to the confluence with the Potomac, and continuing below Harper's Ferry, the place where John Brown's body lies a-molderin' in the grave. This 10-mile run was supposed to be beautiful, with some challenging rapids and good camping—all the major ingredients of what I perceived to be an important weekend.

Saturday morning was clear and crisp as we loaded the blue canoe and headed downriver through a navelike arch of silver maples and sycamores. The river here had sawed away at the mountains as they rose up, embedding itself 1,200 feet or more in the Blue Ridge. I was wearing my new letter jacket, which I had been awarded for the dubious honor of managing the soccer team. Still, it was a badge, and I wore it proudly with hopes it would impress Arlene. It was a beautiful day, brimming with adventure and romance, and I could tell Arlene shared the thrill of feeling a live vessel beneath us sliding silently over brawling water. An ad for Canadian Club had been running that fall showing a couple canoeing in rapids. The woman in the bow looked very much like Arlene. And though I bore no resemblance, I felt like the man in the stern.

As we eased our way down the river the sun's rays reflected off the water, and I began to get warm. I took off my letter jacket and bundled it in front of my knees. At lunch we pulled over beneath a spreading willow, and I prepared a sumptuous repast with Pouilly-Fuissé, brie, and French bread. As we took our first bites, a pint-sized bark came from behind, and a little puppy bounded into our picnic. She was a mongrel with the biggest brown eyes I'd ever seen and a wiggly, irresistible appeal. For Arlene it was puppy love at first sight. She fed the little mutt all of her meal, and some of mine, and then asked if we could bring her along. "But he must belong to somebody," I protested. "Please go check," she implored, and I got up to make a search. Sure enough, I could find no evidence of owners within a mile of our mooring and came to the conclusion that the puppy was, indeed, hopelessly lost.

So we perched the puppy on my letter jacket and continued downriver. As the day wore on it began to cloud and the temperature dropped. The puppy was asleep, so I didn't bother to put on my jacket, but instead paddled harder to keep warm. By late afternoon, we approached the river-wide ledge of Bull Falls, which the guidebook rated as difficult but doable, although it recommended a portage for boaters who were less than expert. Checking my watch, I saw we were at least an hour behind schedule; the puppy adoption had taken up precious time. The guidebook said the portage around Bull Falls took an hour—one that we didn't have on a short midwinter day. If we portaged, we'd have to paddle the final miles after dark, a dangerous proposition in December. And after a full season of canoeing I figured I was more or less an expert, and could make this run.

So, we rammed ahead into Bull Falls. Our entry was perfect, gliding between the boulders as though on a track, slipping down the drop as though by design. At the bottom I held the canoe paddle above my head and screamed, "We made it!"

But I was a bit premature. Tail waves at the bottom of the rapid continued to wash over the bow of our canoe, and the boat filled with turbid Potomac. By the time we reached the last wave, we were swamped, and the canoe phlegmatically rolled over, dispatching us into the icy river. The current was swift here, and the cold punched my breath away. With one hand I hung onto the canoe; with the other I tried to paddle, all the while yelling for Arlene to swim to shore. Then I saw my letter jacket surface a few feet away. The jacket meant the world to me, so I started paddling toward it. Then, a feeble yelp. The puppy was spinning in an eddy in the opposite direction. For a quick second I weighed my options. I could retrieve only one. I went for the puppy.

A few hundred yards downstream I managed to grapple the canoe to shore, the puppy still held above my head with my free hand. Arlene was there, shivering violently, and she gave the dog a hug that would crush a bear. Both Arlene and I had lost our paddles in the capsize, though I had one spare strapped to the center thwart. I emptied the canoe, turned it over, and tried to tell Arlene to get back in . . . but my speech was slurred; I could barely form words. I was becoming hypothermic. So was Arlene.

I knew we couldn't stop here. We had nothing dry, it was getting dark. We'd die if we stayed. I pressed Arlene into the bow of the canoe, and she crouched over the trembling puppy, while I pushed us off. I had just the one paddle, but I dug in with all my strength. The sun dipped behind the trees, and a chilling wind blew up the valley. Barely able to see the rocks, I propelled us into the last rapids, the mile-long Staircase. We scraped and bumped and banged every few seconds, but somehow emerged in one piece at the Route 340 Bridge below Harper's Ferry, where I'd parked my car.

My plans for a romantic camp-out, needless to say, were scrapped. Rather than a hero, I was a bungler who almost cost us our lives and, worse, the life of the puppy, who won the contest for Arlene's heart hands down, becoming her constant companion.

I still remained hung up on Arlene, as did Ricky. But it was unrequited love. As the school year wound down, she started dating a Young Republican, a radical act in the Vietnam era. When Ricky and I independently asked her to the senior prom, she turned us both down for her radical right-winger.

We'd been left, as it were, high and dry. Neither of us found other dates for the most socially significant event of a teenager's life. So we turned to one another and said, "Let's go run a river."

We picked the Smoke Hole Canyon section of the South Branch of the Potomac in West Virginia for two reasons: We'd never done it before, and it was as far away from the prom as we could get and still be on our river. It was a section George Washington described as "two ledges of Mountain Impassable running side by side together for above seven or eight miles and ye River down between them." So, as the senior class was slipping into crinoline and tuxedos, we were putting on kneepads and life jackets; as carnations were being exchanged, we were trading strokes on the upper Potomac. Mockingbirds called from the woodsy cathedral through which we passed, though hardly giving us solace. It was spring, and the delicate pink blossoms of the laurel and the notched white flowers of the dogwood dappled the greening banks. We moved to music—not the Motown our peers were enjoying, but the haunting whistle of the lordly cardinal. The river here was shallow and stinging cold from the spring runoff. Some miles below our launch we struck a moss-encrusted rock, jutting out into the current like some miniature Lorelei. The siren rock punched a hole the size of my fist into our fiberglass hull.

We didn't have the materials or the time to properly repair the hole in our boat, so we stuffed the puncture with spare clothing and continued downstream. It was slow going. We'd paddle 10 minutes, then pull over for 10 more to bail. At twilight, when we emptied the canoe at camp, we discovered our neoprene duffel bag had not been waterproof; all our gear, sleeping bags, tent, food, had been soaked. We dragged everything up a knoll of weathered limestone overlooking the river, erected the wet tent, and lay the rest of our effects out to dry in the waning minutes of daylight.

It was quickly evident that our attempts to dry the gear by natural means would not work, and that it was to be a nippy night. We had several packs of matches, but they were all saturated and wouldn't light. We gathered wood and, with our knives, trimmed paper-thin shavings that ought to light at the least spark. But we went through several packs of matches and couldn't get the spark. With nightfall the air became brittle, and we jumped up and down, slapping our sides, to keep warm. Our classmates were doing the Jerk in the Whitman gym as we flapped in the dark. But I knew we couldn't do the Freddy all night. We needed to build a fire, as much as any Jack London character ever did. If we failed at that, we might perish, and we both knew it.

Then Ricky literally got a bright idea. The flashlight still worked. Why not unscrew the lens covering the bulb and put the remaining matches inside the glass, against the filament bulb, where they could dry from the heat of the light? We had five matches left, and inside they went. The flashlight remained on for 20 minutes as we continued our jumping jacks; then it started to fade. We unscrewed the top, took out the matches, and tried to light the first one. In my haste I tore off the head of the match. The second actually lit, but before I could touch it to the kindling it blew out in the cold wind. I cupped my hand around the third as I struck. It spat to life, and as I touched it to the shavings, the fire took. In minutes we had a bonfire, around which we sat and dried our clothing and sleeping bags. We bathed in the warmth all night, continuing to feed the fire, and occasionally looked down the hill at the Potomac meandering in the moonlight.

Its curves somehow evoked Arlene's.

As it doubtless was for our classmates, that was a special night, one filled with danger and promise, with rites of passage, with friendship and warmth. The Potomac had dealt some blows since our first assignation, but it had given me some of the most exciting and some of the most exquisite moments of my existence. On that prom night, high on a limestone ridge, I realized how much I loved the river, deeply, wholly, and that I had found a consort for life.

I discovered, as Tom Sawyer finally said to Huckleberry Finn, that all I really wanted to do was "have adventures plumb to the mouth of the river." On that prom night I lost and found a certain innocence, and readied myself for the adventures of tomorrow, the great adventures cached just around the next bend, just out of sight.

TRIP NOTES

The Potomac flows deeply through American history. It's been a highway for communication and commerce, yet it also served as a barrier to military forces in a previous century. Nowadays the Potomac has newfound celebrity as a whitewater destination, with rapids of all degrees of difficulty.

When to go

Some of the runs on the Potomac are seasonal and some are year-round (weather permitting). There is no single formula that can guide all people to all runs, particularly since individual skill levels vary. The best advice is to research matters carefully, then try the easiest sections first. Part of such research is assessing river flows, which has a direct impact on difficulty. In general, the more water running through a rapid, the tougher it will

be. The Potomac's level is monitored at the Little Falls Gauge; to get a reading, call the National Weather Service gauge recording at (703) 260-0305. The Potomac is never too low, but when the gauge reaches four feet, greater river skills will be needed. Ten feet is flood stage, when you shouldn't be anywhere near the river.

How to go

The first order of business is to become adept with a watercraft, be it a canoe, a small raft, or one of the new inflatable kayaks. The American Canoe Association certifies instructors who teach classes at many locations around the country; to find one near you, call (703) 451-0141.

Next, make sure you acquire the skills for staying dry (or at least warm) in a river environment. These range from knowing what to wear to knowing when and why and how to build a fire, and how and when to treat hypothermia.

Then get your gear and companions together (experienced personnel preferred) and hit the water.

Where to go

• The first river section described in my story lies between Great Falls and the tidal estuary in Washington, D.C. The C&O Canal follows the river along the Maryland shore between Washington and Cumberland, with access and parking at many points. The Virginia side is mostly privately owned, and public access is rare.

Between Great Falls and Washington, D.C., the major entry points are below Great Falls, at the Old Anglers Inn (the access to Bear Island), and at Lockhouses number 6 and 10, on Maryland's George Washington Memorial Parkway and Canal Road. These points can be reached off the Capital Beltway via the Clara Barton Parkway exit.

Warning: The largest rapid, along the north border of Virginia, is the Great Falls of the Potomac. Stay away—it is extremely hazardous and hundreds of people have died here.

One put-in for the much safer and more popular Class III-to-IV canoeing and kayaking stretches is below Great Falls. But again, be forewarned: A final hazard downstream, before the takeout, is Little Falls, with its low concrete dam. Smooth flow over this three-foot barrier

creates a lethal hydraulic at the base. From upstream, the dam is not easily seen, but the concrete pump building on the left is your clue. When this structure becomes visible, start moving left to exit the river well above it.

Immediately below the concrete dam is an older, rock-filled dam, built to divert water for the canal on the Maryland shore. This dam has no hydraulic force, but often the rocks are thinly covered by water and iron bars poke through the rubble. Choosing the proper channel is crucial.

At this point the river narrows and drops over several small ledges before reaching Little Falls proper. These rapids have a straightforward ledge at the lowest levels, but even a slight rise in water can turn Little Falls into a monster. At high water levels, the Class III drop becomes a Class VI killer with 15-foot exploding waves stretching for up to half a mile.

Maps: USGS quadrants (or "quads") for Falls Church and Washington West.
Skill level: Beginners to experts, based on the section and water level.
Months runnable: All year.
Difficulty: Great Falls proper, VI; below Great Falls to Little Falls, II to IV; Little Falls proper, III to VI.
Gradient: 14 feet per mile.
Runnable water levels: Minimum, none; maximum, 15,000 cubic feet per second.
Areas to scout: The S-Turn, Yellow Falls, and Little Falls rapids.
Portages: Great Falls, Little Falls Dam.

- The middle river section in my story lies on the Shenandoah River tributary, just above its confluence with the Potomac at Harper's Ferry. At the put-in on Bloomery Road, launch underneath the power lines located by the transformer station on the outskirts of Millville, West Virginia. The first three miles are easy. But at Bull Falls, pull over and scout. After running the drop, point your bow downstream: at low levels, a hydraulic of about 25 feet below can flip those who drop in sideways.

Maps: USGS quads for Charles Town and Harper's Ferry.

Skill level: Guided novices and intermediates (at moderate water levels); advanced paddlers (high water).

Difficulty: Class II to III at moderate levels; Class III to IV when high.

Gradient: 10 feet per mile; 3.5 miles at 15 to 20 feet per mile.

Runnable water levels: Minimum, 1.8 feet at Millville Gauge; maximum, 5.5 feet at the gauge. For a reading, call the National Weather Service, Millville Gauge, at (703) 260-0305.

- The third river section in my story lies on the Smoke Hole Run of the South Branch of the Potomac in West Virginia. This 43-mile-long, expert-level run has a put-in in Franklin, West Virginia, and a takeout at the Petersburg Bridge.

  This is a small, clear stretch and can be run only until about June in normal weather. Its deep canyon is among the most spectacular on whitewater runs in the United States. However, this one is for experts only.

Maps: USGS quads for Onego, Circleville, and Petersburg, West Virginia.

Skill level: Expert.

Difficulty: Class IV to V. Some portaging is recommended.

Gradient: 18 feet per mile.

Runnable water levels: 1 foot to 2.5 feet, as marked on the Petersburg Gauge. The river gets vicious, complex, and difficult when the water level is over two feet.

Areas to scout: Most of the first 22 miles can be scouted from the road, but some of the most difficult rapids are not visible from the road. The last 21 miles are a bit easier, but around seven miles below the Smoke Hole campground a landslide has created a dangerous waterfall. The slide is plainly visible on the left side—a definite portage. For more information and advice, call the Game Warden in Pendleton County at (304) 358-2154.

What to bring

The right gear for a river trip varies widely, depending on the temperature of the air and water and such factors as the current and windchill. Unless the air temperature exceeds 90 degrees Fahrenheit and the water exceeds 80 degrees, do not wear cotton. Generally, you'll want fabrics that don't absorb water, such as polypropylene, nylon, and polyester. Wear these garments in layers to add warmth, and, if necessary, add waterproof pants and a waterproof jacket. If temperatures sink below 65 degrees Fahrenheit, it's time to start thinking about wearing neoprene garments (they're made of wet suit material), and at temperatures below 55 degrees, consider a dry suit. No matter what you wear, it should always be topped off with a Coast Guard–approved life jacket (flotation becomes very desirable when you've been separated from your watercraft). In rapids rated above Class III, wear a helmet, too.

Other items to pack include water-resistant sunscreen gel, sunglasses (you may not wear them while paddling, but at the end of a bright day they can bring welcome relief), and a bottle of fresh drinking water (just because a river runs clear and cool doesn't mean it's free of microbes). And don't forget your emergency kit, packed with fire-starter gear stored in a waterproof bag, a portable water filter, a flashlight, a space blanket, and a small first-aid kit.

Additional information
Contact the Canoe Cruisers Association, 4515 Evansdale Road, Dale City, VA 22193; (301) 656-2586.

Voices
in the Lake

by Paula J. Del Giudice

I discover that I have been ambushed. I've hiked down to a viewpoint below Glen Canyon Dam to shoot a few photographs, images to file for stories on the area. But once I'm down there, unpredicted emotions well up inside me. Instead of just admiring a view, I am suddenly aware that beautiful Lake Powell, formed by this dam, is also a vast graveyard. I realize that much is lacking in my knowledge of this place. I must learn how to pay homage to the canyon's ghosts.

Up on the Highway 89 turnout where our truck is parked, my husband and our young son, Kevin, quietly await my return. We are on our way to join other family members for a houseboat vacation on Lake Powell. It's early spring, a time when the lake is serene and relatively uncrowded. Even though

I've lived in Nevada my whole life, this will be my first voyage on this lake—that great aquatic sprawl that reflects so many hues of blue into the desert sky.

I am now at a spot simply called Photo Point. It's perhaps a half mile downstream from the dam, about 400 feet below its high crest, and 200 feet above the river. You have to walk down a long staircase to get to this platform. When you reach it, there's a rather nice pavilion, which looks as though it were built as a shrine or altar to help us admire the work of the engineers.

I sit alone, looking up at the 580 vertical feet of concrete. Beneath that soaring arch, the Colorado River is squeezed down and choked off to a blue-green trickle. Tears involuntarily come to my eyes. My throat begins to tighten as I consider all that "management" has wrought on one of the most beautiful river systems in the world.

Incredible lost canyons lie drowned below the lake and behind the dam. There are ruins here, too, including great homes and artifacts of bygone native people. The brilliant dream of mid-nineteenth-century pioneer and explorer John Wesley Powell is also buried here, under the unimaginable tons of water.

This dam certainly wasn't the first insult flung at the Colorado River. But it does form the concrete icing on a grandiose cake of human schemes, including this project devised by engineers and sanctioned by Congress to give modern humans copious water storage, and to control sediment, abate floods, increase recreational opportunities, and generate power.

Lake Powell is the youngest and the largest of the five man-made reservoirs—the Havasu, Mohave, Mead, Powell, and Flaming Gorge— that were created by damming the Colorado and Green Rivers. It boasts 1,900 miles of shoreline, which is longer than the entire West Coast of the United States.

Like many Americans living in the Southwest, I have used water and power generated from these facilities for years. I thought I had been aware of the consequences of the dam's installation, but as I sit here at Photo Point, I realize there's a whole new level of understanding to reach and that I must grasp these matters more fully and more clearly. This seems to be the minimum that those canyon ghosts require of me.

I wipe my tears, sigh, and climb back up the long staircase to the turnout. I mumble something to my husband about there being more to the lake than meets the eye, and we drive on to begin our vacation.

Our group is a modern-day extended family, and we're gathering together at the Wahweap Lodge and Marina, one of four marinas serving the lake. We meet my husband's three offspring from a previous marriage: Mike, and his two kids; Tim, and his wife, Colette; and Jessica. We board a well-appointed 50-foot Commander houseboat that we've rented along with an outboard skiff for touring side canyons. We motor across the blue vastness of the lake, glorying in the sunny skies and clear desert air, and find our first cove to camp in for the night.

After the kids get bundled into bed, I lie down and listen to the quiet, even breathing of my family as they sleep, unencumbered by a paradox that torments me. I'm enjoying our time on the lake, yet I'm still haunted by those voices I heard, voices of natural wildlife and native men, whose lives were abruptly changed by the descent of tons of concrete.

Yet ancient night conceals all modern works. Darkness feels like a salve applied to this new wound in my heart. Outside, a gentle breeze blows wavelets softly against the side of the houseboat. It rocks peacefully.

I wish I could see this part of the Colorado as John Wesley Powell saw it when his party first explored the area. I imagine what the river might have been like before the placid expanse of rising waters came.

Maps of the Green and Colorado Rivers—near Lee's Ferry and down through the Grand Canyon—were mostly marked "unknown" prior to Powell's expeditions, which began in 1868. (The only other breakthrough had come in 1776, when, just below Padre Bay, the Franciscan priests Escalante and Dominguez found a shallow river crossing that was later dubbed the Crossing of the Fathers.) Powell was a celebrated Union soldier who had lost an arm in the Civil War's battle of Shiloh. He emerged from the war with a thirst for knowledge of the unexplored regions of the West. This scrappy veteran was determined to navigate the Colorado River and wrote, "The thought grew in my mind that the canyons of this region would be like the book of revelations in the rock-leaved Bible of geology. The thought fructified and I determined to read the book."

I decide to read Powell's "book," an account of his first expedition from Green River, Wyoming, to the mouth of the Virgin River in Nevada, a journey that took three months. Powell's determination and tenacity sustained the expedition through many tribulations, including back-breaking portages, swamped boats, near starvation, and extreme weather, including 120-degree heat.

Powell wrote in 1875 that Glen Canyon was a high point of his journey:

> *August 3. Start early this morning. The features of this canyon are greatly diversified. Still vertical walls at times. These are usually found to stand above great curves. The river, sweeping around these bends, undermines the cliffs in places. Sometimes the rocks are overhanging; in other curves, curious, narrow glens are found. Through these we climb, by a rough stairway, perhaps several hundred feet, to where a spring bursts out from under an overhanging cliff, and where cottonwoods and willows stand, while, along the curves of the brooklet, oaks grow, and other rich vegetation is seen, in marked contrast to the general appearance of naked rock. We call these oak glens.*
>
> *Other wonderful features are the many side canyons or gorges that we pass. Sometimes, we stop to explore these for a short distance. In some places, their walls are much nearer each other than below, so that they look somewhat like caves or chambers in the rocks. Usually in going up such a gorge, we find beautiful vegetation; but our way is often cut off by deep basins, or pot-holes, as they are called. On the walls, and back many miles into the country, numbers of monument-shaped buttes are observed. So we have a curious ensemble of wonderful features—carved walls, royal arches, glens, alcove gulches, mounds, and monuments. From which of the features shall we select a name? We decide to call it Glen Canyon.*

Our modern houseboat rocks on the vast lake. What would Powell have thought of this huge reservoir named after him? Why was it even named for him? In tribute? As a mockery?

This whole region drew Powell like a magnet. He convinced political friends in Washington, D.C., to fund a second expedition and was granted a $10,000 appropriation in 1870.

On the second trip, his interest turned from the great river to the native people. He knew the aboriginal culture would be destroyed by the advancing tide of modern civilization. In the terraced Moqui towns—Moqui is the term used by the Spanish explorers to describe the Hopi Indians who lived nearby—Powell spent months collecting, documenting, discovering.

He had the gift of winning the respect, admiration, and trust of both the white settlers and native people. Because of this, he was asked to act as an emissary between the Navajos and the Mormon Church. In a pact prepared by Powell, the Navajos agreed to make no more raids on Mormon settlements. The Mormons, in turn, would open their doors to trade with them.

The survey from Powell's second expedition was an unqualified scientific success. As an outstanding explorer, he became a hero and a celebrity. But more importantly, he developed an intuitive sense of how the West should be settled. His views were considered radical and, unfortunately, were not well accepted.

Powell hoped his document "A Report on the Lands of the Arid Region of the United States, with a More Detailed Account of the Lands of Utah" would bring the country to its senses. Powell stressed in his report that settlement and farming of the arid West could not be undertaken as it had been in the humid East. He favored a scientific and environmental approach to settling the West. He also told Congress that two-fifths of the United States had a climate that couldn't support farming without irrigation. And even with irrigation, only a small portion could be reclaimed, he said.

Marc Reisner, author of *Cadillac Desert,* wrote that Powell's views of riparian water law were "revolutionary." Powell believed that if everyone had a neat little square parcel of land, some would have more stream footage than others, thus property boundaries should be split to give everyone a fair portion of the stream. He also thought that all who held water rights should have to use them, or else relinquish them to the public trust.

In addition, Powell said straight-line fences were nonsense and a waste of a resource. He thought farms should be clustered together and should share a common fence. And why shouldn't boundaries follow nature? Too often the boundaries of states followed rivers for convenience; too often they bisected mountain ranges and dissected watersheds. Powell believed the entire watershed should be in one state.

He was interested in seeing a careful, slow, and well-thought-out expansion in the West. But the rest of the country was in no mood for that. While Powell wanted to conduct broad topographic surveys of the region before settlement and irrigation occurred, development forces were eager to pounce. Powell eventually lost the confidence of Congress and was denied the funds to create his irrigation plan.

Unable to stop the Washington, D.C., forces unleashed on the West, Powell withdrew to the Bureau of Ethnology, where he was at least able to help document the dying native cultures.

On the big houseboat's comfortable berth, I stretch and close my eyes. It is time for sleep. Tomorrow will be a day full of fun and family activity. And perhaps there will also be more quiet moments to contemplate a little more truth.

Powell's first, exploratory voyage down the Colorado in wooden boats was an epic of glorious discovery, harrowing danger, harsh conditions, and narrow escape. Cruising on a houseboat, high above the old riverbed, is clearly a different way to experience this region. If one is just there for fun, renting a houseboat on a large lake is an excellent way to take a family vacation. Every comfort and facility you need is on board, from a bathroom with a shower to a kitchen with a stove and fridge. And there's no need to worry about anyone wandering off, since we're all contained in one place. There isn't even a sense of confinement or claustrophobia because we are surrounded by vast desert-shore vistas and wind-riffled expanses of lake.

I love the lake, yet I mourn the drowned canyons. But what can help me with this trenchant sense of irony?

On the third day, we visit some of the last visible remains of the ancient native cultures above Lake Powell's shore. Curiosity fills me; I want to see how the old ones lived and what their culture contributed to the world around them. And what do these artifacts suggest of their fate?

The Anasazi (Navajo for "the old people") arrived around 200 B.C. Archaeologists divide prehistoric people into cultural phases and groups based upon such factors as location, methods of subsistence, and distinctive tools or household items. These earliest Desert Archaic people had just entered into a phase of cultural development called the Basketmakers. Although primarily hunter-gatherers, they used tightly woven baskets for cooking. During the Pueblo period of the Anasazi, beginning about 750 A.D., they began devising ingenious cliff dwellings. Irrigation systems were installed along the river to assist their agriculture.

The Anasazi disappeared from the Colorado Plateau by the late thirteenth century. Some speculate that prolonged drought, famine, soil depletion, and marauding tribes led to their demise. Others believe the Anasazi were absorbed into other cultures.

Some of their most spectacular remains are in the Lake, Moqui, and Forgotten Canyons on the Escalante River. The arms and fingers of our modern lake reach deep into the ancient canyons, providing convenient boating highways for exploration. Since we launched at Wahweap Marina, we have to keep our search for ruins in Lower Glen Canyon since we won't have time to travel to the other end of the lake. Most of my family comes with me as I scoot along these waterways in the outboard-powered skiff.

We trace the ancient steps that can be seen in several places along the lake. These are Anasazi hand- and toeholds, pecked out with stone tools. They provided a primitive ladder of sorts, for climbing up and down the steep canyon walls from places of habitation to the river.

Although it's good to get on shore and hike a bit, and show the kids these shards of ancient history, I am disappointed. Little is left of the

Anasazi along the Lake Powell shore, aside from petroglyphs, some ruins, and a few sequences of stone steps. These smudges and carved notches are so subtle, and don't tell much about what old-time life must have been like on the Colorado River. What stories lie beneath the lake? And why do I feel those stories seeping upward into my mind? Chief Seattle of the Suquamish tribes of the Northwest said in a famous speech that the American landscape would remain forever haunted by the spirits of those who had gone before. Does everyone who glides along the surface of Lake Powell feel a little of this, whether or not they acknowledge and understand it?

Because the Anasazi dispersed before the advent of the white man, there is little about their demise for which we need to feel guilt or remorse. For many, their disappearance is more of a curiosity. After the Anasazi, the Southern Paiutes may have occupied the canyons along the river on a sporadic basis until the Navajos drifted in during the 1800s.

The Navajos used the area in much the same way as the Anasazi: They planted a little corn and hunted available game. They also enthusiastically adopted the sheep brought by the Anglos, and this river area was important for watering and feeding the flocks. Navajo trails and steps, created by enlarging those Anasazi handholds, can still be seen; many are used today.

At one point, we beach the houseboat on Lake Powell's San Juan Arm at the back of Navajo Canyon, not far from the northern part of the Navajo Indian Reservation. It's impossible to visit Lake Powell without contemplating or confronting the fate of Native Americans. For me, out here on this first voyage, the confrontation feels particularly strong. We've squeezed Native Americans into a reservation to manage them— just as we have the Colorado River. The Navajos are tenacious and persistent, however. Though reduced to a trickle, I think their blood yearns to flow strong, proud, and free, much like the Colorado.

Darkness falls gently once again. On this evening, my 28-year-old stepson, Mike, decides to fish. He disappears over the hill carrying a lantern. Soon he returns with a five-pound striped bass. With great enthusiasm, some of us grab our fishing rods and follow.

We leave the lanterns away from the shore, so the light won't spook the fish. The cover of darkness seems less healing tonight. I want the light to aid us in the simple tasks of tying a knot in a line, baiting a hook, and casting a line. It seems very awkward in the dark, even though I've done it a thousand times before. I am apprehensive and wish I felt more secure in this shroud of inky night.

I cast my line and am reassured by the kerplunk of the fat worm hitting the water. One by one, we catch five- to seven-pound stripers and attach them to stringers.

After I catch my fish, I pick up my rod and carefully scale the rocky shoreline. I want to say goodnight to my two-year-old, Kevin. Anxious for his strong hug and squishy bedtime kisses, I find him enjoying a bedtime story with his daddy.

My husband finishes the story and sends Kevin padding to the stern of the houseboat, where I'm baiting another hook. I kiss him tenderly and tell him to go to bed. I toss the line over the rail of the boat and let the line uncurl off the reel. After a few moments, I feel a very big tug on the line and set the hook. I carefully reel in the biggest fish caught on our trip—an eight-pound striper.

Great fishing is another reason why modern folks like to come to Lake Powell, yet the striped bass is one of the Colorado River's ironies. After a landlocked population of stripers was successfully established in the Santee-Cooper Reservoir in South Carolina, great interest grew in establishing striped bass in western reservoirs. Stripers were introduced into reservoirs on the Colorado, even though it was believed they couldn't successfully spawn. But they did spawn. And now they are the most populous game fish in Lake Powell.

The stripers are at the top of the lake's food chain. When their populations boom, populations of their prey shrink. There's a tremendous cyclic effect on the striped bass. As prey populations shrink, striped bass begin to lose body condition and don't reproduce well. Their numbers shrink. Then the prey species recover, and things take off again. It takes about 10 years to complete each cycle.

In boom periods, stripers provide tremendous opportunities for anglers. They are easy and fun to catch—and great to eat. But the

Colorado River's original piscine denizens are having a tough time. The Colorado squawfish, razorback sucker, bonytail chub, and humpback chub were all once abundant in the river basin. Now, they're endangered because of the changes in their habitat.

Dams built to tame the once wild and unpredictable flows of the Colorado restricted fish to 25 percent of their range, blocked some migration routes, and destroyed some spawning habitat. In addition, nonnative fish were introduced, and they compete for food and space with the endangered natives.

It won't be easy to save these fish. What we've done to the Colorado River won't go away. The fish may not be able to survive in a system that was once a mighty stream of turbid, raging waters and is now mostly a collection of tame reservoirs, with clear flows directed between them based on humanity's timetable.

Another one of Lake Powell's ironies is that the desert sands on its shore have been transformed into many beautiful beaches. Toward the end of our trip, I sit on one of them and let the fine grains of sand roll through my fingers. With them roll many thoughts. I cannot right the many injustices of white man's pioneering spirit that demanded control of nature, regardless of the consequences. I'm an infinitesimal unit in this web of life, nearly inconsequential. However, if injustices continue without my help to block or interfere them, I most certainly must bear some blame. So much change happens without protest or forethought. I would like to be able to reconcile my feelings about the past, so that I might help plan a better future for what remains of the river.

The building of Glen Canyon Dam didn't come without controversy, but opponents were few and vastly outnumbered. The Colorado River Storage Project Act authorized construction of the Glen Canyon Dam and three other dams, among other projects. Before the law was passed, a site for this huge, new storage facility had to be chosen, and two sites were proposed: on the Colorado River at Glen Canyon, and on the Green River at Dinosaur National Monument.

Conservationists, horrified at the proposed damming of the magnificent river canyons, were led primarily by the Sierra Club's only full-time employee at the time, David Brower. He waged battles over the impact the proposed reservoir would have on a national monument. An argument was also made that less surface evaporation would occur at the Glen Canyon site than at the Dinosaur site. Apparently, they were resigned to accepting one last plug in the river. In a compromise designed to prevent any further damming in the Grand Canyon or the flooding of any national monument, conservationists also agreed to support the building and operation of coal-fired power plants—a decision they later rued.

Even the Bureau of Reclamation was torn over the location of the site. Hydrologists feared that the Navajo sandstone at the Glen Canyon site would make a leaky, porous foundation for a dam. But the scheme became law when it was signed by President Eisenhower in April 1956. And work on the Glen Canyon Dam site began in 1957, the year of my birth.

Lake Powell evokes the strongest sorts of emotions. One's feelings about the environment and the fate of Native Americans can't easily be separated from the landscape—no matter what those feelings are. One can't view the dam without feeling either remorse or awe or maybe both. One can't view the Anasazi ruins or the Navajo Reservation without a sense of somber wonder. Even *our* bold and boisterous civilization will one day pass from the earth, just as theirs did.

Sometimes, while peacefully motoring up the lake, even in a houseboat, a passion for this magical place sweeps over, just as surely as if you'd witnessed a classic symphonic performance. What evokes that passion? Maybe it's the variety of sandstone, limestone, and gypsum changing texture as the landscape unfolds—layered, jagged, rough, smooth, weathered, and eroded. Then throw in some special-effects lighting from the sun as it rises and sets, casting a low-level glow upon the strata, changing the hues as it fades in and out. Or perhaps it's the lake's clear water (although it's not clear enough to expose all the mysteries of the canyons that are now submerged).

As our long weekend winds to a close, the calls of waiting jobs and midterms pull my stepkids toward homes scattered around the West.

I'm sorry to see them go, though I am happy we've had a good family reunion on the lake. We get to keep the houseboat for another night, so we decide to head for the most isolated cove near our final destination—Wahweap Marina.

I'd like to sample the fishing one last time. We have the Honey Hole near the dam to ourselves, and we fish it from the skiff. Though others try to fish nearby, they are skunked, and watch in amazement as my husband and I haul up one five-pound striper after another. The moment is light and airy; we laugh openly as we share the enjoyment of our success. Kevin amuses himself quietly, playing with toy cars in the boat. Mike and I continue to reel in our dinner—and then some.

Once back at the houseboat, I recline in a sun chair on the deck and relish the delicious warmth of this spring day. Heat washes over me like the first sip of a good cognac.

With Kevin in bed for his nap, it's the first time there's absolutely nothing to do: no photos to capture, no fish to catch, no dinner to prepare, no dishes to clean, and no deadlines to meet. That's when I learn about another precious attribute of this lake: there can't be anyplace on earth that's as quiet as Lake Powell. Until you've experienced the silence, you don't realize how welcome it is. But if you *really* listen, in the background you can hear the voices of the past.

TRIP NOTES

Glen Canyon Dam, a 710-foot-high concrete arch, stopped the waters of the Colorado River in 1963 and created Lake Powell. This vast desert reservoir is 186 miles long and bordered by 1,900 miles of shoreline. The lake makes a smooth highway for boaters to explore the fingers and arms of side canyons, which harbor beautiful, natural rock structures and Native American ruins. Unfortunately, many more natural wonders and remnants of the past lie drowned below the surface of the dammed lake, never to be seen again.

Glen Canyon Dam is located near Page, Arizona, just off Highway 89; however, most of Lake Powell extends upstream into Utah.

When to go
Lake Powell is accessible year-round, but the most popular season is late spring through early fall. For a tranquil trip, visit midweek in the off-season. If you want

to rent a houseboat and are on a tight budget, your best bet is to go between November 1 and March 31, when houseboat rentals are reduced by 40 percent. From April 1 to mid-May and from mid-September to the end of October, the rental fees are reduced by 25 percent.

How to go

A houseboat is the perfect vessel for exploring Lake Powell. It's not as inexpensive as camping, but if you have a large group of people it's often less costly per person than a week in a hotel (especially in the off-season). Houseboats are also comfortable, convenient, and easy to use. For details on renting a houseboat, see "Where to go" below.

Where to go

The best map of Lake Powell is created by Stan Jones, better known as "Mr. Powell," and it features descriptions of everything there is to see on and around the lake. The map also provides a primer on the navigational system used here. To purchase a copy, send a check for $4.50 (or $9 for a flat, laminated copy) to Stan Jones, P.O. Box 955, Page, AZ 86040.

Local lodgings include motels, houseboats, an RV park, and a campground. To make houseboat rental reservations or order a brochure on houseboats, contact Lake Powell Resorts and Marinas, P.O. Box 56909, Phoenix, AZ 85079-6909; (602) 331-5200 or (800) 528-6154 (phone), (602) 331-5294 (fax). Houseboats depart from Wahweap Lodge and Marina near Page, Arizona; and from Hall's Crossing Marina, Bullfrog Resort and Marina, and Hite Marina in Lake Powell, Utah (addresses and phone numbers are listed below).

Houseboat rentals include:

- **The Admiral.** A luxury 59-footer; sleeps 10. Summer (i.e., peak season) rates are about $2,085 for three days, $2,780 for four days, and $3,984 for seven days.

- **The Captain.** A 50-foot executive model; sleeps 12. Summer rates are about $1,515 for three days, $2,020 for four days, and $2,832 for seven days.

- **The Commander.** A standard 36- to 50-foot houseboat; sleeps 6 to 12. Summer rental rates range from $759 to $1,198 for three days, $1,006 to $1,581 for four days, and $1,445 to $2,240 for seven days.

- **The Commodore.** A 56-foot deluxe model; sleeps 10. Summer rates are approximately $1,746 to $1,907 for three days, $2,329 to $2,542 for four days, and $3,255 to $3,405 for seven days.

Also available to rent are 16-foot skiffs, 18- and 19-foot small boats, patio boats, and other water toys. If you plan to rent a houseboat and spend a lot of time exploring or fishing, consider renting a small tow-along craft, too.

For information on motels, contact the Wahweap Lodge and Marina, Box 1597, Page, AZ 86040, (520) 645-2433 (phone), (520) 645-0731 (fax), or the Lake Powell Motel, at the same address, (520) 645-2477.

Three-bedroom mobile homes are available at Bullfrog, Hall's Crossing, and Hite Marinas. For information, contact:

- **Bullfrog Resort and Marina,** Box 4055-Bullfrog, Lake Powell, UT 84533; (801) 684-2233 (phone), (801) 684-2355 (fax).

- **Hall's Crossing Marina,** Lake Powell, UT 84533; (801) 684-2261 (phone), (801) 684-2319 (fax).

- **Hite Marina,** Box 501-Hite, Lake Powell, UT 84533; (801) 684-2278 (phone), (801) 684-2358 (fax).

Boat tours of Lake Powell, including a paddle-wheel cruise, depart daily from Wahweap Marina. Half-day Colorado River float trips are also available. To make reservations more than seven days in advance, call (800) 528-6154 (or, in Greater Phoenix, call 602/278-8888); to make reservations fewer than seven days in advance, visit the office of Wilderness River Adventures, 50 South Lake Powell Boulevard, Page, AZ; (520) 645-3279 or (800) 992-8022.

Whitewater rafting trips are popular here, and must be booked very far in advance. For details, contact Wilderness River Adventures, P.O. Box 717, Page, AZ 86040; (520) 645-3279 or (800) 992-8022.

What to bring

The beauty of houseboat travel is that you don't have to pack the kitchen sink (the houseboat already has one), yet you can bring nearly anything else you could want, because there's plenty of room for stowage. Bring a wide array of clothing with an emphasis on garments that provide solar protection (light, long-sleeved shirts and pants, and broad-brimmed hats). Sunscreen gel and high-quality sunglasses make smart accessories.

Anglers after Lake Powell's striped bass can use bait to good effect; ideal lures are anything resembling a shad, crank baits, and rattletraps. Few trout are left in the lake, but there are good populations of largemouth and smallmouth bass, as well as crappie.

Those planning side hikes are well advised to bring light, Vibram-soled hiking boots for traction. Because the area is home to Western diamondback rattlesnakes, a handy first-aid item is the Sawyer Extractor, a reverse syringe for sucking snake venom out of puncture wounds—very effective if used in the first few minutes following a bite.

Finally, to take advantage of the awesome scenery, pack a video and/or still camera and plenty of tape or film. Binoculars will also prove entertaining and useful.

Additional information

For general information on Lake Powell, contact the National Park Service, Glen Canyon National Recreation Area, P.O. Box 1507, Page, AZ 86040; (520) 608-6200. If you'll be cruising the lake on a houseboat, read Bob Hirsch's "Houseboating on Lake Powell" for trip pointers; to order a copy, send a check for $7.95 to Bob Hirsch, P.O. Box 644, Cave Creek, AZ 85331. And to learn more about the nation's quest for water in the West, read "Cadillac Desert," by Marc Reisner (Penguin Group, 1993).

Anglers, please note: An Arizona fishing license is required from Wahweap downstream to Lee's Ferry, and a Utah license is required uplake from Wahweap. Licenses are available at marinas and in nearby communities. For more information, call the 24-hour fishing hot line: (800) ASK-FISH, and press AZ (for Arizona) and UT (for Utah).

THE QUEEN
CHARLOTTE ISLANDS

The Place of Wonder

by Tim Cahill

A guidebook I once paged through at a Prince Rupert newsstand opened with an admonition that read, as I recall, "In the Queen Charlotte Islands, you should put your troubles and cares in your pocket, but leave plenty of room for high spirits and adventure." I had puzzled over that bit of advice. Was I supposed to have high-spirited adventure in the same pocket that contained my troubles and cares? Why couldn't I have a couple of adventures in an entirely different pocket altogether?

As it was, I was enduring an unexpected and out-of-pocket adventure. We'd pretty much killed the bleeding last night—my head wound was taped shut—but the pain in my back was excruciating. This morning, I had managed to hobble through thigh-deep water to get to a floatplane that would take me to the hospital in Queen Charlotte City, about a 45-minute flight north. I had been hiking in the wilderness of South Moresby Island, and it doesn't really pay to be stupid in such places.

And I had been really, really stupid. High-spirited, but stupid.

It was, I suppose, a good day for a flight over the Queen Charlottes. In late June, at the 53rd parallel, there were still a few patchy bits of snow on peaks that rose to 3,000 feet. The sun was burning its way through a scudding layer of low clouds, and slanting shafts of light fell across the otherwise gray North Pacific just as light falls in a cathedral. The islands themselves were almost black with vegetation, except where those purely religious shafts hit them like celestial spotlights, and then the ancient mossy forests seemed to glow from within, emerald luminescence anchored in a tenebrous misery of unrelieved gray.

From above, I could almost make out the shape of the Queen Charlotte archipelago. It looked a bit like a giant fang: the broad expanse of Graham Island in the north, then Moresby Island curving down south and east, tapering off to a point at Cape Saint James in the far south. Interspersed among these two main islands were at least 150 others— some little more than rocky hummocks—located from 31 to 95 miles off the coast of British Columbia.

The islands were separated from the mainland by Hecate Strait, a shallow and treacherous body of water one early sailor described as "a black-hearted bitch" that seemed charged, in the sailor's opinion, with the task of "protecting the Queen Charlottes." This archipelago sits at the very edge of the continental shelf, so the rocky western headlands are pounded fiercely by the Pacific's full force.

Back somewhere in the frosty reaches of geological time—during the ice ages, when much of the world's water was frozen at the polar caps—sea levels were much lower, and the Queen Charlottes were probably connected to the North American mainland by a land bridge. Enter a few mainland species, both plants and animals. Exit the ice age. The land bridge was drowned in meltwater and became the black-hearted gatekeeper we call Hecate Strait.

The Queen Charlottes, in turn, became islands, with Hecate on one side and the inhospitable North Pacific on the other. These rough waters have kept the islands isolated over the millennia since the last ice age. No new plants or animals. No new genetic information. The former mainland species isolated on these islands have been forced to respond to local conditions, and have sometimes evolved survival strategies quite different from those of their mainland cousins. According to Dr. J. Bristol Foster, director of the British Columbia Ecological Reserves Program, the Queen Charlotte Islands are "an evolutionary showcase."

Down there, in those undisturbed ancient forests of spruce, cedar, and hemlock, are species of flora and fauna that exist nowhere else on earth. The largest black bear in North America (*Euarctos americana carlottae*) roams the forests of the larger islands, and there are subspecies of woodpecker and owl unique to the Queen Charlottes, along with several species of moss and flowering plants, including the alpine lily (*Lloydia serotina ssp flava*). The sheer volume of endemic species—those peculiar to one place—is, according to Dr. Foster, astonishing. The Queen Charlottes are sometimes called the Canadian Galapagos.

So that's what I had been doing when it happened: hiking through the South Moresby National Park Reserve, looking for endemic species. Alone. Didn't tell anyone at the camp where our kayaks were beached or exactly where I was going. Just took off. I had made my way through the dim forests, looking for bears, the saw-whet owl, and the hairy woodpecker. I had come across a few tiny orchids, an insectivorous plant, and any number of mosses that I couldn't identify (the Queen Charlottes are the moss capital of Canada, if not the world).

South Moresby is a temperate-zone rain forest. I was trekking through country that had never heard the scream of the chain saw. The spruce, hemlock, and cedar stood like monarchs, and only about 10 percent of the available light filtered through to the forest floor. The canopy above acted like a giant sponge, so the forest seemed to be dripping water even under clear skies. There was a strange, green, subaqueous quality to the light. The mosses underfoot were six or more inches deep.

There were fallen trees everywhere, covered in moss. Spruce saplings grew out of every horizontal surface. Old-man's beard, a kind of wispy green moss, hung from the branches of the living trees, and there were standing dead snags everywhere. The cedars, in particular, were spectacular in death: 100 feet of soaring silver wood, like monuments on the land. No wonder the local Indians, the redoubtable Haida, used cedar to make their totem poles.

I was looking for woodpeckers in one particular dead cedar when the thread of linear thought abandoned me, as it sometimes does in the wild. The tree was standing at a Tower of Pisa slant. What if I were that tree? And what if I retained some shred of consciousness, even in standing death? My life span had stretched out over several centuries, and now, here I was, falling, slowly, toward the forest floor. Given my life span, it would seem to be happening very fast. It would be like catching your foot at the top of the stairs: the arms windmill about, there's a brief shout, then thump-thump-thump.

And what did I, as a conscious cedar, have to look forward to on the forest floor? Over the span of several months—to me, the blink of an eye—I'd be covered in moss, fungus, parasites. Insects would penetrate to my core and eat my cells from the inside out. Other living trees would colonize me with their seeds, and the saplings would suck the last living thought from my marrow.

Now, I know that this is all part of the biological cycle of regeneration. Perfectly natural. Perfectly healthy. My problem is that I tend to personalize everything. You're a tree, you fall, everything on the forest floor feeds off your body. It would be like a slow-motion horror film.

I was indulging in this eccentric train of thought when the forest right-of-way presented me with a mossy cliff wall about 15 feet high. Easy climb. I even took my walking stick with me. I recall reaching over the top of the cliff, but then—and this seemed totally unacceptable at the time—I seemed to be falling face first toward the mute forest floor. Happily, I landed in a thick bed of moss. Unhappily, I gashed my forehead rather deeply, probably on my own damn walking stick.

I lay there for a while, assessing the extent of the damage, and wondering how badly I had hurt my back. What if I couldn't move? It would be the whole cedar scenario, that slow-motion horror film of rot and decay, with my human body in the lead role.

This thought, I suppose, got me onto my feet and kept me moving for four hours until I got down to the seashore where my kayaking companions were already at work, searching for me. A radio call was placed to the hospital.

And now, here I was, being medevaced out of a place I considered an earthly paradise because I had been stupid enough to put my adventures in the same pocket as my problems.

The Queen Charlottes, like Nepal or Tibet, are one of those places people go for emotional renewal or spiritual enlightenment. In the 1960s and 1970s, the islands had been a little-known hippie mecca, and survivalists, known as coasties, had colonized some of the more remote areas. In those years, several timber companies were hard at work clear-cutting the ancient forests.

There had been an acrimonious controversy. Conservation-minded locals, the hippies, the coasties, and the Haida had all banded together to stop the logging. After almost 15 years of bitter argument, on July 11, 1987, the Canadian government saved a substantial portion of the Queen Charlottes from the saw by making the southern part of Moresby Island a National Park Reserve. This reserve includes 138 islands, and comprises about 15 percent of the Queen Charlottes' land area. Gwaii Haanas, it's called in Haida talk—"place of wonder."

An article I read in the *Queen Charlotte Islands Observer* said there was a movement afoot to change the name of the islands to the aboriginal appellation Haida Gwaii ("place of the Haida"). There was going to be a referendum. After spending three weeks in the islands, I had a sense that it would pass.

About 6,000 people of various ethnic descent live on the islands. They still make a living logging the northern islands. Halibut and salmon are plentiful, and many folks fish to earn their daily bread, too. Tourism is in its infancy.

The soul of the Queen Charlottes—the wilderness of Gwaii Haanas—is accessible by floatplane or chartered boat. I chose to kayak South Moresby with Grant Thompson of Tofino Expeditions, out of

Vancouver, who had invited me along on a scouting trip to the place of wonder. There were 10 of us in the party.

We camped, for the most part, on Moresby Island's southeast coast. The gray cobblestone beaches were piled, at the high tide line, with gigantic heaps of drift logs that had escaped logging booms. Stacked at the base of the logs, or flung past them, were the flotsam and jetsam of the North Pacific; the Japanese current tosses material that's three years old up on the beach.

Hawaiian garbage takes a bit longer to get to South Moresby, about five years. There were plastic detergent bottles, disposable diapers, and beer cans (from Canada, Japan, and Hawaii, judging by the labels), along with treasures such as the handblown glass balls that Japanese fishermen use to float their fishing nets.

Sometimes the beaches were covered with a slick glaze of tiny transparent jellyfish—small disks with protruding dorsal fins that catch the ocean breezes and give these organisms their other name: by-the-wind sailors. There were broken dolls staring up from the drift logs, and huge plastic floats that boomed loudly when kicked and hence were handy for impromptu soccer games. Indeed, I was standing on a beach, booting one of these beach-ball-size affairs around, making a lot of noise, when my friend Linnea asked me to stop: "Shhhh. . . ."

A bald eagle was sitting atop one of the dead spruce trees that fronted the ocean. This was pretty much par for the course. There are more eagles per square mile in the Queen Charlottes than anyplace on earth, with the exception of Alaska's Admiralty Island. I looked closer and saw that there were, in fact, two eagles, sitting shoulder to shoulder, high up on the bare branches.

I got my binoculars and watched an odd performance. Each eagle seemed to be pretending that the other one wasn't there. Each scanned the beach and ocean, and through the glasses I could see the stern eyes, the hooked beaks, the implacable nobility. And then both eagles turned at the same time, and their heads collided with an almost audible thump, like two humans stooping to pick up the same sheet of paper. They regarded each other with visible annoyance, staring fiercely at the other as if to say, "You dork!"

One day we paddled for several hours to the head of Rose Inlet, where a freshwater stream ran through a grassy meadow. The tide was high, and we paddled up the meandering stream. A small harbor seal with a friendly, doglike face frolicked beside us for a time. The grass in the meadow was knee-high, and I could just barely see the tops of my companions' heads gliding through an undulating lake of greenery. A black-tailed deer, drinking from the stream, glanced up to watch us pass. I was close enough to touch it with my paddle. The deer just stood there, watching.

That day we gathered clams and a large bag of sea asparagus, a kind of thick-stemmed grass that grows at the edge of the ocean. We cooked the sea asparagus with butter and garlic, wolfed down the clams, and sat, sated, at our campsite while the sun took about four hours to set.

The next day we paddled through a flotilla of purple jellyfish the size of volleyballs and past a rocky island where red and orange starfish larger than my head clung to craggy rocks just under the surface of the sea. Ahead was a point of land that caught the worst of the ocean swells. Booming plumes of spray exploded off the rock, and for a moment, with the sun before me, the great wall of seawater scattered the light, and dozens of tiny rainbows fell across the rock.

We gave a wide berth to the rainbows and came back along this small island, a sloping hummock of rock where several dozen sea lions were basking in the sun. The males weighed more than 2,000 pounds, and they grunted at us like foghorns as we passed. I had never heard a grunt sound lordly before.

One day, a pod of killer whales passed under our kayaks, and we could hear the great glottal pop of their breathing. My friend Linnea was so excited that she kept drumming her feet on the hull of her boat. We didn't see any gray whales. A local boatman told us that the last one he had seen making the long southern migration had passed through more than a week ago.

Our campsites, just up above the drift logs, near freshwater streams, were hard to leave. We had pitched our tents on beds of moss a foot thick. During the long twilight hours—the sun didn't set until almost 11 o'clock—we talked about what we had seen that day, and the incredible journeys the Haida made, and still make, in 40-foot-long cedar canoes.

Indeed, early on, a few of us had even seen some of these canoes being built.

Soon after I had arrived on Graham Island, several of us drove from Queen Charlotte City north to the town of Old Masset, an Indian village the local people prefer to call Haida. We stopped at the White residence, a functional, boxy affair, to see the canoes Morris White and several friends were making. The canoes would be paddled to a great meeting of the Northwest tribal bands at the mainland town of Bela Bela at the end of June.

Morris White, the patriarch, appeared to be in his early 50s. He spoke slowly, with a kind of throat-clearing stutter. He introduced his son, Christian, a handsome and rather cosmopolitan young man (a handshake for me, a continental hand kiss for Linnea). Christian's son, a boy who looked to be about 12, dozed on the couch while a Saturday afternoon kung fu movie blared away on a small color TV.

"Haida canoes, like the ones we're building?" Morris White asked. "In the old days, Haida paddled these canoes to California." He cleared his throat. I expressed amazement on this point and mentioned that I had never read anything to corroborate such a boast in the historical record.

"Oh, no one knows about it," Christian said.

"The elders tell us," Morris added, "that we paddled to Chile. In South America."

"Japan," Christian said.

In point of fact, early Euro-American explorers were forever pointing out that the Haida people were fairer of skin than the coastal tribes. They are also bigger; the men still tend toward a certain Polynesian immensity.

"Hawaii?" I asked. There was general agreement among the White men on this point.

"The Hawaiians are our relatives," Christian said. "Our cousins."

We stepped out back to visit a huge wooden barn. Here, the Whites and three friends had been working nonstop on the ceremonial canoes for several months. Morris White had lost so much weight that his clothes hung loosely on his large frame. Three huge boats, each more than 40 feet long and each made from a single cedar log, lay upside down on huge sawhorses. The place smelled like Grandma's hope chest.

The canoes, even before they had been carved and painted with totemic symbols of the Haida people—bears, eagles, beaver, ravens, and killer whales—were beautiful works of art that had been built over the centuries.

Later, over a beer in the White house, we sat chatting while Asian people kung fu'ed each other on TV. The Whites, it turned out, were remarkably talented: Morris carved silver bracelets similar to those I had seen selling for $500 apiece in Queen Charlotte City, and Christian carved traditional figures out of argillite, a soft slate, and his sculptures sold for as much as $8,000 each.

Still, the Whites weren't rich. Morris was bitter about the clever white men who somehow cheated the Haida out of their fishing boats in the mid-1950s. Worse, the forest all around them was being cut down, with hundreds of millions of dollars extracted from the land, and the Haida people weren't being compensated (a good percentage of the village of Haida was dependent on public-assistance programs).

"If we had lawyers and chartered accountants," Morris White said, "then we'd be a wealthy village." Christian nodded over to the couch in front of the television, where his young son was sucking on a Tootsie Pop. "My son," he said, "is going to be my lawyer."

The boy glanced up from the television. "I said I was going to be *a* lawyer," he replied. "I didn't say I was going to be *your* lawyer."

Our kayak party camped for a time at Fanny Bay, near the southern tip of Moresby Island and only an hour's paddle from Sgan Gwaii Island (called Anthony Island on some maps). On Sgan Gwaii ("red cod") stand the remains of Ninstints, a Haida ghost village, abandoned late in the last century. Here, magnificent totem poles still tower against the sky. In 1981 the United Nations recognized the totemic art at Ninstints as a World Heritage Site.

We decided to visit Ninstints at dawn, and notified the resident Haida caretaker of the plan by radiophone from Fanny Bay. It was a clear night when we set out, with a full moon low in the sky. By the time we reached Ninstints and pulled our kayaks up above the high tide line, a fog bank obscured the rising sun. The world was pearly-gray, and wisps of mist floated low among the sacred poles. It was very still; even the birdcalls seemed subdued.

The great cedar poles were silver-gray, and the faces carved into them—bears, eagles, ravens, and killer whales—grimaced in decay. They stared out to sea with rotting, ruined eyes.

The Haida caretaker's name was Wanagun; his wife, Dja Da Unn Koo Uss, invited us to call her Bernice. Wanagun wore gray jeans, a red sweatshirt, and sunglasses. He walked us among the poles, answering our eager questions. He told us the totemic animals weren't gods or demons; they represented family crests, just as a European coat of arms does, and were built to front long wooden houses that no longer exist.

Every Haida, Wanagun explained, was either a member of the Raven family or the Eagle family. There was no intermarriage within either family: Ravens married Eagles; Eagles married Ravens. The children joined the mother's family.

Wanagun was a Raven, and he had married Bernice, an Eagle, here at Ninstints, in the space between the largest eagle totem and the largest raven totem.

Most of the totem poles, Wanagun said, were actually funerary poles: Great men of the olden times were "buried" in the small carved boxes at the top. He pointed out that a pole had fallen and was propped up at about a 45-degree angle. The coffin lid had broken open. We could just barely make out the white, rounded shape of a skull protruding from the dirt and the grasses that grew inside.

Wanagun was a storyteller. He told us about the long wooden houses that could only be entered by a single oval doorway. "You had to put one arm through, and then your head," he explained. Once, the villagers had killed a number of enemies simply by clubbing them over the head as they entered the long houses. "The dead people had thought they were going to a party," Wanagun said. And then he laughed. "Hee-hee."

And when new poles were put up in front of the homes of important families, slaves were sometimes stuffed in the hole first and crushed to death with several tons of magnificently carved cedar. "When they tried to get out," Wanagun said, "we poked them with sharp sticks. Hee-hee."

Then there was the story about a massacre. The only survivor of the attack was a Haida boy who was so young he didn't know which coastal tribe had attacked the village. So the rest of the Haida had simply paddled up and down the coast, from Alaska to Vancouver, killing everyone, hee-hee. Even today, Wanagun said, some coastal chiefs refuse to meet with the killer Haida.

Another party of visitors arrived on a chartered boat, and Wanagun met them at the shore. We decided to take a walk. Our party moved silently through the mist, with the poles towering overhead. We followed a trail to the west through a tunnel of giant spruce. The ground was a series of mossy hummocks.

The trail led through old-growth forest and emptied onto a gravel-and-cobblestone beach. It rose through a stand of spruce that included a few giant cedars, then wound its way through a narrow rock canyon whose walls were covered with lichen and moss.

The walls rose 60 to 80 feet above us, and they led us, willy-nilly, into a dead end, a great rounded horseshoe of stone. We found ourselves staring into two caves at the base of the rock wall. Both were shaped like upside-down Vs. The rock walls on either side were festooned with tree roots, twisting down from the spruce that grew at the lip of the cliffs, 80 feet above. These immense roots wound down over the irregularities of the rocks like great woody snakes, some of them as big around as a 55-gallon drum.

A rope was stretched across the mouth of the caves. Wanagun had told us the main cave was "where we used to burn our bodies." (I hadn't been there to hear that particular statement, but I suspect it might be more accurately transcribed as, "burn our bodies, hee-hee.")

It was dark in the shadows, and the lazy, drifting mist took on a greenish hint of the forest above. As we stood at the rope, a light, drizzling rain began to fall. I flipped on a flashlight and directed the beam into the maw of the central cave. There was a momentary backscatter of light, silver-bright in the gently falling rain, and then we could see into the cave, which had been blackened by the smoke of innumerable fires. There were ashes scattered across the floor.

Presently, the rain let up and we could see a bit more clearly. In the center of the opening was a large boulder, shaped a bit like a pyramid. Certain projections on the rock gave it the look of a face. The sun was higher now, the sky had cleared a bit, and shafts of sunlight poured down through the trees.

The face, we decided from our position behind the rope, was natural, not manmade. It was eerie, and just vaguely menacing.

"I thought they buried people in those boxes on the tops of the poles," someone said. A theory was advanced that the ancient Haida burned the bodies first, for sanitary purposes. "Not enough poles to bury everyone," I offered. "Ten thousand years of Haida occupation? The whole island would be nothing but a stand of funerary poles."

The more satisfactory explanation was that ordinary people were cremated, and that important people, chiefs, were buried in the funerary poles. We contemplated these theories for a while, in the gloom, with the tree roots snaking down like giant arthritic hands and the stone face glaring out at us from the ashes.

This was just real damn spooky, and I'm obliged to report that we began throwing pinecones at one another—throwing pinecones and laughing out of sheer nervousness. Whistling past the graveyard. This was wrong. We knew it. All at once we knew it. There was another long silence. But maybe, I thought, it wasn't entirely incorrect behavior. Perhaps we had absorbed a bit of the traditional Haida outlook on life. And death, hee-hee.

The Haida, I fervently hoped, might be inclined to forgive our brief bout of pinecone dodgeball. They might even have approved.

It was just after that visit that I had my little setback and was medevaced out. After a day of recuperation in the motel, I found myself well enough to repair to the one local bar in Queen Charlotte City, where I met a young woman who dressed like a logger and talked like a hippie.

She lived with her husband and child in a log cabin near Port Clements, about an hour-and-a-half's drive north. She had no running water or electricity, but she pitied folks who had to live all packed together like ants in places like Prince Rupert. The young woman said she was in favor of calling the islands Haida Gwaii.

A mildly intoxicated white carpenter sat down and demanded to know, "Whoever said the Haida had no sense of humor?" I told him that no one had ever said that, as far as I knew. And then the carpenter told me a story.

It seems that several years ago, one of the greatest of all Haida artists carved a magnificent canoe, to be displayed in a great museum. The canoe was very big, and it was covered in exquisitely carved totemic symbols.

The canoe had to be lowered onto its stand with a large crane, and the young operator, a white man, worked hard to arrange everything just so, because the Haida artist had a specific idea of exactly how it should be placed. The crane operator imagined there might be some religious symbolism at work that he didn't understand. The artist would look away, ponder some internal problem, then gesture minimally for the operator to, say, turn it just a bit to the east. They worked together in this way for hours.

Later, when the canoe was finally placed to the artist's satisfaction, he invited the young crane operator to have a drink. They spoke for some time. The artist was, as many Haida are, politically active. He was angry at the United States at the moment because some decision by the president of that country would, indirectly, affect him and the forest he loved.

Finally, the crane operator asked the question that had been burning inside him. The artist should forgive him, he said, but he saw very little difference in the various placements of the canoe. Why had it been set, just so, on its stand?

"On the canoe," the carver explained, "there is a bear."

"I saw it," the crane operator said.

"Look closely," the artist said. "The bear's asshole?"

"Yeah?"

"It points toward the White House."

I hobbled back to my motel room, appreciating the Queen Charlotte Islands in general and the Haida people, hee-hee, in particular. My companions had another three days of kayaking left. And me, I had a long, lonely wait, and a bunch of packaged soup to eat. It had cost a fortune to be airlifted out of the place of wonder. That alone, I suppose, qualifies my fall as a pretty good out-of-pocket adventure.

TRIP NOTES

The elongated triangle formed by the Queen Charlotte Islands lies in the North Pacific Ocean, about 80 miles west of Prince Rupert in Canada's province of British Columbia. The three largest islands are commonly referred to as Graham, Moresby, and Louise. The chain is 190 miles long, 65 miles wide at the north end at Masset, and tapers to a point at the southern end at Cape Saint James.

The islands are home to the indigenous Haida people, who continue to carve what many consider the finest totem poles ever created. The residents, who number about 6,000, prefer to refer to the islands by their Haida name, Haida Gwaii, and have instigated a referendum to make it official.

When to go

Summer is the best season here, even though the weather can be capricious. You could encounter a seven-day string of sunny, 70-degree weather, but most likely you'll also get a rainstorm or two. The storms are worst from October through January.

How to go

The islands are accessible by air or ferry. Canadian Airlines International has flights from Prince Rupert or Vancouver in British Columbia that land at the Sandspit airport, near Queen Charlotte City, at the center of the island chain. For reservations, call (800) 426-7000.

Ferries depart from the port at Prince Rupert five times a week during the summer; these six-hour crossings are often booked well in advance, so be sure to reserve early. For reservations, contact the B.C. Ferry Corporation in Victoria, (604) 386-3431, or Vancouver, (604) 669-1211.

There are various means of getting around on the islands. Bicycles can be rented in Queen Charlotte City, and boat and small plane charters and helicopter tours are available at the Sandspit airport. The government's Travel and Information Center in Queen Charlotte City, (604) 559-8316, can help arrange tours and rentals.

Sea kayak tours are the best way to explore Moresby Island, the largely wild southern island. Costs for guided tours range from $125 (Canadian) for one day, including all gear and lunch, to $1,130 for a six-day outing with all meals. Sea kayak rentals cost about $180 for a week for a single-seater, $310 for a double. Some recommended outfitters include:

• Moresby Explorers (rentals only), (800) 806-7633.

- Queen Charlotte Adventures (tours and rentals), (800) 668-4288.

- South Moresby Kayak Charters, (604) 559-4748.

- Tofino Expeditions, (800) 677-0877 (phone), (604) 687-8525 (fax).

For more outfitters, contact the Travel and Information Center, (604) 559-8316, or the park offices listed below.

Where to go

The northern large island, Graham, is the most settled and populated, and has the widest array of activities. The island's towns of Masset and Old Masset (population 2,000) offer museums, shops, fishing opportunities, and even golf, while Port Clements (population 600) has the Heritage Museum. The Rose Spit Ecological Preserve offers hiking trails that wind from forest to beach; the preserve is administered by Naikoon Provincial Park, (604) 557-4390, which also has information about other natural sites on the north islands.

Lodgings tend toward the simple and sparse. If you plan to arrive in the summer, make reservations well in advance. Two recommendations: Searaven Motel, in Queen Charlotte City, (604) 559-4423; and Sandspit Inn, in Sandspit, (604) 637-5334.

The southern large island, Moresby, has the largest share of natural attractions, including some of the best examples of old-growth temperate forest left on earth. The Gwaii Haanas National Park Reserve–Haida Heritage Site encompasses 568 square miles, including about 992 linear miles of shoreline. The park contains the southern part of Moresby and more than 100 adjacent islands. Visitors need to register at park offices in either Queen Charlotte City or Sandspit. There are no user fees at present, but they may be instituted soon. Park staff can show you where camping is permitted (Hot Spring Island, Tanu, Anthony [Sgan Gwaii] Island) and where it is not (native cultural sites, primarily).

Park staff, working with the Haida Band Council, can issue permission to visit the Haida village on Sgan Gwaii (also known as Anthony Island). This village is a World Heritage Site. The park also mails out information on request; call (250) 559-8818.

What to bring

The weather is changeable, so pack warm, insulating garments (artificial piles are best) and a wind- and waterproof outer shell layer. Sea kayakers will enjoy having wetsuit booties and windsurfers' gloves handy.

All visitors should tote along a passport or some other proof of citizenship, such as a copy of a birth certificate. Note: Credit cards are not a widely accepted form of currency on the islands, so equip yourself with a roll of Canadian dollars on the mainland beforehand.

Additional information

For general travel advice and assistance, contact the Travel and Information Center in Queen Charlotte City at (604) 559-8316, or the Tourism British Columbia office in Vancouver at (800) 663-6000.

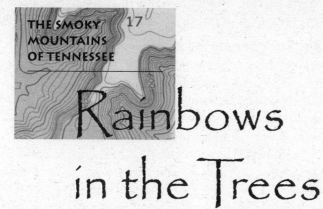

Rainbows in the Trees

by Bob Marshall

O ur trip was only four hours old, but Karen Rodrigue
seemed ready to give up on backpacking and
the Smoky Mountains.

Her hands and knees were bruised from several falls on the
rocky, overgrown trail. Her pack and clothes were soaked from
the constant downpour that had dogged us from the start, pen-
etrating the thick canopy of trees, leaving a film of trail grime
that covered everything from boots to hair. Her face was a
mask of frustration and pain. She was tired of the wall of forest always around her, tired of the never-ending up-and-down.
A young grammar school teacher from a New Orleans suburb, Rodrigue had been lured by the prospect of this Fall Colors Trip offered by a New Orleans outfitter, which had seemed

to guarantee something different from the flat, evergreen marshlands surrounding her hometown.

But if these were mountains, where were the vistas? Where were the great wide valleys? Where was the fun? Then the sun came out, and wonder began to light the edge of Rodrigue's eyes.

"Oh, look how beautiful," she said, pointing to a ridge half a mile away. Freed from an overcast sky, the sun had sent beams racing up a slope on the opposite side of the cove, revealing tides of red, gold, and yellow flooding the hardwoods. As the beams shifted, the light fell on wave after wave of brightly colored mountains and hills rolling to the horizon.

The pain and frustration fled Karen's face. Now she was glowing.

"Have you ever seen anything so pretty?" she asked. "Just being right here to see that is worth all the trouble."

Pain. Pleasure. Discovery. They are the central themes for what may be the most cherished ritual among outdoor-minded Southern folk: a Smoky Mountain autumn.

This is a place where residents of a generally flat landscape can find adventure in the high and wild, where outdoor-loving hearts trapped in the spreading urban centers can beat free and easy. This is a land where the skyscrapers are trees, where the noise of tires on concrete is replaced by the music of water over rock. And fall is the time when we enjoy it most.

From the first week of October through the second week of November, we flatlanders often head for the South's Four Corners—southwest Virginia, western North Carolina, northwest Georgia, and eastern Tennessee. This is where the Appalachian Mountains spread in all their glory, a great verdant splash on the map that includes the Great Smoky Mountains National Park and a corridor of wilderness areas in the surrounding national forests. This is our true high country, Dixie's cordillera. It reaches up to 6,000 feet, as wild as it gets in a land that has felt the clutching grasp of human development for nearly three centuries.

We realize these mountains get casually dismissed by our western brethren, who view them with the same disdain they have for many things eastern: charming, perhaps historic, but basically old and boring. After all, most trailheads in the Rockies are higher than the Appalachians' tallest peaks. And granted, anyone who has traveled both ranges won't argue the point on spectacular beauty or size.

Take a hike in a western range and you're jolted by the scenic punch of raw rock against a blue bowl of a sky, with yawning vistas that seem to place the planet at your feet and set your imagination soaring.

Take a quick look at the Appalachians and you'll see a gentle sea of rolling, forested waves, smooth tops, quiet valleys, sleepy hamlets.

Big, bold, and wild versus sleepy, old, and verdant. What's to choose? Plenty.

Dedicated Smokyphiles would say that haughty grandeur doesn't necessarily outclass subtle substance. Step inside the Smokies' green curtain and you may find that quiet forests, like still waters, can run deep, holding many secrets. The western mountains shout a message for everyone to hear. The Smokies whisper theirs in a soft drawl, heard only by those willing to lie back and listen.

"It's natural for people who have been out west before they've been east to look at the Appalachians and be a little surprised, maybe a little disappointed," said Byron Almquist, owner of New Orleans–based Canoe and Trail Outfitters, who led the trip I was on with Karen Rodrigue and eight other clients.

In a career spanning three decades, Almquist has guided adventurers to wild spots from British Columbia to the Everglades. "There tends to be a preconception about mountain beauty that includes snowcapped peaks—the typical Rocky Mountain scenery," Almquist said. "So when they see the Appalachians for the first time, it's not what they might have been expecting. But once they get out of the car, get past that first look, they're surprised. The Smokies are really fascinating. There's a lot to learn."

They came into the world as a child of geologic ages, the offspring of a planet-shaping collision at a time before man, before dinosaurs, when history was being written by minerals and gases and shifting volcanic forces. It was a time when crises were truly great; when clashes were not between armies and nations, but between continents.

WILD PLACES

It was a time when North America and Scandinavia were part of the same landmass, an immense island surrounded by a sea that was growing shorter, pulling the island-continent of Africa ever closer. The cataclysmic meeting took place between 225 million and 250 million years ago, and along the line of that collision the force of its impact pushed all surface deposits toward the sky. When it was over, a monument had been left to mark the site, a range of mountains higher than the yet-unborn Rockies, longer than the Andes. A range that extended from Alabama to Sweden—the original Appalachians.

Since then, a relative peace has settled over the southern end of that range. Below the reach of the ice ages, the Appalachians were protected from the mountain-eating glaciers that shaped portions of the Rockies and flattened the central plains. Rather than being hammered by ice, they aged slowly, gracefully, under the soft hand of water. Rain and rivers have been their main sculptors, gradually mellowing the towering vigor of their youth, changing their personality from a sky-scraping fence of rock and snow to a rolling green ocean of trees. And water has given it a name that sticks: The "smoke" of the Smoky Mountains are the clouds of water vapor snaking through its valleys and crawling across its peaks.

Reduced in size, they have grown in wisdom, living a more complex existence as a plant world soaked with rain, filled with an unending parade of life, giving birth to a forest as famous as the mountains. Oak, birch, chestnut, maple, ash, poplar, basswood, and buckeye are a few of the species known as deciduous trees—those that lose their leaves in the fall. They dominate the range and provide a canopy for the plants below, a world of laurel and rhododendron, of moss, lichens, and ferns, of gooseberry and holly.

It is the type of environment that wildlife love to call home, and these trees shelter black bears, white-tailed deer, boars, wild turkeys, raccoons, wildcats, mink, weasels, rabbits, skunks, warblers, owls, eagles, snakes, and grouse.

They may have come to life with noise and fury, but today's Smokies live a much different life. This is a land of quiet times, of whispering creeks and the murmur of rain—the soothing voice of experience.

E ven poets can party, and there is one time of the year when the complex personality of these quiet mountains is turned inside out, when the beauty hidden behind the waves of summer green suddenly bursts skyward with a force that will make even the most jaded western rock jock take a second look: autumn.

In the course of four weeks in October, the constant green of the mountains gives way to a riot of color. The transformation is startling, like watching a symphony orchestra trade its tuxedos for wild skateboarding garb.

The change has a magical pull on Southerners, drawing them from the steamy deltas and urban centers, from the college campuses and suburban malls. During the summer many will stay away, intimidated by the heat, turned off by the drive-through tourist crowds. But fall has a liberating effect, prompting the most timid to put their dreams to the test. People who spend most of their summers wrapped in the cocoon of air-conditioning or basting on Gulf Coast beaches emerge as born-again hikers, fresh-baked backwoods explorers.

The migration includes both innocent novices and veteran backpackers who know what lies ahead. They probe deep into the mountains for an experience that can't be sampled from the roadside, and they leave with memories that will never fade to black and white.

But they pay a steep physical price. The southern Appalachians are the highest and meanest part of the range. Mountains pushing up to 6,000 feet are stacked together like firewood, and the challenges they present can scorch the enthusiasm of the unprepared. Steep switchbacks turn thighs to jelly, icy-cold stream crossings freeze feet, and inevitably, rain and mist hang in the coves for days, turning human bodies into chilled sponges. It's all part of the bill for an intimate look at the great forest.

Karen Rodrigue, 23, was one of a group of city folk who had left the Big Easy behind for a chance to learn what all the Smoky yarns were based upon.

"The fall trip is always one of the most popular," Almquist said. "It seems like everyone has heard about the fall colors, and they all want to see it. People who wouldn't normally think about backpacking are willing to give it a try."

That includes Ash Tabir, another trekker, a physician whose native country was Pakistan. "When I first came to this country, I flew into the Northeast," he recalled. "It was the fall, and as we circled the countryside I saw all these incredible colors. It was unbelievable. I had never seen this before. I didn't know what was happening. I remember asking if these Americans painted their trees this way."

The color magic happens as a matter of survival, during a process botanists call abscission. When the shorter days and cooler temperatures signal winter's approach, trees, like animals, prepare for the coming rigors by building a wall of protection. Animals store fat, seek shelter, and retreat into various states of slowed animation. The great hardwoods of the deciduous forest follow that pattern by closing all openings, all spots vulnerable to freezing cold.

It begins at the stem of the leaves. Sensing the threatening chill, the tree closes off the stem by forming a layer of cork, a small yet strong wall that blocks the flow of water from the roots. That one miraculous step stirs the palette that eventually paints fall's colors.

Each leaf contains many coloring pigments, but the most dominant by far is the green of chlorophyll, the vital food-producing chemical. Chlorophyll, however, cannot be sustained without water from the roots. When the cork layer seals the stem from the tree, the chlorophyll begins to break down.

As the chlorophyll dissipates, other pigments that had been masked take over, and the show begins: Reds, yellows, oranges, and a staggering combination of the three turn a quiet withdrawal into a wild celebration.

That party is standing-room-only in the Appalachians, where deciduous trees dominate mountainsides for hundreds of miles.

Almquist steered Rodrigue and her friends to the heart of the show, aiming for the Nantahala National Forest, just south of the Great Smoky Mountains National Park. While the park has made the name Smoky famous, it also made it generic to the entire southern half of the range. When Southerners say they're "going to the Smokies" it could mean either the park or the wild and beautiful folds of the range that surround it. Much of the region is managed under restricted use, as wilderness areas, national forests, or other state and federal preserves.

In 1970 most of the area was included in the Southern Appalachian Biosphere Reserve, part of a United Nations program that seeks to balance development with protection of this important and unique ecosystem. It came not a moment too soon. Since 1980, theme parks and time-share condos have spread like cancer, consuming every unprotected valley.

The park always draws the most attention, feeling the press of nine million visitors each year, the most popular spot in the national park system. Most simply drive through, spending less than six hours within the park boundaries, even during the fall. But many others come for extended stays, drawn by the park's 800 miles of trails, including a section of the famed Appalachian Trail. During the peak summer and fall seasons, trail shelters and designated campsites along this and other popular trails can be filled for days on end.

But the surrounding national forests and wilderness areas offer just as much beauty, plus one overpowering reason to avoid the park: far fewer people.

Almquist likes the Joyce Kilmer–Slickrock Wilderness, a 17,013-acre preserve just south of the park that offers a sampler of the best aspects of this landscape. Straddling the Tennessee–North Carolina border, it protects some of the highest and wildest sections of Nantahala and Cherokee National Forests, with peaks topping 5,300 feet. There are even "balds"—mountaintops covered with rhododendron instead of trees, offering that rare eastern mountain treat: a vista.

The Kilmer-Slickrock name is a giveaway to the beauty of the area. Joyce Kilmer was the soldier-poet of World War I, immortalized by his poem "Trees." His wilderness includes some of the last virgin stands of hardwoods in the east, woodland giants that do his poem justice.

Slickrock is the name of a wild creek whose beautiful waterfalls cascade over rocks wearing slick suits of algae and moss. Its watershed is among the wildest patches of habitat left in the nation east of the Mississippi River, twisting and turning through draws thickly forested by virgin timber, tumbling into pools harboring wild trout.

Almquist's 14-hour drive has brought our group to the edge of the wilderness at a spot named Deal's Gap, where U.S. Highway 129 reaches the south side of Calderwood Lake. A local hiker listening to the flatlanders' enthusiastic oohs and aahs gives a small sniff of disapproval.

"It ain't as purty as usual," he offers. "We had a rail dry year. That hurts the colors. Makes 'em fall early, too."

To less accustomed eyes, though, the show is a hit. The trip will start up Ike's Branch Trail, and the group is tripping over each other in the excited rush to head into the forest and sample the colors.

The other inhabitants of the forest must think we humans are a strange species, running in reverse. For them, fall is a time for hurried, even desperate preparation. Enzymes and hormones urge them to prepare for a meeting with their greatest natural predator: winter. Given a choice, squirrels would not hoard acorns, bears would not hibernate, and ducks, geese, and many other animals would not undertake long, treacherous migrations. For that matter, trees would not change their leaves. But they have no choice. They can't adjust the thermostat, order a pizza, or drive to the grocery store.

If plants and animals could talk, the sight of changing leaves probably would not elicit oohs and aahs but "hells" and "damns" or something even stronger. For wildlife, fall color means the fat days of summer are running out, and the thin, desperate days of winter lie just ahead. Sensible residents of the planet don't celebrate autumn, they fear it.

Humans are the exception.

To us, fall is a time for change worth rejoicing, a time when nature puts on a show whose acts move us in strange ways. Trees burst into color, the skies become dotted with the sights and sounds of migrating birds, and the forests and mountains become busy with the traffic of mammals seeking food, moving to winter range.

So while animals flee the fall season, we humans rush to meet it. In the northern Appalachians, cabins and campgrounds are booked for October a year in advance. Rates double. Backpackers, paddlers, cyclists, and campers struggle to squeeze a few free days from work and school schedules.

In the steamy South, fall is welcomed with open arms. An audible murmur of excitement runs through a community when you can simply step outside and suck in a lungful of air that doesn't carry a gallon of water, when the sun stops leaning on the skin with such brutal weight, when a breeze stops evoking the Gulf of Mexico and instead brings visions of Canada.

And there is something more than the sensual. Fall is the most visible sign on a microchipped planet that a natural world does in fact still exist. Computers may race faster, human life may be created inside a bottle, and people may be solving the riddles of the universe. But there are certain things you can count on that will never change.

Fall tells us, despite gloomy headlines on the course of human events, that the earth, tilted on its axis, still orbits the sun. And as long as it does, trees will drop their leaves every fall and ducks will fly south—and there's nothing humans can do about it.

And that's worth a few oohs and aahs all its own.

The forest floor already is covered with a thick padding of freshly fallen leaves, but there are plenty left above. Crowding the thin trail, the hardwoods of the heavy forest cross branches above our heads, forming a thin latticework of yellows, reds, pale greens, and orange, colors that will be our companions for the next four days.

Our path will take us along Ike's Branch Creek to Yellow Hammer Gap and a base camp on Nicholl's Cove Creek. Day hiking will bring us to Big Fat Gap, then down through the lush, green, almost tropical setting of Wildcat Falls, a series of major drops on the cascade-studded Slickrock Creek.

For the newcomers, the environment is a sudden surprise. The words *mountains* and *wilderness* do not mean the same thing here as they do elsewhere. Nothing they have seen fits the western clichés that dominate wall calendars and coffee-table books.

Where the western mountains reward the hiker with frequent vistas of majestic peaks and endless blue skies, the Smokies are more grudging, more secretive; their theme isn't spirit-soaring highs, but a calmer, deeper mood, one of introspection. The crowding forest shuts off the sky, closes the door on horizons, and forces the traveler to look inward.

Creeks tumble down every cove, bouncing white against the green wall of the forest. Rock-hard trails with roots and stones force eyes downward, helping the visitor discover the Smokies' most unique gift, a perpetually damp forest floor that nurtures an endless mass of mosses, ferns, and lichens growing in cloistered communities. These tiny rain forests and plant cities spread across rocks, crowd creek banks, and encircle the trunks of the massive hardwoods.

Our group is surprised by the difficulty. The Smokies might be half the size of the Rockies, but some people consider them twice as difficult to travel. Because they are packed so tightly together, these mountains charge a lot for even a short hike.

"There's a lot more up-and-down here, a lot more switchbacks, and not nearly as much level ground," Almquist said. "The West has high altitudes, but the Smokies make you work almost constantly."

None of this country is a place for beginners. Trails are often poorly marked, and the countryside is a maze of heavily forested hollows and ridges that confused even Daniel Boone. The shortage of overviews means leaving the trail may be an adventure; everything can look the same in a hurry. It's always better to travel in groups.

Our group of Big Easy trekkers labors through the maze, plowing through rain showers, clawing up mountainsides, and plunging into hollows. It is already growing dark when we finally stagger into the base camp at Nicholl's Cove. Like the rest of the terrain, this hillside is heavily forested, and a yard-wide stream, swollen by the rain, is crashing toward Slickrock Creek. Tents are pitched on whatever level ground can be found between the trees. The spot is marked by the remains of an old cabin featuring a crumbling grave site with a headstone. The simple inscription conveys immense sorrow:

Twin Daughters of
John & Margret Dotson
Born Dec. 14, 1914
Died Dec. 20, 1914
At Rest

For the proud citizens of the Cherokee nation, the Appalachian Mountains were a comfortable, natural home, rich in game and rich in their history. For the white men who began pushing these people aside in the 1790s, life in the Appalachians was hard. The forest was a dense jungle, and the land it sheltered was so full of stones that farming was a pitched battle in itself.

But they came anyway, seeking the personal freedom offered by a subsistence lifestyle on the frontier. When that frontier passed them by in the mid-1800s, they were left behind, isolated in their mountain homes. Their culture and history began to resemble their environment: rugged, punishing, hard by any standards. The rewards remained the same: freedom to live as one wanted, to gain from life whatever one could earn from the mountains.

Finally, by the 1920s, the cycle was ending. Pressure to create a national park in the east eventually forced farmers such as the Dotsons out of the hills, returning the land to the forest.

For two days, we used the Dotsons' old farm as a headquarters for explorations deep into the mountains. We followed Slickrock Creek on its bouncing course through the valley, watching trout feed in its pools and deer browse along its banks. We followed bear tracks into laurel thickets, and ascended a ridge top where the forest changed from hickory and beech to deep-green towering spruce and a meadow of rhododendrons. And we enjoyed what many consider the Smokies' greatest gift: quiet.

The trees above and the lush growth below filter out sounds from beyond the forest walls. Follow a creek a few yards off a trail, take a seat on a moss-covered rock, and listen. Within minutes the whisper of the creek over its rocky bed combines with the soft dripping of rainwater through the canopy to create a hypnotic spell. Muscles begin to relax, thoughts drift away, and the mind empties in complete surrender to the peace of these old mountains and its woods.

On the last day, our group hiked out on a forgotten trail that Almquist resurrected from a light trace along a mountain spur, bringing us to Big Fat Gap—the trailhead for the last challenge: the Hang Over Mountain Trail.

Hang Over peak is one of those rare balds. Those who reach the top are promised an unhindered view of the Kilmer-Slickrock watershed and the eastern rim of the park beyond—a real western-style vista.

Like every part of the Appalachians, however, this treasure doesn't come easy. It is guarded by a trail that rises 2,000 feet in 2.6 miles. The start is almost vertical, climbing through cove hardwoods for half a mile before leveling slightly in mixed hardwoods and firs. At 5,000 feet, the trail breaks into the open in an ocean of rhododendrons that rises to a uniform eight feet. Hikers have a clear view of the sky above, but there's only the green tangle of rhododendrons on either side as the trail continues climbing through ankle-deep, boot-sucking mud.

By the time the summit is reached, two hours after the first step, hearts are racing, legs are on fire, lungs are screaming for rest. Our group clusters around the highest rock. Before us the Appalachians roll to every corner of the horizon in seemingly endless folds. In the valleys, the sun is striking colors. Hickory trees are brilliant red, maples bright yellow.

Karen Rodrigue remembers the deep mud of the rhododendron stands, the rock climbing, and the pain of that first day.

"I'm glad we did it," she says. "This was worth it." The bright, always green swamplands around New Orleans are a jewel, an emerald in their own right. But there is nothing back home like the wonder of this, standing among all the broad rainbows that lie tangled in the fall forests of the Smokies.

TRIP NOTES

Everyone is reasonably sure where the Smoky Mountains are—the national park headquarters is in Gatlinburg, Tennessee—but no one is entirely sure how far outward the designation really extends on either side. It's safe to say that all 520,409 acres of the park are Smokies. In the park, there are 800 miles of trails, including 72 miles of the famed Appalachian Trail, providing ample opportunities to explore. What we may call the Smoky Mountain vicinity of the Appalachian Range also has other terrain, including designated wilderness areas, in adjacent national forests.

When to go

Fall colors usually start to appear in the southern Appalachians around the first of

October, peaking during the third and fourth weeks of the month. Much depends on rainfall; good summer showers create excellent fall displays. Dry years produce an earlier, shorter, and duller color season. A heavy storm after the second week of October can knock many leaves to the ground.

The busiest time at Great Smoky Mountains National Park is between mid-April and November first, when 70 percent of the 9 million annual visitors drop by; hence, winter is actually the best time to find solitude here. The 60 inches of annual rainfall is spread fairly evenly throughout the year, though March through May sees the heaviest concentration. During the winter, low elevations can receive a dusting of snow and high elevations (above 5,000 feet) may accumulate a pack of up to five feet in depth.

How to go

Even experienced hikers will encounter a moderate-to-serious challenge here. Although lower in elevation than western ranges, the Appalachians offer much more up-and-down terrain, and many trails gain a lot of altitude over short distances. Trails also tend to be rocky, and slippery when wet (a common condition).

An alternative to backpacking is car camping. The Great Smoky Mountains National Park holds 985 sites in eight campgrounds. During the busy summer season, the three main campgrounds—Elkmont, Smokemont, and Cades Cove—take reservations via Destinet at (800) 365-2267.

In addition, there are numerous primitive National Forest Service campsites around the edges of the wilderness areas. You can set up at one of these sites (generally available on a first-come, first-served basis), then go on long day hikes to explore the backcountry. To avoid the crowds, stay away from the Great Smoky Mountains National Park and the Appalachian Trail. Check with Forest Service district supervisors for seasonal tips on the most uncrowded areas.

Where to go

For information on the national park, contact the Superintendent, Great Smoky Mountains National Park, 107 Park Headquarters Road, Gatlinburg, TN 37738; (423) 436-1200.

The park is surrounded by national forests that also contain parts of the southern Appalachian Range. These forests hold wilderness areas for recreation, sometimes sharing jurisdiction with adjacent forests. For example, the Cherokee National Forest holds all or part of 11 wilderness areas: Bald River Gorge (3,721 acres), Big Frog (8,000 acres), Big Laurel Branch (6,251 acres), Citico Creek (16,226 acres), Cohutta (36,942 acres), Gee Creek (2,573 acres), Joyce Kilmer–Slickrock (17,013 acres), Little Frog Mountain (4,666 acres), Pond Mountain (6,665 acres), Sampson Mountain (7,992 acres), and Unaka Mountain (4,700 acres).

For more details, contact the Cherokee National Forest, 2800 Ocoee Street NW, P.O. Box 2010, Cleveland, TN 37320; (423) 476-9700.

Other ambient national forests can also provide recreation information in their areas. Some options include: Chattahoochee-Oconee National Forests, 1755 Cleveland Highway, Gainesville, GA 30501, (404) 536-0541; Jefferson National Forest, 5162 Valleypointe Parkway, Roanoke, VA 24019, (540) 265-5100; and Nantahala National Forest, Supervisor's Office, P.O. Box 2750, Ashville, NC 28802, (704) 257-4200.

What to bring

In the fall, temperatures generally run into the 60s and 70s by day, dipping into the 30s at night. Occasionally, early cold fronts will drop those readings by 10 degrees. And the humidity makes temperatures feel colder. Bring several light layers of clothing, topped off with an outer shell of good rain gear and top-quality boots. Rainproof tents and reliable drinking-water filters are essential. A lightweight tarp that can be used as a cooking fly is also recommended.

Additional information

Thanks to a wealth of guidebooks to this region and the well-established trail systems, self-guiding is easy here. Guidebooks, maps, advice, and gear can be obtained at the Nantahala Outdoor Center, 13077 Highway 19 West, Box 41, Bryson City, NC 28713; (704) 488-6737. Nantahala has discontinued its own land-based guide service, but the staff can put you in touch with independent local guides and naturalists for day or overnight hikes.

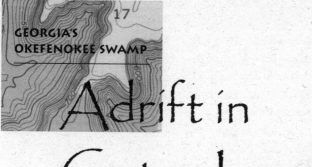

GEORGIA'S
OKEFENOKEE SWAMP

Adrift in Gator Land

by Linda Watanabe McFerrin

W hen I was a blithely disobedient little girl, my father
would threaten, with a malignant air, to throw me
into the Okefenokee Swamp. He doesn't know to
this day, I'll bet, how thrilling a prospect that seemed. O-ke-fe-
no-kee. The very name was magical, and I rolled it around in
my mouth with other delicious words like Ubangi and
Kilimanjaro. It is possible, in fact, that my unspoken desire
for that forbidden place was the secret font of all my future
misbehaviors.

Years passed, and I almost forgot about the Okefenokee and
about swamps in general. That is, until I arrived one midnight at the Valdosta airport on an all-important corporate
assignment. Dead tired and cranky, I sarcastically (that's how

I channeled my hostilities in those days) asked my cabdriver what sights there were to see in Valdosta.

"Well," he drawled, "not far from here, there's the Okefenokee Swamp." He said this, I think, with the same tone that my father had used on his ill-behaved daughter, but the subtlety was lost on me at the time.

I had enough sense not to insist that the cabdriver, to whom I'd just been so rude, drive the 120 miles west so that I could try to wander into a swamp at midnight. But a flame had been fanned on a very old fire. A new Okefenokee fever consumed me.

The Okefenokee Swamp is one of America's largest wetlands, covering 438,000 south Georgia acres—an area approximately one-third the size of the Everglades. It fills, flows, and drains an enormous watershed basin that centers at an elevation of about 12 feet above sea level, and is the source of two large rivers, the St. Marys and the famous Suwannee (read "Swannee").

The name Okefenokee is of American Indian origin and it means "land of trembling earth." As the Indians discovered, "land" in the Okefenokee is not land as we commonly know it. The swamp is composed of more than 60 spongy, peat-moss-formed islands, bearing colorful names such as Black Jack and Roasting Ear; a similar number of lakes; innumerable watery glades called homes or hammocks; and about 60,000 acres of grass-covered marshland.

You'll know when you're getting near the Okefenokee Swamp. If you drive up from Orlando, through well-manicured north Florida, for example, the scenery will go through a dramatic transformation: On either side of the road, you will notice narrow channels widening into still ponds of mahogany-colored water. You might see the fat, snake-like silhouette of an otter clinging to the trunk of a skimpy cypress that rises from ash-colored muck. Or an egret, neck curled into a perfect question mark, poised on the grassy marshland.

The Okefenokee Swamp has four entrances (see the Trip Notes at the end of this chapter). All are wild and beautiful points of ingress that offer picnic areas, nature trails, guided boat tours, canoe rentals, and interpretive centers where you can gather an assortment of literature. And you will need such information to penetrate the swamp's mysteries. You can also gain information via one of the boat tours, with a naturalist and ranger such as Pete Griffin guiding you through this watery world. Pete's story arsenal includes tales about moonshine, hidden stills, and gator counts, along with lectures on swamp etiquette.

"They still have stills here?" I asked during his presentation. It seemed so anachronistic.

"'Course!" Pete responded definitively. "Fella's gotta have a drink now and then."

Pete also had plenty to say about alligator behavior.

"We catch folks feeding gators bananas, Doritos, Cheetos, Oreos, marshmallows, and vanilla wafers," he reported. "Now a gator's brain is not big, but it's loaded with common sense. He thinks, 'Why should I work for a living anymore? I'll just follow these folks around.'"

"Have you ever lost anyone to an alligator?" I asked.

"Of course not," Pete replied with pride. Then he laughed. "That is, no one who's come back to tell us about it."

To really learn about the area, gather most of the literature, study it, walk the trails, bring a picnic, and take one of the guided boat tours. Beyond that, you will need all of your senses, for the swamp is a soup of flora and fauna as rich as a great bouillabaisse—and as profoundly satisfying.

If you are a more adventuresome spirit, rent a canoe and paddle along one of the aquatic trails. Some of these run the breadth of the swamp and take up to five days to traverse; platforms along the way at 5- to 10-mile intervals have been set up for camping. The longer trails are regulated and are limited to one canoe group a day.

My journey into the Okefenokee Swamp finally began at the Okefenokee Swamp Park, a privately run entrance situated to the north of Cowhouse Island, just 15 miles from the town of Waycross. My constant companion Lawrence and I went the adventurous route, renting a two-person canoe and paddling out into the web of narrow channels. These wind around the park entrance, then lead ever deeper into the swamp.

"Look, Lawrence," I said before we got going, "shouldn't you give me a quick canoe lesson or something?"

"Oh, don't worry," Lawrence answered in his usual self-possessed manner. "You'll pick it up as you go along."

His confidence short-circuited my prudence. I hopped into the boat, and we set out.

A waterway filled with poisonous snakes and carnivorous reptiles is not the best place for canoe lessons. It's like learning to drive on the Grande Corniche. I kept trying to focus on improving my skills, on using the paddle properly, on attempting to steer, but the surroundings proved too distracting.

The world around us mixed the dreadful and the sublime. It's a strange place. Three-hundred-pound black bears plod the same cypress and mulberry glades through which white-tailed deer delicately spring. Seven-hundred-pound alligators cruise canals in which egrets, ibis, herons, and sandhill cranes gingerly wade. Regal flags of purple iris spring from the same mud that nourishes the hairy bowls of carnivorous pitcher plants, filled with narcotic venom. Lilies open like celestial white crowns next to the sticky tongues and yellow-lipped chambers of sundews and bladderworts.

It was easy to get diverted by such wonders, yet it seemed a wandering focus could be deadly. Embankments on both sides of us were lined with alligators. They looked awkward and sluggish as they dreamily soaked up the sunlight. But earlier, under Pete Griffin's tutelage, we'd seen how quickly a gator can move. He'd motor up close to one, and I'd focus it in my camera lens, only to have it suddenly swing around, dart, and dive, avalanching us in water from the slap of its tail.

Ever try to catch a tiny lizard? Mostly, they elude you. They're just too quick. That is how chillingly fast even a very large alligator moves.

In spite of my best efforts with the paddle, our canoe kept heading straight for those gator-governed embankments. The tangled snarl of cypress knees formed a natural canoe trap.

"Listen, Lawrence," I said, my voice dripping with stress. "Let's just stay in the center of the channel, OK?"

Lawrence complied, and had just given a mighty stroke to send us around a bend in a careful course, dead-center in the creek, when I saw the 14-foot alligator waiting ahead, right in the targeted zone. We were on a collision course.

"Paddle back," Lawrence, my companion-at-oars, faintly breathed behind me.

Paddle back? I hadn't even mastered paddling forward. Thankfully, Lawrence managed to put the canoe into reverse.

Then, less than a paddle-length away, the alligator watched us suspiciously as we tried to maneuver past. He snorted water from his nose flaps and submerged himself like an enemy submarine until only his eye knobs showed above the water. Hmm. Large. Long. I imagined I would fit quite comfortably into that vast gullet. More so after just a few snaps, and perhaps a chew or two.

I kept chanting a subliminal mantra: "Do not let it smell your fear. It thinks you are part of the canoe. It thinks you are as big as it is." I was also trying hard not to splash as I rowed, lest I be mistaken for a dog. Ranger Pete had advised us that dogs are one of the alligator's favorite foods.

"Wow," Lawrence whispered as we glided by. "That was close. Did you get a picture?"

After that fright, we capsized in a bog. We were on a dotted-line trail that Lawrence had promised not to take. But at the marker and trail junction he was seized with a sudden amnesia. Despite my protests, he took the ominous (yet infinitely more exciting) path less paddled. I was trying to force our retreat when our canoe flipped. I watched my journals, tape recorder, and camera sink below the tannic, ocher surface. Fortunately, we had tied down almost everything in the canoe, and recovered most of it when we hauled the waterlogged craft to shore.

The water was warm and brown and I couldn't get out of it fast enough, finally finding a foothold on spongy earth. The experience lent new meaning to the old expression "up to your armpits in alligators." The illumination was one that I do not regret but do not care to repeat.

As we stood, boots filled and bodies covered with mud, on the shaky ground of land and relationship, Lawrence asked, with utter innocence, "Are you OK?"

I considered for one moment only.

"Yes." I said. "Yes, I'll be OK. But what I need now, what I really need, is a glass of cold, crisp Chardonnay."

"Right," said Lawrence, eagerly grabbing at hope. "Right. We'll get you one. As soon as we get out of this swamp."

But as we eventually discovered, we were in the Bible Belt South, where a form of Prohibition called blue laws is still in force. It would be days before I would finally get that glass of wine. During that stretch I would think ruefully of Ranger Pete ("fella's gotta have a drink now and then"), and the wisdom of that simple statement began to reveal itself.

Meanwhile, I'd lost a roll of film on the muddy bottom. We had to right the canoe and paddle on, to recapture some of the shots.

We didn't have to go far. Almost immediately the swamp fever seized me again, snakes and gators be damned. As we moved down one channel after another, the delirium took hold, and I let myself drift, disoriented, absorbed by the molasses-dark mirror of the waters and their labyrinthine, hypnotic twist.

(In a way, the experience fulfilled an old prophecy. "Dear Dad," I later wrote on a postcard. "Well, I finally made it to the Okefenokee. Canoe capsized. I fell in. I guess it was destiny.")

I was awestruck by the operatic grandeur of the curtains of Spanish moss, the golden carpet of grasses, and the wildlife cast of thousands. Our small boat felt pulled toward the center.

Silence surrounded us, broken only by the "skreek" of insects or the muffled splash of an alligator dumping itself into the water. The swamp's languor is delectable, soporific. You lose track of time. You lose track of yourself. It's easy to get lost in the Okefenokee. Once you do, it's easy to stay lost, even when you think you have left it behind. Even when you remember you were there quite some time ago, and that you are now thousands of miles away.

TRIP NOTES

One of America's largest and most primitive wetlands, the Okefenokee Swamp covers 438,000 acres in south Georgia and houses a wild and exotic cast of critters that includes alligators, water snakes, black bears, otters, deer, ibis, ospreys, spiders, and some very aggressive flora. It is home to more than 40 species of mammals, 50 species of reptiles, and 60 species of amphibians, and it's a popular hangout for more than 200 species of birds. Consisting of more than 60 spongy, peat-moss-formed islands, innumerable watery glades, and acres of marshland, the Okefenokee Swamp has no real "land" per se. There are limited boardwalk trails around the entrances, but the best way to visit the swamp is to paddle in—just as the Seminole Indians used to do.

When to go

The best time to visit is from late fall to mid-May, when heat, humidity, and mosquitoes are not too intense (but you'll still need insect repellent). Alligator activity also dies down a bit in the cooler weather, and migratory birds are out in force.

How to go

There are four official points of entry into the Okefenokee National Wildlife Refuge, as the swamp is more formally known. The western entrance at Stephen Foster State Park is just off U.S. 441 near Fargo. The northern entrance is at Kingfisher Landing, off U.S. 1/U.S. 23, south of Waycross. The eastern entrance is at the Suwannee Canal Recreation Area, headquarters of the Okefenokee National Wildlife Refuge. And visitors can also enter via the Okefenokee Swamp Park, a privately run facility 15 miles south of Waycross.

Your route will depend on your angle of approach. Study a good map and chart your course accordingly.

Where to go

Travel within the refuge is restricted to designated areas during posted hours. Guided boat tours are available, and canoe trips can be launched from any of the entrances. Reservations are required for trips into the Okefenokee lasting two to five days; for bookings (which must be made in advance), contact: Refuge Office, Okefenokee National Wildlife Refuge, Route 2, Box 3330, Folkston, GA 31537; (912) 496-3331 (Monday to Friday, 7 A.M. to 10 A.M.). Overnight camping is permitted only at designated stops, which generally consist of constructed platforms to which campers are wisely restricted from sunset to sunrise. Designated canoe trips are as follows:

- Kingfisher—Bluff Lake—Kingfisher. Two days, 16 miles.
- Kingfisher—Maul Hammock—Big Water—Stephen Foster. Three days, 31 miles.
- Kingfisher—Bluff Lake—Floyd's Island—Stephen Foster. Three days, 24 miles.
- Kingfisher—Bluff Lake—Round Top—Suwannee Canal. Three days, 30 miles.

- Kingfisher—Bluff Lake—Floyd's Island—Canal Run—Stephen Foster. Four days, 29 miles.

- Kingfisher—Bluff Lake—Floyd's Island—Canal Run—Suwannee Canal. Four days, 31 miles.

- Kingfisher—Maul Hammock—Big Water—Floyd's Island—Bluff Lake—Kingfisher. Five days, 43 miles.

- Kingfisher—Maul Hammock—Big Water—Floyd's Island—Canal Run—Stephen Foster. Five days, 38 miles.

- Kingfisher—Maul Hammock—Big Water—Floyd's Island—Canal Run—Suwannee Canal. Five days, 41 miles.

- Kingfisher—Bluff Lake—Round Top—Canal Run—Stephen Foster. Four days, 31 miles.

- Suwannee Canal—Canal Run—Stephen Foster. Two days, 17 miles.

- Suwannee Canal—Canal Run—Suwannee Canal. Two days, 20 miles.

- Suwannee Canal—Round Top—Floyd's Island—Stephen Foster. Two days, 24 miles.

- Suwannee Canal—Round Top—Floyd's Island—Suwannee Canal. Three days, 32 miles.

- Suwannee Canal—Round Top—Floyd's Island—Bluff Lake—Kingfisher Landing. Four days, 33 miles.

- Stephen Foster—Canal Run—Stephen Foster. Two days, 14 miles.

- Stephen Foster—Craven's Hammock—Stephen Foster. Two days, 18 miles.

- Stephen Foster—Flood's Island—Canal Run—Stephen Foster. Three days, 20 miles.

What to bring

Mosquito repellent, rain gear, waterproof hiking boots, and binoculars are a good idea no matter when you visit. If you plan on wilderness canoeing, also pack a rope for pulling the canoe, drinking water, mosquito netting, more mosquito repellent, a first-aid kit, litter bags, a flashlight with extra batteries, a pop tent and/or jungle hammock, and a sleeping bag. Although the temperature rises to about 90 degrees Fahrenheit through most of June, July, August, and September (this is also the rainy season), the rest of the year it stays in the 50s and 60s.

Additional information

There are no restaurants or hotels within the refuge, but camping facilities are available at or near all four entrances.

For more information on attractions and accommodations, contact: Tourism & Conference Bureau, Waycross–Ware County Chamber of Commerce, 200 Lee Avenue, P.O. Box 137, Waycross, GA 31502; (912) 283-3742.

To visit or camp in the Okefenokee, contact: Stephen Foster State Historic Park, Fargo, GA 31631, (912) 637-5274; or Okefenokee Swamp Park, Waycross, GA 31501, (912) 283-0583.

For details about sportfishing, contact: Resources Division of the Department of National Resources, South Central Region, 108 Darling Avenue, P.O. Box 2089, Waycross, GA 34502-2089.

Dances with Crampons

by Richard Bangs

*Doubly happy, however, is the man to whom lofty
mountaintops are within reach, for the lights that shine
there illumine all that lies below.*

—John Muir

On May 12, 1992, a record 32 people stood on the summit of Mount Everest. One was Skip Horner, another, his client, Louis Bowen, an American businessman based in Hong Kong. They shared a supremely satisfying moment on top of the world.

For Skip, 44, who had been a professional guide for 20 years, it was the cap of a long quest: to be the first to guide the Seven Summits, the highest peak on each of the seven continents.

Six weeks later, at a National Press Club gathering in Washington, D.C., Sir Edmund Hillary, conqueror of Everest, gave a talk. In it he recalled his emotions when he and Sherpa Tenzing Norgay first stood on the crest of Mount Everest on May 29, 1953. "We felt a satisfaction, and a little humbled, too," he said.

But then, in a chiding tone, he commented on the deeds of the previous month: "Everest, unfortunately, is largely becoming a commercial money-making opportunity. You didn't need to be a schooled mountaineer, not this year. If you were reasonably fit and had $35,000, you could be conducted to the top of the world. How thankful I was that I was active in a pioneering era when we established the route, carried the loads, all worked together for the ultimate objective. The way things are now, I don't think I would have bothered."

Skip Horner had climbed with Sir Edmund's son, Peter, on a Karakoram peak called Rimo in 1986, and counted him a friend. And in March of 1992, Skip had finally met the world's most famous mountaineer in Chaunrikarka, Nepal, where he paid respects and expressed feelings of honor. Thus, when he heard Ed's lament, Skip was disheartened. So he wrote to Ed: "I am disturbed by your well-publicized comments disparaging the ascents that were made on Everest this year. Certainly the climb is not now the adventure it was in '53, due to improvements in knowledge and equipment. Still, it takes an extraordinary amount of ability, persistence, and luck to reach the top of Everest, as the weather and snow and ice conditions are as unpredictable and treacherous as ever." He added that "to minimize our achievements does the international climbing community a disservice and does more to minimize the mountain than the climbers," and that "to reach Everest's summit still requires all the physical and mental virtues possessed by you and your mates in '53 . . . Mr. Hillary." He concluded: "I will always have deep respect for you, but I wonder if you have had the chance to ponder your remarks about us?"

There was no reply.

Somehow Ed's words jostled me as well. It seemed there was a ring to his rave. Hadn't Yosemite, the Grand Canyon, Kilimanjaro, and Victoria Falls lost some transcendence because of their manufactured, commercial accessibility? When you can hire a guide to do much of the work, doesn't that diminish personal commitment, and thus the quality, the profundity, of the experience? Then again, isn't it elitist to deny others what you have experienced, to seek to preserve in private sanctuary the apotheosis that came with a special effort, time, and place?

In my years as a river guide I had escorted blind children, senior citizens, and paraplegics down the Colorado River, and I can warrant that the transformational aspects of the experience were as vital for them as for the young, hearty do-it-yourself expeditioneers. It may be less of a feat now to climb Everest than in 1953, what with better gear and well-described routes. But is the adventure really less for the guides and the clients who feel the same elation and sense of personal achievement on top?

I decided to explore the issue on my own. I had never summitted a peak requiring real mountaineering impedimenta: ropes, crampons, nylon slings, carabiners, ice ax, and such.

Everest was not in the stars for me. However, the dormant volcano the first American Everest climbers trained upon was: Mount Rainier, in Washington state. Born of fire and carved by ice, Rainier shoves the rim of its still-steaming volcanic crater 14,410 feet into the atmosphere southeast of Seattle. And as much as I might have wanted to, I could never attempt such an enterprise on my own. I needed someone to show me how, just as Ed Hillary was first guided when he started climbing on Mount Cook. So I called Skip Horner in Montana.

As it turned out, he, too, had never climbed the most heavily glaciated mountain in the continental United States. In the spring of 1989, he had made it to the parking lot on the north side, with hopes of a climb up the Liberty Ridge. But the clouds were so heavy, the rain so thick, he never made it out of the car. Skip was ready to try again, and to lead the way.

So it was that we gathered at the parking lot in Paradise, 5,400 feet up Rainier's southwest slope, on a Saturday in September. There were now eight of us, all friends ready to carry the loads and work together for an ultimate objective. With our 50-pound packs snugly shouldered, we headed up the hill. We stepped lightly through the brooding evergreens, trees that were giants when British navigator George Vancouver sailed the Washington coast in the spring of 1792, presumptuously naming the grand inland peak after a rear admiral in the Royal Navy who had captured an American privateer during the Revolutionary War.

The trees gave way to subalpine mountain meadows, where several marmots, perched trailside, fattened themselves on flowers. A mere fingertip away was the bright volcanic crown, high and lordly as a god. The Indians of the Pacific Northwest had always known its true name: Tahoma, "the mountain that was God." Now a lenticular cloud bannered across its pinnacle, indicating high winds and the possibility of trouble. However, I began to think this was not going to be difficult, as I quickly bounded ahead of the pack. It seemed my mere three weeks of running and swimming prior to this venture were paying off.

Some 8,000 climbers attempt Rainier annually, and about 50 percent make it at least to the crater rim. Yet there have been fatalities: more than 20 in the last dozen years, and overall, at least 75 since the summit was first reached in 1870, and it's as certain as bad weather that there will be more. Still, though I no longer felt the immortality of my twenties, I did feel strong, and confident I would succeed, perhaps even without Skip's help. At Pebble Creek the trail sank into a pocked snowfield, and I continued to plod upward at a good pace.

At a rest stop called by Skip, I paused to look around. A chill came with the view. The frosty fingers of 26 glaciers gripped the cone of Rainier, forming a wonderland of wide snowfields, crevasses, snow bridges, gleaming seracs, and awesome icefalls. This was a world unfamiliar, fantastic, and frightening.

When Camp Muir finally came into view, I downshifted, while Skip and three others passed me and steamed on up. Maybe I wasn't in such great shape, I thought, as I dragged myself up the pumice-strewn ridge, halfway to heaven at 10,188 feet, and spilled the pack off my back. It was four o'clock, six hours after we'd bounced out of the parking lot. Clouds were boiling up from below, while above, the mountain wore a cap of gray cloud. Wind knifed across the ridge, cutting the temperature down, and Skip directed me into the low, public shelter built of rocks that squatted in the gap of a ridge between the Nisqually and Cowlitz Glaciers.

After choosing a wooden bunk by tossing my gear onto it, I followed Skip over to the ranger's station, an A-frame hut not much larger than an outhouse. Here we met mountain ranger Joe Dreimiller, who told us that of the 50 or so who attempted summit climbs that day, none had made it. The winds were simply too high, 60 miles an hour at times, enough to blow a man off the mountain. And he warned us about getting onto Disappointment Cleaver. The ice was separating from the rock at the base, cutting through a route marked by a yellow line the rangers had laid. The ice bridge was on its last legs and would break sometime soon. It was a dangerous crossing.

An hour later I emerged from Joe's hut into a hailstorm to negotiate the 200 yards back to our shelter. I saw a dim, solitary figure struggling up the embankment. I called down, but no reply. I called again, and he stopped in his tracks. I stepped on down, and recognized Howard from our group, who looked dead exhausted, glasses missing from his wan face, sweat gleaming on his scalp like Mylar. I asked if I could help with his pack, and with an affirmative shake of his head it was off his back and onto mine. Looking at Howard's fallen shoulders and spent eyes, I knew then he wasn't going to make it.

With all safely in the hut, Skip whipped up a dinner of Lipton's Parmesan noodles as we recuperated. He announced we would not try for the summit tomorrow. The weather was too bad, the team too tired, and climbing skills were notably lacking. We would spend the following day learning the ropes, so to speak.

All night the wind, with the wrath of a living thing, sandblasted our shack with ice pellets. At times it seemed we might be picked up and hurled to California. It would be impossible to climb in this wind, and I began to think of how to deal with the failure of our adventure.

But by daybreak the weather had calmed, though the mountaintop remained stubbornly wrapped in clouds. After a leisurely breakfast— during which I was reminded that water hot enough to boil at two miles high is not very hot at all to a cup of hot chocolate—Skip brought us out onto the glacier for some essential training. We learned crucial techniques of self-arrest, using the ice ax to halt a fall, and how to walk "like a cowboy" in the 12-point crampons so they wouldn't snag on an inseam, and the rules of team survival, including, "Never step on the rope."

By day's end, Howard announced he wasn't going to try for the summit. That left the seven of us.

At 1 A.M., Skip woke us up. The close, stove-fuel air in the shelter was stuffy. We had melted snow the night before and filled all the water bottles, so it was just a matter of dressing: two layers of Thermax long underwear, Polartec pants and top, a Gore-Tex expedition suit, a parka, inner and outer gloves, two pairs of wool socks, double plastic boots, steel crampons, a harness (the same type used in the opening accident scene in the movie *Cliffhanger,* someone pointed out), and a hat. I had brought my Walkman and two books-on-tape, but Skip said no. This was too dangerous an ascent; one had to be alert to the sounds of falling rocks, to the cries of falling team members.

It took an hour before we were on the snow. We roped into two teams, and I was second on the string, just behind Skip, a link in a four-man chain. As we waded across the Cowlitz Glacier toward the bare rock bluff of Cathedral Rocks Ridge, I couldn't help but think the rope was not only a protection against falls, but also a prevention against running away. The wind was low, the sky clear.

I had put a set of fresh batteries in my headlamp the night before, and now I followed a little yellow puddle at my feet. On our left, the mountain loomed—felt more than seen. Pale snow-light glowed from the empty space below us to the right. We few, fragile climbers were caught between the dark mass of the mountain and the reach of vacuous space all around us.

We started up the loose rockfalls of Cathedral Gap, the metal claws of our crampons sparking and scratching against the stone. The path was a dribble of small rocks among the boulders, and about 50 yards into the debris my left crampon came loose. Embarrassed, I pulled the line, like stopping a bus, and Skip turned around, then patiently backtracked to help me reattach the crampon. Then we were off again, clattering up the rocky trail.

Our column of climbers crested the rocky ridge and stepped down onto the ice of the Ingraham Glacier, the frozen river we would follow to the top. We were on the mountain's ice-scoured east face, and the wind blew black. A trail was more evident here, the alternating pattern of boot holes in the snow, beaten out by climbing parties over the preceding weeks.

And then we crossed our first crevasse—a long gash less than a yard wide at the top, but cutting hundreds of feet into the ice. Stepping over the black crack, it was easy to envision the tensed 9-mm rope dangling me in the hungry mouth, bait for the catch.

Not long off the rocks, we reached a level stretch known as the Ingraham Flats. Here Skip picked up the pace. But Steve, just behind me, and recovering from a bout of flu just two days before, was lagging, so I found myself in a constant tug-of-war between the two.

For another hour we walked through the hostile dark, a team in silence, chained souls floating upward together yet alone in thick thoughts. Finally, we came to another rocky section—the infamous Disappointment Cleaver. We followed the yellow rope across the narrow ice bridge, dimly aware that inches away, on either side, gaped a bottomless abyss.

Then we were on the Cleaver, another jumble of rotten rock, and we continued up a steep grade of loose scree. Now my other crampon released, and I scraped the ground for purchase, wrenching my ankle. There had been much in the news lately about how Rainier was going to begin charging climbers for a rescue. "Great," I thought. "Not only will I fail in this summit attempt, I'll have to pay a small fortune for the privilege." I wished I could divorce my crampons on grounds of metal and physical cruelty, as well as inadequate means of support.

With infinite patience, Skip waited as I reattached the crampon in the stinging cold and stood up. My ankle hurt, but I could still walk, so I signaled thumbs-up, and Skip's rope went tight. Not too long afterward, Skip's lamp abruptly died, and Tom, on the rear of our rope, passed his to the front. I was glad I had inserted fresh batteries in my lamp, and mechanically trudged onward behind Skip. But then, not 30 minutes later, my lamp went out.

I knew morning light was close at hand, so I volunteered to proceed torchless, not that I had a choice. Now the faint glow from a fingernail moon, the green flashes of the northern lights, and the sparks created by my crampons were my only light. I used my hands a lot now, scrambling up the scree.

Finally the darkness dissolved. The mountain looked the same in the pale morning as it had felt in the pitch of night: angular, distant, coolly impersonal. As the sun crawled up to the horizon, a thick line of crimson neon bled along the edge of the earth. It hung there a long time—it seemed like an hour—before one spot bloomed with intensity and the sun rose. In the meantime, distant layers appeared in the rest of the sky, as if glass plates separated the pink morning air from the indigo shadows left over from night. Mount Adams, Oregon's Mount Hood, and the open throat of Mount Saint Helens floated like islands in a sea of clouds on the southern horizon.

Less than an hour after sunrise we reached the upper end of the Cleaver and stopped for a rest before breaking back into the snow. The wind engulfed us. I was sucking the thin atmosphere deeply, expelling it forcefully. I had no appetite, but drank water like chocolate. When it came time to bundle up, I couldn't zip my parka, and felt like a helpless child heading into a winter playground. I asked Skip for help, and like a tolerant proctor, he pulled off his glove and zipped me up. I wanted to give him a hug.

Joe Dreimiller had said it was an easy haul beyond the Cleaver, and I kept reminding myself of those words as I kicked the front points of my crampons into the ice on a near vertical section. As instructed, we carried our axes in the high-slope hand, the rope in the other, and made the awkward switch from one to the other at the elbow of every switchback. Now that it was light, Skip often turned around to check our progress at these switches, and it seemed every time he checked I was tangled in the rope or, worse, stepping on it. I felt like a daft and moonstruck tyro.

Rainier seemed all steep pitches now. We crunched along the glacier's more impressive flotsam. We tramped beneath a skyscraper serac, its sleek sides curving skyward. We jumped the narrow slit openings of crevasses, peering down into the sculptured dark walls that fell away forever. Towering blue ice cliffs curled over us like giant glacial tidal waves, mumbling and groaning as we skirted the edges. Their voices sounded hollow, tubular, and for a moment I felt I was negotiating the barrel of a gun.

One such wall collapsed near here in 1981, sweeping 11 climbers into oblivion.

Skip had instructed us at the start to keep a coil in one hand, to adjust the slack in the rope between climbers. But as Skip continued, with the pigeon-toed gait of an athlete, he pulled the rope taut between us, and I couldn't maintain a coil. The rope went tight as a banjo string, and I realized in my dull brain that Skip was literally pulling me up the mountain. I couldn't keep his pace, and he refused to back off. Exhaustion blanketed my thoughts and limbs, and I began to wonder if I had the endurance to make it. I felt like Howard looked when he reached Camp Muir two days ago. I fought for every breath. I was so bone-deep tired I thought each step might be my last.

"Can we stop for water?" I finally cried, although it seemed to dribble out of my frozen mouth as, "Caweesopfoater?" Skip ignored my pleas, or couldn't understand them, and continued to keep the rope taut. I could do nothing but follow. I was too numb to resist. Then, almost without warning, we leveled out at a low wall of brown rock, and Skip dropped his pack.

I folded to the ground like a kicked tent and pulled out my last water bottle. The water was frozen. Between breaths I looked around, and saw we were at the brow of a huge crater. On the other side, the western rim, a small, rounded hump rose less than 300 feet above us. There was nothing beyond. That must be the summit.

So, after perhaps a 15-minute break, we re-roped and began the final walk in the high winds of near-summit. We crossed the crater caldera, and clambered onto a last staircase of bare rock, steam-cleaned of snow and ice by hissing fumaroles. And, at 9:40 A.M., we made the last steps to the 14,411-foot Columbia Crest, kings of the Cascade Range we.

Suddenly, the simple act of being present assumed a sense of gathered immediacy. I was overcome with some sort of inchoate emotion. I lost control of my face, and felt a kind of crazed delight that had me laughing and crying simultaneously. Though thousands, tens of thousands, had stood here before us, I felt this was the first morning on earth, and we the first to bathe in its beauty, unbounded by geography or history. It was a fragment of a cycloramic dream to be on top, and as

WILD PLACES

I hugged the other team members, just as Tenzing Norgay had hugged Ed Hillary on Everest, I felt a satisfaction, and a little humbled, too. I knew acutely I would never have been here without Skip's help, without a thaumaturgic leader who could lift spirits to new heights. In a world shorn of magic, it was the guides who still carried the power. And I knew: There is nothing wrong with guiding people to the upper limits; in fact, there may be nothing more right.

TRIP NOTES

Mount Rainier, near Seattle, is the most extensively glaciated volcanic peak in the continental United States. It offers limitless mountaineering possibilities to the aspiring or experienced mountaineer. This unique training ground is demanding and at times relentless. The combination of altitude and cold challenges the climber to readily adapt his or her skills to an ever-changing environment.

When to go

Portions of the park remain open year-round, but activity is sharply reduced in the winter. During the winter, some guided attempts on the peak occur when and if the weather permits, but success is uncommon. The primary climbing season runs from May 15 through September.

How to go

Alpine mountaineering is a physically demanding sport. Mount Rainier is considered the longest endurance climb in the lower 48 states. It is thus imperative to undertake—well in advance of your trip—a rigorous conditioning program to maximize your aerobic power and leg strength. Walking up and down hills while carrying a backpack is especially recommended as a form of training. However, if there are no hills in your vicinity, put on a pack and try climbing flights of stairs, stadium steps, or Stairmaster machines in gyms. Also helpful are good jogging, running, cycling, and swimming regimens. In season, both Nordic and downhill ski workouts will build strength and acclimatization.

It is also important to get good clothing and equipment, plus some experience and instruction in its use prior to your trip. Only one outfitter is commercially licensed by the park to take clients up to the peak: Rainier Mountaineering, Inc., which has been in operation since 1968. The company offers a series of three-day summit climbs (including one day of instruction) starting at about $400. Trips depart from June through September. In the summer (May 15 through September), contact Rainier Mountaineering, Inc., at: Paradise, WA 98398; (360) 569-2227. In the winter, contact the organization at: 535 Dock Street, Suite #209, Tacoma, WA 98402; (206) 627-6242 (phone), (206) 627-1280 (fax).

Where to go

The 14,411-foot peak is the centerpiece of 235,612-acre Mount Rainier National Park. Besides making attempts on the peak, visitors can enjoy the mountain by hiking portions of the 93-mile-long Wonderland Trail, which rings the mountain's base at elevations ranging between 3,000 and 6,500 feet. The Wonderland has numerous spur trails that explore various features. There are 300 miles of trails in the park.

Local lodgings are limited to two hotels in the park: National Park Inn (open year-round) and Paradise Inn (open mid-May through early October); for reservations, call (360) 569-2275. Five campgrounds in the park offer a total of 577 individual campsites; group camps are available, too. Only one campground is open year-round; the rest are seasonal. Fees range from $6 to $10 a night.

What to bring

Required equipment for a Rainier summit climb includes lug-soled climbing boots with gaiters; rain- and windproof shell garments; glacier sunglasses with side shields; sunblock cream and lip balm; a headlamp with extra batteries; a medium-to-large backpack (an internal-frame pack is best); a sleeping bag (rated to freezing temperatures or below); a parka (down or synthetic pile); two sweaters (wool or pile); a wool or synthetic watch cap or warm hat; two pairs of wool or pile gloves, plus shell overmitts; eating utensils; and two water bottles. The primary tools you'll need are an ice ax and boot crampons. Taking classes and gaining some expertise in using the ax and crampons prior to your trip is essential.

Additional information

Call Mount Rainier National Park at (360) 569-2211 for information on camps, trails, visitor centers, and park naturalist programs and seminars. Printed material and books can also be ordered by calling this number.

MANITOBA PROVINCE, CANADA

17

Finessing the Seal

by W. Hodding Carter

H ap was in the midst of explaining how careful we would have to be on our canoe trip through the Canadian wilderness when he spied Andy, his fellow river guide, strolling into the bar.

"Where have you been?" Hap asked Andy, looking pained.

"Well, you know, I was at the Wal-Mart getting some last-minute things," Andy explained. "When I came out, these four Indians in the parking lot called me over." Andy sat down and cuddled a tin of Player's tobacco. He tried not to look Hap in the eyes. " 'Hey,' they asked, 'you want to try some Finesse?' "

"Finesse?" Hap asked loudly. We were sitting in an empty, darkened bar and there was no chance of anyone overhearing, but I couldn't help glancing around anyway.

"Yeah. Liquid hair spray," Andy said. He seemed to pay a lot of attention to the job of rolling a cigarette. "So I said, 'Sure, why not.' I took three hits, mixed with some water. The label said it was 20 percent alcohol."

"Why'd you do that?" Hap demanded.

"Don't know. Never had it before." He paused, as if tasting the stuff again. "It was awful."

Suddenly, Hap, who at age 42 was Andy's senior by 14 years, added a new twist to our itinerary: "We're also going to sail across Hudson Bay," he announced. "You know, strap the canoes together and push straight through to Churchill. Have either of you ever sailed before?"

A few minutes later, Hap and Andy left—to buy some more Finesse, for all I knew. Russell and I retreated to our hotel room. We were in Thompson, Manitoba, assembling our gear the night before heading north.

"What the f—— are we getting ourselves into?" Russell exploded. He began fidgeting with his wire-rimmed glasses. I didn't know how to answer. We'd been sent by a magazine to do a he-man wilderness story, and had met for the first time only hours before.

If I could have seen into the future, I might have replied that we were about to embark on a whitewater canoe trip for hundreds of miles with two crazy Canadians on a river patrolled by polar bears. I might have added that we'd be chased by forest fires, blackflies, and mosquitoes, and—for a grand finale—suckered into a night of paddling hell on Hudson Bay.

"Who are these guys?" he continued. "Can we trust them? Do you think we should go?"

I thought it best to give Russell my Manitoba Natural Resources flyer. It bubbled with enthusiasm for the Seal River's "undeveloped, wild, and rugged" nature. However, it also warned that the river is "fast, shallow, and ice-cold. Capsizing and hypothermia are very real possibilities. Rapids are often long, shallow, and boulder strewn . . . portage paths do not exist at present. Travel on the estuary and Hudson Bay requires prior knowledge of tide charts and healthy respect for unpredictable weather, ice, and polar bears."

This flyer repeated all the information Hap and Andy had told us. In other words, we now knew as much about the Seal River as they did.

The Canadian government dubbed the Seal a Heritage River in June 1992. This means the government will supposedly preserve the river's "natural, cultural, and recreational values." The little information that exists on the Seal—a few newspaper articles, a government report, and some canoeists' diaries—paints a picture of an undisturbed river. No dams or pollution, but lots of white water, aromatic spruces, and, of course, seals.

White men gave the river its present name because there are so many seals that dine on the river's trout and arctic grayling. Seals inhabit marine harbors around the world, but there are only a few places where they swim hundreds of miles into fresh water.

The allure of the seals, the sheer wildness, and a rumor that beluga whales linger at the river's mouth made it impossible for me to pass up the adventure. But I wasn't so handy in a canoe. Russell Kaye, my photo-snapping cohort, was also a novice. Yet we had to paddle 200 miles of turbulent lakes, Class IV white water, and then a bit of treacherous Hudson Bay to reach Churchill, our ultimate destination.

Only a few dozen canoeists attempt the Seal each summer, and hardly any try to cross Hudson Bay. Instead, they arrange for a pickup at the river's mouth.

Enter the two Canadian guides, Hap Wilson and Andy Pepall, our wellspring of expertise. Hap is a best-selling Canadian guidebook writer who has been classifying whitewater rivers for decades. Andy has not been guiding as long, but has apparently made up for it in enthusiasm.

Within 24 hours of meeting each other, we were all wandering in a land where burnt pine needles showered the ground. The town was called Tadoule, a reservation for the Déné tribe. It was created by the government amid miniature black spruce trees and blankets of dust on the edge of Tadoule Lake in northeastern Manitoba.

We had flown in on a two-prop plane that serves as the town's only link with its southern neighbors. I believe what threw me off from the beginning were all the forest fires we saw during our flight, as well as the smoke surrounding the town. No one had said anything about a plague of forest fires. But in the Déné language, Tadoule means "floating cinders lake." Every summer the spruce, lit by bolts of lightning, burn like kerosene-dipped matches. And the government almost always lets the fires run their course.

We wandered the dusty town, trying to make some sense of our surroundings and ourselves. Navajo healers (the Navajo and Déné are related) were also visiting Tadoule. This was a time for spiritual cleansing—a festival for the whole village.

Blackflies crawled up our shorts and down our socks, feasting on soft, white skin. Dust drifted above our knees like sifted flour wherever we walked. Drums beat loudly from the town hall, where men played the Hand Game—a fast-paced, traditional gambling event that hurtled along, with more than 30 different signals.

The night before we left, Hap and I sought out the Navajo healers. Hap said we needed to pay proper respect to the river spirits. We went from building to building, starting with the town hall, where people were beating drums. No luck. Eventually, we found the healers in a closed-up, forbidding house.

Hap knocked on the door. No answer. He tried again. "Come in, come in," someone called, in irritated English. There were three men inside, watching TV. Hap told them what we wanted. They talked it over in Navajo (I presume). Finally, one man said, "Sure, we'll do it."

Hap gave them presents of tobacco and $50. They told us to sit down in front of the TV. Gleeful men sung from the screen. It was *Robin Hood: Men in Tights.* Somehow, it wasn't what I expected. Hap seemed unaffected.

The healer set out sweetgrass (sage and cedar), an eagle feather, and a Styrofoam cup filled with water. For the next five minutes, he chanted. The healer eventually lit the sweetgrass and, with the feather, swept the smoke from it into and over the Styrofoam cup. He held the burning grass above my head and feathered the smoke around my body, then did the same for Hap.

"I've asked that your trip be blessed and told them that you travel through here with respect—for the land and the people," the healer explained. "This prayer will provide you with health, strength, and safety to finish your journey. I've also asked that you be returned to your kinfolk at the end. And now, I want you to share this water, saving some for your friends."

Hap and I drank half the cup.

"One last thing," he said. "Be sure to make a tobacco offering before you leave here and at the beginning of each day. You must give a present to the spirits."

We awkwardly thanked them and left. I could hear *Men in Tights* again as we made our way back to camp with the Styrofoam cup.

O h, boys. . . . Time to wake up," Hap chirped, much too early the next morning. He had already cooked a hearty breakfast and packed all of his and Russell's gear into their canoe. He was ready to go at 7:30.

Andy rose last, rubbing his bushy beard as if that alone might take care of his chores. He rolled a cigarette, stretched his lanky body, ate a leisurely breakfast, and cleaned the dishes while singing a little out of tune.

It nearly drove Hap out of his mind with impatience. Hap snapped the spray skirt (the canvas that stretches over the canoe to keep out high waves) over the gunwales of his canoe, told Russell to hop in, and shoved off. Two-foot-high swells smashed against their bow as they left with nary a good-bye.

We did not catch up with them until lunch. After Andy spent two minutes teaching me all the strokes I'd need for two weeks, we set out. The swells seemed intent on obtaining a canoe sacrifice and rose to nearly four feet in minutes.

The spray skirt, however, defeated the waves. Although they washed over the bow and soaked me, our canoe remained intact. We paddled madly for five hours, trying to keep Hap and Russell in sight.

After noon, we met for lunch on an island nine miles from Tadoule. My back ached, my right elbow throbbed from tendonitis, and my crotch, navel, and ankles itched from blackfly bites.

We stayed together for the rest of the day, and I liked watching the waves bash into Russell. Soon, however, we reached the northern end of the lake and the shore held the wind and waves in check. We also realized the day's goal: our first rapids. They weren't very strong, a technical Class I.

The rapids carried us a little more than a half mile before Hap chose a campsite. We'd canoed 14 miles our first day—most of it against a head wind. Once everything was unpacked, we had to clear a space, set up the tents and tarp, saw some logs, then split firewood. Nearly two hours later, we finally sat down, just in time for a blackfly and mosquito onslaught.

A steady rain began, driving away most of the bugs, cooling us off, and falsely leading me to believe that Tadoule would be spared from the fires.

Our leaders whipped up a tasty chicken stir-fry for dinner. It was a good night. The assorted twentieth-century artifacts of beer cans, bottles, and plastic whatnots left behind by hunters and fellow canoeists lulled me into believing all was well. After all, how much danger could we be in with so much *civilized* trash around?

The next day, the weather had cleared enough so we could set out around noontime. Rapids quickly shot us into Negassa Lake, where wind, waves, and spray lay in ambush. The whitecapping swells stood three feet high, and the wind blew at 35 to 40 miles per hour. For two hours we fought the elements and lost. We traveled two miles, and that included zigzagging to find a safe harbor to spend the night.

The weather didn't clear until the next afternoon, when we were hit by a horde of biting mosquitoes. "Oh, good. The mosquitoes are back," Andy said.

"Yep, it's clearing up," Hap added. "Time to go." I never thought I'd be glad to feel a mosquito's proboscis, and I still wasn't too sure. Already, I had some 57 bites from them or their buddy *Simulium aureum* (the blackfly). I was just glad we weren't farther south, where biting blackflies release worm larvae that swim through the body, eventually settling in a person's eyes, causing a complete loss of eyesight known as river blindness. There is no known cure.

I told Russell and Andy all about the disease, omitting the fact that it's only found in more southerly climes.

We departed at 3 P.M. and crossed Negassa Lake in a half hour. We'd been warned that the rapids there would be tough. We landed our boats in a thicket of beech trees and went out to scout the route.

The going was nearly impossible. We hiked on spongy mounds of peat moss that sunk a foot into pools of black water. "This is stupid," I whined. As the mosquitoes mercilessly zeroed in, I fantasized about knocking Hap and Andy around. When we reached the end of the island, Hap pronounced the rapids runnable.

Suddenly, though, on our hike back to the canoes, all our troubles seemed worthwhile. We found three plump black bear scats not far from someone's winter camp. And one of them rested atop a wolf dropping. How wonderful!

We ended up skirting most of the bigger rapids, but the others were a fun ride, lasting nearly 10 minutes. A mile farther, we reached a more difficult set. Hap rated them a Class III. I suggested to Andy that we just run right through them. I seemed to be paddling well enough to avoid danger until one huge boulder jumped at us. Andy screamed, "Draw right!" but I couldn't figure out what direction that was quickly enough. We hit the boulder sideways. Thanks to the spray skirt and some fancy balancing on Andy's part, we only took in a few gallons.

Those rapids brought us to Shethanei Lake, where we were greeted by more wind and waves. Nighthawks and Bonaparte gulls darted by, and Andy spotted an immature bald eagle. As we rested at an island, Andy pointed out a tall outcrop of boulders on a nearby shore and asked Hap to let us explore them. Once we made the crossing, Russell, Andy, and I mutinied, convincing Hap to stay there for the night.

Delicate white lichen carpeted the ground around the boulder tower, and moss bogs stood guard just beyond. When we climbed to the top of the boulders, we could see nearly all of Shethanei Lake. Squiggly orange ptarmigan droppings, hairy wolf loads, and piles of bear dung waited beside every rock. It had to be a holy place.

We returned to the boulders after supper. A few minutes before the sun dropped below the horizon, the light glowed yellow on our hands and faces. It seemed like we were bathing in golden water.

"Even if we see nothing else on this journey, this is worth it," Hap declared.

After the sun set, we gathered in a hole on top of the boulders and sat on lichen pillows. Hap lit some sweetgrass. "I was talking to the shaman, and he said these wild, undammed rivers still have their spirits. He said once they get their dams and progress, the spirits leave. That's why it's important to be aware of these things and visit places like Tadoule and these rocks."

For some reason, that didn't seem hokey.

We only paddled 1.5 miles on our fourth day out. The wind and waves were bad, but we stopped for other reasons. We'd reached our first esker.

Before leaving for our trip, Andy called me at home one day. "We'll be hiking eskers every day," he said. "It'll be amazing."

I said I couldn't wait, but in truth, I had no idea what eskers were. My dictionary described them as glacial sand deposits. Now I saw that they were ridges of sand dozens of feet tall (sometimes even 100 feet tall) that ran from one end of a landmass to the other in this watered country.

We had learned in Tadoule that eskers were the Déné's highways. Traditionally, the people followed the caribou that migrated that way: When the caribou reached water, they swam across to the next esker. The Déné made small caribou-skin boats to cross in pursuit. At one time, the animals were the Déné's supermarket: Caribou bones, skin, meat, and organs provided shelter, food, clothing, and tools. The caribou and the eskers defined the Déné. Dwindling herds and government restrictions, though, have kept the Déné off the eskers in recent years.

We hiked the esker in the evening. We came across countless tracks of moose, wolf, and bear and also found two human graves. A small stand of aspens quaked and I felt an eerie longing that always overwhelms me when I smell and hear rustling leaves.

That night, we ate more fish—a four-pound lake trout Andy and I had caught while canoeing to our campsite.

Hap woke us at 5:45 A.M. The lake was calm, and we paddled 12 miles before noon. "See what you can get done when you wake up early?" he said. After lunching next to another esker, we paddled eight more miles—on a lake that had become hot and flat as a desert. At some point, I noticed we were paddling toward the billowing smoke of another forest fire.

We stopped at the Wolverine River, a colder stream where we'd been told to fish for arctic grayling. Russell had been yammering about them ever since we met. Finally I asked him, just before setting out to catch some, "So, they're great fighters, huh?"

"No, I don't think so," he said.

"But they taste really good?"

"I haven't heard."

"Then what's so great about them?"

"They have a beautiful multicolored dorsal fin."

We managed to land two keepers.

Just after floating past the Steel River, we spotted our first seals. They swam below some small rapids and kept a good 50 yards between us. These harbor seals have adapted to living in fresh water for protection and better foraging, but they return to Hudson Bay every winter—a 200-mile round-trip. We wanted to stay and play, but the current quickly carried us past.

We hit a slew of rapids and riffles that day. The longest one lasted seven miles; the strongest was a Class III.

Sometime after noon, we rounded a bend in the river and were confronted by a flaring fire less than a stone's throw away. It wasn't very large, maybe 100 yards wide, so it felt safe enough to stop and watch.

Spruce and small aspens flared like gunpowder before our eyes. A 60-foot tree was demolished in three to four seconds. Needles splattered on the boats. Sunlight filtered through the smoke, turning the water a golden orange. It looked as if the water were on fire. And the smoke swirled into a wavy dance of brown, black, white, yellow, and mustardy clouds.

When it got too hot, we pushed off. The rapids did all the work the rest of the day and we pulled onto the beach at Great Island around 4:30 P.M. Wolf tracks led straight up from the shore. A trail of huge bear prints looked big enough for a polar. Most likely, though, they were black bear prints enlarged in loose sand. The polar bears seldom travel more than 40 miles inland, and we were well beyond that.

We spent two nights camping at Great Island. Russell was looking worse off than anyone else, which made me immensely happy. His predicament even seemed to diminish the itch of my bites. His ears, neck, belly button, and the skin under his eyes bled. So many bites covered his arms that it looked like he had poison ivy.

"Has anyone ever died from blackfly bites?" Russell asked, trying to sound casual. Hap said he didn't think so, but he knew that animals agonizing from their bites would sometimes start running into trees.

After our one-day rest, we ran 9-Bar, a 2.2-mile stretch of Class III and IV white water. Traveling through the high water made the canoeing a breeze because we never had to portage.

After the rapids, a mile-wide forest fire waited for us on the left shore. The black smoke seemed to be heading straight toward us. Hap started to steer his canoe toward the fire, but I screamed that we might want to take pictures from a more distant vantage point. He agreed and paddled toward the opposite shore, a good distance away. The river had almost widened into a lake.

For the next four or five miles, I paddled harder than I had in a few days, checking the smoke over my shoulder every few seconds. At first, it seemed to stay with us, but after 30 minutes or so, we had outrun it—for the time being. I eased up, exhausted.

About then, we came across the water station—a government outpost used to monitor the river's water level. Of course, we had to check it out, because diary entries from other canoeists and water-station guys waited inside.

A silence hung over the little water station—no birds, no rustling leaves. The place felt doomed. Inside, it was a cramped and cluttered one-room cabin. Four bunks, a generator, a Coleman heating stove, a carpet sweeper, and a boat engine lay scattered about.

"Is it eerie today or is it just me?" Russell asked. "Of course it's eerie," I wanted to scream. "We're being chased by a forest fire!" I remained calm, though, and only replied, "Yes."

While the rest of us pored over the diaries, Russell wandered outside.
He was excited by the danger. The trip was definitely changing him. Suddenly, we heard knocking at the window. Hap, Andy, and I jumped, but it
was only Russell. "You can hear the blasting caps go," he said. We ran
outside and sure enough, they were popping like firecrackers.

"Good thing we didn't go to the old mine," Hap said. The blasting
caps were left over from a mine located not more than a mile away
on Great Island—a mine we had meant to visit. The fire was right on
our tails.

"Okay," Hap said, "Let's grab these diaries and get out. We'll figure
out who to mail them to later. I think this whole place is going up."
Andy wanted to take a few more things, since the fire was going to
torch the place. He and Hap argued. Hap won.

We bugged out of there and stroked pretty hard, until we decided to
eat lunch. We couldn't pull over or the smoke would catch us, so we
used bungee cords to fasten the boats together and floated. Hap made
salami sandwiches with bannock and served them on his paddle. If
you were going to be chased by a fire, this was certainly the way to go.
A couple of seals popped up, but none came close. They'd have a look
and then disappear.

The next morning, Russell woke up and yelled, "Bring on Deaf Rapids!" Those hard rapids wouldn't come up for three more days. What
was happening to him? "Did you see us go over that ledge yesterday?"
he said. "I want to do 9-Bar again." I expected him to thump his chest.
He was becoming a man while I was withering away into a cowering
chipmunk.

It was a work day. We canoed 28.5 miles, most of it in slack water.
The only thing I liked was a gregarious seal showing off in a set of
rapids. He repeatedly rode the waves, and stared at us as we sat on a
nearby boulder eating lunch. The other good thing was that the blackflies no longer bothered me. They still bit and caused itching and swell-
ing, but I had become used to them—the same way you get used to the
noise, muggers, and trash of New York City.

We took it easy the following day. We were about 38 miles from the
mouth of the river and the landscape was slowly changing. Tree-lined

shores gave way to rolling hills of peat, sporadically shaded by skinny spruces. The soil was cold to the touch when I dug a few inches down, and probably turned to ice just a few inches farther. Clumps of boulders dotted the land.

That afternoon, we finally had time to look over the water-station diaries. Russell approached me a little later. "I noticed in the journals that one guy who was on his second trip here said he wasn't going to try to paddle the Hudson Bay again. Gives you a clue, huh?" A mosquito net covered his head so I couldn't tell if he was truly worried. "Big bodies of water scare me, especially in a canoe with two guys who hate each other. I used to be worried about the white water. Now, I just want to get to Churchill without Hap shooting Andy." Ever since the water-station argument, our guides had not stopped bickering.

The next day went pretty well, except when Andy and I flipped our canoe. After a hearty lunch of Italian-herbed bannock stuffed with Velveeta, I had taken over in the stern. I wanted to work on my sweep and J-strokes, but I felt unsteady. "Let's catch as many eddies as we can," Andy told me when we were under way. "I like to look back at the rapids."

"Uh, yeah," I responded. I didn't see a single boulder with a good eddy. A wide, sharp ledge loomed on our right, with a boulder just beside it. And the water seemed to be frothing and bubbling a hell of a lot more than when I sat in the bow.

"Let's do that one," he ordered. The waves rolled big, and the thunder from the hydraulic was deafening. "No way," I yelped and cut her downstream. A minute later Andy saw another he liked, with a large ledge beside it.

"Here we go," he coaxed. "We'll cross into it." Our speed did carry us over the ledge wave, but the second we entered the eddy, we toppled over the upstream side. The spray skirts kept everything in the boat, but water ran underneath the attachments. It took us a half hour to unload, drain, and reload the boat.

That night, we camped on a tiny island across from the aptly named Tamarack Island (every square inch appeared to be occupied by one of those odd trees) and we were visited by a brave little vole. He scampered in our bags and under our feet, showing no fear.

Near dusk, the sun shone a bright yellow line along the water to our camp and the tamaracks filtered the light, illuminating our site in an airy glow while Hap cut and stripped four spruce poles to rig a sailboat with our canoes.

We pushed off the next morning around 10 A.M. It was our tenth day out and our last on the river. Russell would finally meet Deaf Rapids. We sailed for the first couple of miles with our boats lashed together, catamaran style.

When we reached Deaf Rapids in the midafternoon, I didn't want to run them. It didn't feel right. Hap gauged them as a Class IV, but they seemed a lot worse. One of the holes from a boulder looked more than 20 feet deep, and the resulting wave towered seven feet above the waterline.

We stood on the rocky shore, surveying the run. "We're not going to run that," Russell said.

"Sure we are," Hap shot back.

"These guys are being macho now," I complained to Russell when they were out of earshot. "They just want to say we didn't have to portage anything." Maybe Hap was too tired to make the right call. A river safety book I'd read about whitewater deaths said that's what usually happens when experienced canoeists die on the water. I tried my best to scare Russell so he'd get them to call it off.

"I don't want to do this," Russell admitted. "How do you vote?" The fact that I could barely hear him over the roar of the rapids had me scared. But I was more afraid of being a chicken. Walking back to our canoes, I found a long white feather on the ground, and when we lined up to run the rapids, I held it in my left hand and some tobacco in my right. I released it all once we were in the current.

"We're getting pulled in!" I yelled at Andy, and screamed for him to keep us to the left, the channel Hap had marked out. We made it quite easily, but we did have to bang our way through the boulders on the left, leaving behind a lot of blue plastic.

We then dropped down fast, and suddenly the river widened. We'd reached the mouth of the Seal. All we had to do was navigate through zillions of boulders while being pushed by the current and the tide. We wanted to get near the mouth but did not want to enter the bay. If we did, there'd be no place to camp.

But we sped past, misjudging everything. We had to turn around and paddle through the boulders against the current to reach a tiny island we thought might be above high tide. Eventually, we climbed out of the canoes and pulled them through the water—hopping from rock to rock and falling into stinging-cold water up to our chests.

Our island rose only a foot above the high tide mark. Smoke moved in, and mosquitoes mercilessly attacked. My Zen feeling about them had evaporated. Hap and Andy bickered. I grumbled that we didn't have enough fresh water for the bay crossing if something went wrong. Russell pointed out that we were perfect polar bear bait: Willows made it impossible to see anything more than 10 feet away. The worst part was that we had to stay there until noon the next day because high tide wasn't until 2 P.M. It was a wasteland.

For some reason, our moods brightened that night and the next morning. Maybe it was because things were so desperate that being in a bad mood seemed like a waste of time.

"I have an intuition that there's a beautiful, blonde Swedish biologist over at the Whaling Station," Russell announced during the night. The whaling station was about a mile away. "Why don't we go there, hang out with her, and then fly out of here on a floatplane? Well?"

Hap woke up at about 6:30 A.M., worked on the sailing poles, packed his stuff, and cooked us breakfast. We embarked about a half hour before noon because he was itching to go.

It would have been a sunny day if there hadn't been so much smoke. Something shined on us, though. Nearly two dozen seals escorted us through the final boulders. They flapped their fins on the water and dove in unison, guiding us through the deeper channels. It was a good omen.

Within 20 minutes, we reached deeper water and saw a pod of ghostly giants beneath our boats. They were the gentle belugas. These whales have been spending their summers at the mouth of the Seal River and other Hudson Bay rivers for thousands of years, but until recently scientists didn't have a clue as to why. The beluga actually go to these river estuaries to grow. Somehow, warmer water kicks their pituitary glands into hyperdrive, and they gain a year's worth of growth in just a season. About 3,000 of them come to the Seal every summer.

They sounded all around us, squeaking, sighing through their spouts, and staring even more intently than we. For the next hour, whales stopped by to pay their respects. Mothers brought in calves riding on their backs. And the little gray babies (they turn whiter every year) paid so much attention to us that they'd fall off their mothers' backs and then quickly squirm their way back on top. We splashed our hands in the water to draw the bigger ones closer; some came within a foot or two before darting off. Eventually, hundreds surrounded us—a daunting situation, considering that the larger ones weighed a ton and were the same length as our canoe. Some whales determinedly made eye contact, holding it for as long as possible. Others squeaked, patiently waiting for an answer.

We sadly said good-bye to the whales and headed for shallower water. As the tide departed, more and more boulders popped up. Around 4 P.M., it was clear we wouldn't make it to land. Mud and sand flats stretched for nearly a mile to shore. By 6 P.M., we couldn't go any farther. Russell anchored the canoes to a rock, and 20 minutes later we were resting on sand. The tide was out.

Since I had already thought the mouth of the Seal River was a wasteland, I couldn't think of a way to describe the sand flat we were stuck on. Our world had become sand, boulders, hazy sky, and an occasional tidal pool. It was a desolate place, except for Canada geese, gulls, and the infrequent common eider.

Hap made coffee and cooked soup for dinner. We had decided to canoe through the night after the tide returned, since there were only four hours of darkness. As long as we kept the shoreline in sight, what could go wrong?

Well, first of all, the tide didn't return as fast as we thought it would. Not until 11:28 P.M. did the water lift us from our anchorage. We started out in high spirits, bragging that we'd reach Churchill before sunrise. In an hour, no one was talking. For four muscle-straining hours, we paddled along the edge of Hudson Bay and around—but more often over—boulders. Every time we got stuck on one, we'd turn in a circle, trying to escape. Around 3:30 A.M., thinking we were farther down Button Bay (the deep bay that leads to Churchill), we raised our sails.

Andy and Hap steered with their paddles, while Russell and I maintained the sails. At some point, Hap dozed off and Andy seized the moment. He headed for the far shore.

"The one thing you cannot do," a denizen of Tadoule had warned us, "is try to cross Button Bay. Too many people have died that way." One newspaper account I'd read about the Seal mentioned four young men who did just that. An investigating officer, referring to the bay and Churchill's distant town lights, said, "It's just an optical illusion. It looks like (Churchill) is only a mile or two away, but as a matter of fact it's closer to 15 or 20 miles away." The officer said the bay can switch from being perfectly calm to being whipped by storm conditions within minutes, and that even experienced canoeists should never attempt a crossing.

Suddenly, I noticed that I couldn't see any shore, and suggested we head back. "But I can see the lights," Andy responded. There were some lights out there, miles away. It could have been a ship. Andy would follow it until we were well past Churchill and heading out to sea. Our water would run out in two to three days. We'd die in a week. I began to blabber to myself.

Hap woke up. "Where's the shore?" he demanded.

"We can't see it," I said.

"I do," Russell piped up. I almost punched him. Instead, I cussed him and Andy both, saying they didn't know what they were talking about. I didn't know what I was talking about either, but I knew we couldn't see the shore.

"Let's get that sail down and head back to shore," Hap said. "We're not crossing Button Bay." I immediately forgave him for all those mornings he had left Andy and me behind. Andy didn't, though, and they had one last argument. Once again, Andy lost and we headed back to shore.

The paddling was hard. I prayed my arms would fall off, so I'd have an excuse to quit. Near dawn, a male common eider swooshed down out of the silent night, missing our mast by inches. It seemed as startled as we were, but it was a good sign. We could now see the farthest shore and we hoisted the sail. A slow steady wind blew us north toward Churchill.

Seven hours later we entered the town harbor, escorted by ghostly whales and flapping seals. After we had landed and returned to civilization, people said we were lucky to have made it across Hudson Bay.

They were wrong. It had nothing to do with luck. Fear and *Men in Tights* saved our lives. And, so, later that evening, worn out from 200 miles of paddling, 42 rapids, and one night of hell, I dumped an entire pouch of tobacco into the bay.

TRIP NOTES

In the Cree and Ojibwe languages, Manitoba means "the place where the Spirit lives." This province, in Canada's exact geographical center, has 250,000 square miles that hold only a million human inhabitants; its one major city is the capital, Winnipeg. Besides forests, plains, and tundra, the province has 100,000 lakes and uncounted rivers and streams. Of its four major river systems, the Seal is the only one that remains completely undeveloped, and it was declared a Canadian Heritage River in 1992. (However, other rivers within the Heritage system have been dammed while under its "protections," so I urge anyone who travels the Seal to wax poetic about the experience to help defend it from dams and other industrial developments.)

When to go

Generally the best time for a canoeing trip is in the summer, when the province is consistently warm and dry. Yet conditions vary depending on the location and elevation of the river you want to run, so consult with professional outfitters and government agencies to determine the best time for your trip.

Two-thirds of this province lies north of the 53rd degree of latitude, so when winter comes, it arrives with a vengeance. That's when cross-country skiing, ice skating, snowshoeing, and whimpering take over as the principal sports. (Then again, fall and winter are the best seasons to view the aurora borealis.)

How to go

Local outfitters offer a variety of canoe trips in this region; see "Where to go" on the following page for trip descriptions. A couple of guides and outfitters include:

- **Del Hartwig, Hartwig Wilderness Adventures,** 512 Airline Road, Saint Andrews, Manitoba R1A 3P3; (204) 668-3234.

- **Doug Weber, Dymond Lake Outfitters,** Box 304, 26 Selkirk Avenue,

Churchill, Manitoba R0B 0E0; (204) 675-8875.

For other recommended guides and outfitters, contact Travel Manitoba (see "Additional information," on the following page).

If you're a very experienced river runner and don't want to travel with a guide down the Seal, at the very least consult with a local outfitter for advice. You should allow yourself two weeks to make a Seal River trip. Fly to Tadoule Lake (the put-in) from Thompson or Gillam. At the end of the trip, charter a coastal airplane or boat from the mouth of the Seal to take you to the town of Churchill. Then you can return to Gillam or Thompson by plane or train.

Please note: I do not recommend attempting to cross Hudson Bay as we did. In the cold light of hindsight, I now say we were very lucky we made it. Two outfits that provide a boat pickup service are Jack Batstone, 90 James Street, Churchill, Manitoba R0B 0E0, (204) 675-2300; and Sea North Tours, 39 Franklin Street, Churchill, Manitoba R0B 0E0; (204) 675-2195.

Where to go

Besides wonderful canoeing streams, the province holds great hunting, fishing, and hiking opportunities, along with chances to view an abundance of wildlife. For example, there are many moose in Hecla Provincial Park, and tremendous numbers of red-sided garter snakes gather to mate in the Narcisse Wildlife Management Area in the spring.

If you plan to go on a canoe trip, here's a sampling of Manitoba's canoe outings (also see "Additional information," on the following page):

- **Gods River.** The four-day trip from Shamattawa on this southern tributary of the Hayes River (see below) is best undertaken in June, just after the thaw. The lower stretch has no rapids but plenty of wildlife, including wolf, moose, and caribou, and is 124 miles in length. Those in search of white water can add on an upper stretch of 130 miles, starting at Gods Lake.

- **Grass River.** This intermediate run can be tailored to your abilities and the amount of time you have. There is a basic eight-day stretch of 118 miles, or add more stretches for a total of 341 miles from the Cranberry Portage put-in. You can run the easily identifiable rapids or portage them. Since sudden storms can occur, good paddling techniques and basic wilderness skills are essential.

- **Hayes River.** A three-week voyage down the river that links Lake Winnipeg with Hudson Bay, this trip goes through a few rapids and a lot of history. The old-time fur traders who used this route had to make 33 portages, but modern-day canoeists can do it with 27.

- **Seal River.** Very remote and very wild, the Seal presents a few tactical problems to the recreational traveler. It's best to travel with guides and outfitters for the voyage, and, as you can tell from my story, these folks can also supply some special entertainment. The upper Seal is surrounded by boreal forest with white spruce and tamarack. During a two-week paddle eastward toward Hudson Bay, it traverses transition forest to tundra. Besides a full panoply of subarctic wildlife, you may also, depending on where you are, encounter polar bears hunting for seals.

Either fly to Tadoule Lake and cross it to reach the river put-in, or fly by seaplane to the put-in at the headwaters.

What to bring

A canoe orientation class will help give you a grasp of the basics. In general, you want to dress as if at any moment you might get dunked. For hot days, that means nylon pants and cotton shirts; for cold and wet days, pile on insulating garments and wind- and rainproof outer shell layers. Rubberized, waterproof stow bags are needed for storing gear. And bring the toughest, meanest bug repellent you can find that will not peel off patches of your hide. One of those net hats may also prove useful when you find yourself swarmed by blackflies and mosquitoes. For more advice on clothing and gear, see "What to bring" in "Following Huck," on page 208.

Additional information

The Manitoba Recreational Canoeing Association publishes a list of 62 classic canoe trips throughout the province. For information contact the association at Box 2663, Winnipeg, Manitoba R3C 4B3; (204) 925-5639.

For information about the Seal River, including the latest on regulations and permits, contact the Manitoba Department of Natural Resources, Parks Branch, 258 Portage Avenue, Floor 4, Winnipeg, Manitoba R3H 0B6.

General travel information on this area is available by contacting the following organizations:

- **Manitoba Lodges and Outfitters Association, Inc.,** 23 Sage Crescent, Winnipeg, Manitoba R2Y 0X8; (204) 889-4840.

- **Tourism Winnipeg,** 325 Forks Market Road, Winnipeg, Manitoba R3C 4L9; (800) 665-0204.

- **Travel Manitoba,** 25 Forks Market Road, Floor 7, Department 3361, Winnipeg, Manitoba R3C 4L9; (800) 665-0040.

A good contact for topographical maps is the Canada Map Office, 615 Booth Street, Ottawa, Ontario K1A 0E9; (613) 952-7000.

About the Authors

Paul McHugh, born during a hurricane near south Florida's Everglades in 1950, grew up hiking, fishing, sailing, and skin diving, studied for the Catholic priesthood for six years in his teens, then left the seminary and finished college at Florida State University with a degree in poetry. Since 1973 he has lived in Northern California, where he has dedicated himself to writing about the environment, resource use, and outdoor recreation. He has independently produced video documentaries for PBS, including "The Eel—Life of a Threatened River" and "Return of the Desert Bighorn." His articles have appeared in *California, New West, National Fisherman, West, Runner's World, American West,* and other journals; a novel, *The Search for Goodbye-to-Rains,* was published in 1980. In

1988, McHugh was a member of Team USA when it won the world kayak-surfing championship on the west coast of Ireland. He has been the outdoor feature writer for the *San Francisco Chronicle* since 1985.

Richard Bangs is one of the world's leading mavens of adventure travel. He began his swashbuckling career in the outdoors by exploring the Potomac River in a canoe at age 15, then went on to work as a raft guide in the Grand Canyon in 1968.

As founder of the Sobek adventure travel company, Bangs has pioneered explorations of more than 30 rivers, including the Bío-bío in Chile, the Zambezi in Africa, China's Yangtze, and the Indus in Pakistan. He has also used his master's degree in journalism to good effect, penning more than 500 magazine articles and 11 books, including *Rivergods* and *Mountaingods* (Sierra Club Books) and his latest endeavor, *Peaks* (Taylor Publishing), produced with his wife, photographer Pamela Roberson.

A popular public speaker, Bangs has given talks for the National Geographic Society, the Smithsonian, and the Explorers Club. He is active in conservation work with the International Rivers Network, Friends of the River, American Rivers, and the Sierra Club.

Now that Sobek has merged with Mountain Travel, Bangs continues to explore and guide trips to the world's wild rivers and exotic places. In between, he resides in Montclair, California, where he and Roberson have begun a new adventure: raising Walker, their infant son.

Tim Cahill, outdoor raconteur nonpareil, may not be the founder of adventure travel, but he's one of its most famed prophets. He has belched greetings to mountain gorillas, surfed waves off calving icebergs, stood in the mist of jungle waterfalls, and dangled himself off the lip of El Capitan while performing the world's longest rappel. Cahill began his illustrious career in San Francisco as a reporter for *Rolling Stone* magazine. In 1976, he became a cofounder of *Outside* magazine, and is now an editor-at-large for the publication.

In addition to publishing his yarns in outdoor magazines, Cahill has written nonfiction books, including *Buried Dreams,* a study of mass murderer John Wayne Gacy, and story collections that include *Jaguars Ripped My Flesh* and *Pecked to Death by Ducks.* Cahill calls central Montana home, but says he still enjoys exploring remote reaches of the globe, such as the Congo's untracked Ndoke Forest.

W. Hodding Carter was born and raised in Greenville, Mississippi. At Kenyon College, he swam on the national championship team and read books that had nothing to do with his classes. After graduating, he became an English and history teacher in Kenya for the Peace Corps, where he befriended a KGB agent, until the agent gave him a small sum of money and asked him to take information off the Peace Corps director's desk.

After returning to the United States in 1986, he held odd jobs—everything from working as a waiter to spying for the Dukakis presidential campaign (presumably having picked up a few tips from his KGB friend)—then became a fact-checker for *Esquire* magazine in 1989. He later worked as a staff writer for *M* magazine, specializing in travel, history, and food.

In 1992, Hodding and a companion traveled the Lewis and Clark Trail from Saint Louis, Missouri, to Astoria, Oregon. His book *Westward Whoa* (Simon & Schuster, 1994) tells all about their adventures on the trail and the weirdos and friendlies they met along the way. Carter now lives and writes in West Virginia and works part time as a whitewater rafting guide.

Paula J. Del Giudice, a writer and photographer based in Las Vegas, writes an outdoors column for the *Las Vegas Sun* and is the Nevada editor of *Outdoor Life.* Her articles have appeared in *Field & Stream, Nevada Magazine,* the *Reno Gazette-Journal,* and other publications. She is also the author of *Microwave Game & Fish Cookbook* (Stackpole Books). Her photographs have been displayed at Nikon House in the Rockefeller Center in New York City.

Del Giudice also serves as volunteer vice-chair of the western region of the National Wildlife Federation, where she's been on the board of directors since 1992, and has been active for many years with the federation's Nevada affiliate, serving as president from 1986 to 1988. She currently edits the federation's newsletter, *Western Sportsman*. In 1986, Del Giudice was awarded special recognition by Congress for her work, and in 1988 she won a Conservation Service Citation from the National Wildlife Federation. An avid hunter and angler, she has pursued game in 11 states and in Mexico and Canada. She and her husband, Mike Wickersham, enjoy family life with their son, Kevin, and daughter, Katie.

Gretel Ehrlich, born and raised on the south coast of California, traveled to Wyoming in 1975 to work as a documentary filmmaker. Enamored of the sprawling landscape, she moved there to live and work on ranches and began writing full time in 1979. Her insights into life in Wyoming resulted in the book *The Solace of Open Spaces* and the novel *Heart Mountain*.

Ehrlich's essays have appeared in the *New York Times, Harper's, Life,* and the *Atlantic Monthly.* The considerable recognition she's won for her work includes an American Academy of Arts and Letters award, a Whiting Foundation grant, and a Guggenheim fellowship. Other notable books have been *A Match to the Heart,* an account of being struck by lightning, and *Islands, the Universe, Home.* She currently resides on a ranch in the coastal hill country above Santa Barbara, California.

Pam Houston's collection of short stories, *Cowboys Are My Weakness* (W.W. Norton), was the winner of the 1993 Western States Book Award and has been translated into seven languages. Her nonfiction articles have been published in *Travel and Leisure, Elle, Food and Wine, Ski, Los Angeles Magazine,* and the *New York Times.*

Houston is a licensed river guide and a horsewoman. She is currently finishing another book of fiction, a collection of essays, and a screenplay, and has recently edited the book *Women on Hunting* (Ecco Press), a collection of fiction, nonfiction, and poetry.

She teaches in the MFA program at Saint Mary's College in Moraga, California, as well as at many writer's conferences in the United States and England. Houston is a member of the 1995–96 National Writer's Voice Tour. She lives in Colorado at 9,000 feet above sea level, near the headwaters of the Rio Grande.

Bob Marshall, a New Orleans native and the outdoors editor of the *New Orleans Times-Picayune,* has spent most of his life fascinated by the wonders of the natural world. Although he specializes in the great wetlands surrounding his home, his curiosity and his writing projects have taken him to Alaska, Central America, and Europe. Besides working in the newspaper business, Marshall has produced feature stories for *Field & Stream* and *Condé Nast Traveler* magazines, and has served as the conservation editor for *Southern Outdoors.* He has also produced stories for episodes of ESPN's *Outdoors Writers.* Over the years, he has received more than 50 writing and conservation awards. Marshall lives in New Orleans with his wife, Marie Gould, and their daughter, Erica.

Linda Watanabe McFerrin is a poet, travel writer, and fashion merchandiser who has been a contributor to more than 40 literary journals, newspapers, and magazines, including the *Washington Post, EcoTraveler* magazine, the *San Francisco Examiner,* and *Modern Bride.* She's also the author of two poetry collections: *Chisel, Rice Paper, Stone* and *The Impossibility of Redemption Is Something We Hadn't Figured On.* . . . When this Northern California resident is not traveling, she directs art projects and consults on communications and product development for apparel manufacturers. She is currently writing a novel.

Tom Wharton was born a dyed-in-the-wool Utahan in 1950 and has been a part of the Great Salt Lake scene ever since. His father was a hunter and outdoorsman, and Wharton was raised to pursue both deer and pheasant, the family passion. His writing career began in high school, when he was a correspondent for the city's evening paper.

During the Vietnam War, Wharton was a public affairs officer with the Utah National Guard, a post he held until 1991 after the end of Desert Storm. He became a sports reporter for the *Salt Lake Tribune* in 1970 and the paper's outdoors writer and editor in 1976. His feature articles have appeared in *Outdoor Life* and *Field & Stream*.

Wharton lives in Salt Lake City with his wife, Gayen, and their four children, Jacob, Rawl, Emma, and Bryer. Gayen, an outdoorswoman, educator, and writer, has joined him in producing several books, including *Utah—A Family Travel Guide; Utah—Discover America; An Outdoor Family Guide to the Southwest's Four Corners;* and the Utah section of the recently released Foghorn Press guidebook *Utah and Nevada Camping*.

CREDITS

Rebecca Poole Forée	Editor in Chief
Stuart L. Silberman	Cover and Interior Design
Michele Thomas	Production Manager
Karin Mullen	Associate Editor
Aimee Larsen	Assistant Editor
Alexander Lyon	Production Assistant
Cynthia Rubin	Copy Editor
Jeanette Good	Research Assistant
Judith Pynn	Acquisitions Editor
Paul Souders, Tony Stone Images	Cover Photo

Acknowledgments

I would like to thank Foghorn Press' former executive editor, Ann Marie Brown, for encouraging me to write for Foghorn Press, and for helping me hatch the inspiration that led to this volume. I would also like to thank the rest of the Foghorn staff for their dedication in making *Wild Places* a quality book. I especially want to express gratitude to Howard Rabinowitz for his patient and perennially imperturbable work on the initial copy edit.

"You Are Cowboy" by Tim Cahill reprinted by permission of the author. Copyright © 1995 by Tim Cahill. This story first appeared in a spring 1995 issue of *Outside* magazine.

"Not Only the Wind" by Tom Wharton reprinted by permission of the *Salt Lake Tribune*. Copyright © 1989 by Tom Wharton. Portions of this story first appeared in the *Salt Lake Tribune*.

"On the Trail of Walking James" by Pam Houston excerpted from *Heart of the Land: Essays on Last Great Places* (Pantheon Books, 1994). Reprinted by permission of the author. Copyright © 1994 by Pam Houston.

"The Source of a River" by Gretel Ehrlich excerpted from *Islands, the Universe, Home* by Gretel Ehrlich. Copyright © 1991 by Gretel Ehrlich. Used by permission of Viking Penguin, a division of Penguin Books USA Inc.

"Ursus Major" by Paul McHugh reprinted by permission of the author. Copyright © 1993 by Paul McHugh. Portions of this story first appeared in the debut issue of *EcoTraveler* magazine in 1993.

"The Lure of Hoodoos" by Linda Watanabe McFerrin reprinted by permission of the author. Copyright © 1995 by Linda Watanabe McFerrin. Portions of this story first appeared in the April 30, 1995 issue of the *San Francisco Examiner*.

"Paddling Off the Edge of the Big Easy" by Bob Marshall reprinted by permission of the *New Orleans Times-Picayune*. Copyright © 1991 by Bob Marshall. Portions of this story first appeared in the *New Orleans Times-Picayune*.

"In Pursuit of the Leaper" by Paula J. Del Giudice. Copyright © 1995 by Paula J. Del Giudice.

"On (Not) Climbing the Grand Teton" by Pam Houston, originally published as "In the Shadow of the Grand" in the May/June 1995 issue of *Ski* magazine. Reprinted by permission of the author. Copyright © 1995 by Pam Houston.

"Home Is How Many Places" by Gretel Ehrlich excerpted from *Islands, the Universe, Home* by Gretel Ehrlich. Copyright © 1991 by Gretel Ehrlich. Used by permission of Viking Penguin, a division of Penguin Books USA Inc.

"The Year of Living Curiously" by Tom Wharton reprinted by permission of the *Salt Lake Tribune*. Copyright © 1991 by Tom Wharton. Portions of this story first appeared in the *Salt Lake Tribune*.

"How I Learned to Hate Thoreau" by W. Hodding Carter reprinted by permission of the author. Copyright © 1992 by W. Hodding Carter. This story first appeared in the January 1992 issue of *M* magazine.

Index

WILD PLACES

Leave No Trace

Leave No Trace, Inc., is a program dedicated to maintaining the integrity of outdoor recreation areas through education and public awareness. Foghorn Press is a proud supporter of this program and its ethics.

Here's how you can Leave No Trace:

Plan Ahead and Prepare
- Learn about the regulations and special concerns of the area you are visiting.
- Visit the backcountry in small groups.
- Avoid popular areas during peak-use periods.
- Choose equipment and clothing in subdued colors.
- Pack food in reusable containers.

Travel and Camp with Care
On the trail:
- Stay on designated trails. Walk single file in the middle of the path.
- Do not take shortcuts on switchbacks.
- When traveling cross-country where there are no trails, follow animal trails or spread out your group so no new routes are created. Walk along the most durable surfaces available, such as rock, gravel, dry grasses, or snow.
- Use a map and compass to eliminate the need for rock cairns, tree scars, or ribbons.
- If you encounter pack animals, step to the downhill side of the trail and speak softly to avoid startling them.

At camp:
- Choose an established, legal site that will not be damaged by your stay.
- Restrict activities to areas where vegetation is compacted or absent.
- Keep pollutants out of the water by camping at least 200 feet (about 70 adult steps) from lakes and streams.
- Control pets at all times, or leave them at home with a sitter. Remove dog feces.

Pack It In and Pack It Out
- Take everything you bring into the wild back out with you.
- Protect wildlife and your food by storing rations securely. Pick up all spilled foods.

- Use toilet paper or wipes sparingly; pack them out.
- Inspect your campsite for trash and any evidence of your stay. Pack out all trash—even if it's not yours!

Properly Dispose of What You Can't Pack Out
- If no refuse facility is available, deposit human waste in catholes dug six to eight inches deep at least 200 feet from water, camps, or trails. Cover and disguise the catholes when you're finished.
- To wash yourself or your dishes, carry the water 200 feet from streams or lakes and use small amounts of biodegradable soap. Scatter the strained dishwater.

Keep the Wilderness Wild
- Treat our natural heritage with respect. Leave plants, rocks, and historical artifacts as you found them.
- Good campsites are found, not made. Do not alter a campsite.
- Let nature's sounds prevail; keep loud voices and noises to a minimum.
- Do not build structures or furniture or dig trenches.

Minimize Use and Impact of Fires
- Campfires can have a lasting impact on the backcountry. Always carry a light-weight stove for cooking, and use a candle lantern instead of building a fire whenever possible.
- Where fires are permitted, use established fire rings only.
- Do not scar the natural setting by snapping the branches off live, dead, or downed trees.
- Completely extinguish your campfire and make sure it is cold before departing. Remove all unburned trash from the fire ring and scatter the cold ashes over a large area well away from any camp.

For more information, call 1-800-332-4100.

FOGHORN ✖ OUTDOORS

Founded in 1985, Foghorn Press has quickly become one of the country's premier publishers of outdoor recreation guidebooks. Through its unique Books Building Community program, Foghorn Press supports a variety of community environmental issues such as park, trail, and water ecosystem preservation. Foghorn Press is also committed to printing its books on recycled paper.

Foghorn books are sold throughout the U.S. Call 1-800-FOGHORN (8:30–5:30 PST) for the location of a bookstore near you that carries Foghorn Press titles. If you prefer, you may place an order directly with Foghorn Press using your Visa or MasterCard or visit our Web site at www.foghorn.com. All of the titles listed below are now available.

THE NATIONAL OUTDOORS SERIES

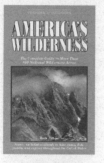
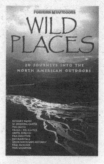
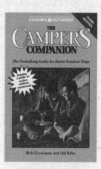

AMERICA'S WILDERNESS
The Complete Guide to More Than 600 National Wilderness Areas
592 pp., $19.95

WILD PLACES
20 Journeys Into the North American Outdoors
320 pp., $15.95

THE CAMPER'S COMPANION
The Pack-Along Guide for Better Outdoor Trips
458 pp., $15.95

AMERICA'S SECRET RECREATION AREAS
Your Recreation Guide to the Bureau of Land Management's Wild Lands of the West
640 pp., $17.95

EPIC TRIPS OF THE WEST
Tom Stienstra's Ten Best
208 pp., $9.95

OUR ENDANGERED PARKS
What You Can Do to Protect Our National Heritage
224 pp., $10.95

THE COMPLETE GUIDE SERIES

The Complete Guides are the books that have given Foghorn Press its reputation for excellence. Each book is a comprehensive resource for its subject, from *every* golf course in California to *every* fishing spot in the state of Washington. With extensive cross-references and detailed maps, the Complete Guides offer readers a quick and easy way to get the best recreational information available.

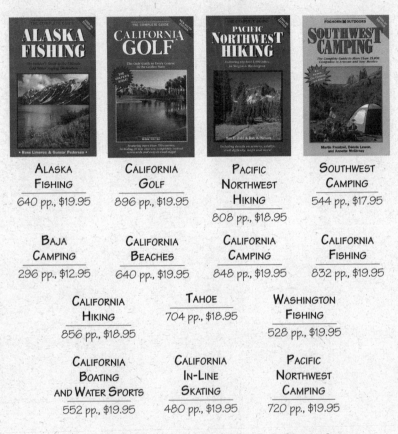

ALASKA FISHING	**CALIFORNIA GOLF**	**PACIFIC NORTHWEST HIKING**	**SOUTHWEST CAMPING**
640 pp., $19.95	896 pp., $19.95	808 pp., $18.95	544 pp., $17.95
BAJA CAMPING	**CALIFORNIA BEACHES**	**CALIFORNIA CAMPING**	**CALIFORNIA FISHING**
296 pp., $12.95	640 pp., $19.95	848 pp., $19.95	832 pp., $19.95

CALIFORNIA HIKING	**TAHOE**	**WASHINGTON FISHING**
856 pp., $18.95	704 pp., $18.95	528 pp., $19.95
CALIFORNIA BOATING AND WATER SPORTS	**CALIFORNIA IN-LINE SKATING**	**PACIFIC NORTHWEST CAMPING**
552 pp., $19.95	480 pp., $19.95	720 pp., $19.95

A book's page length, price, and availability are subject to change.

For more information, call 1-800-FOGHORN,
visit our Web site at www.foghorn.com,
or write to: Foghorn Press,
555 DeHaro Street, Suite 220
San Francisco, CA 94107

Foghorn Press
BOOKS BUILDING COMMUNITY™